Screening Scotland

Screening Scotland

Duncan Petrie

 Publishing

For Val and Neil

First published in 2000 by the
British Film Institute
21 Stephen Street, London W1P 2LN

The British Film Institute promotes greater understanding of,
and access to, film and moving image culture in the UK.

Cover design: Lisa Swerling/Default
Cover images: (front) *Ratcatcher* © Pathé Fund Ltd (dir. Lynne Ramsay, 1999)
– image by Tom Townend; (back) *Whisky Galore!* © Canal Plus (Ealing Studios)
(dir. Alexander Mackendrick, 1949)

Set in Minion by ketchup, London
Printed in Great Britain by St Edmundsbury Press, Bury St Edmunds

British Library Cataloguing-in-Publication Data
A catalogue record for this book is available from the British Library
ISBN 0–85170–785–8 pbk
ISBN 0–85170–784–X hbk

Contents

Acknowledgments

A considerable number of people assisted this project in a variety of ways. First of all, I would like to thank Andrew Lockett of BFI Publishing for inviting me to write a book on Scottish cinema in the first place. The process of tracking down and viewing copies of films was both arduous and pleasurable and could not have been accomplished without the generous help and patience of Bryony Dixon and Kathleen Dickson at the National Film and Television Archive, Janet McBain at the Scottish Film Archive, Sine Foster at BBC Scotland, Isabella Edgar at Scottish Screen and Patrick Brennan at the University of Glasgow's Department of Theatre, Film and Television Studies. Thanks also to Mike Alexander and Ian Sellar for lending me personal copies of their work, and to Robin Macpherson for giving me access to his invaluable unpublished thesis on independent Scottish production. I am especially grateful to the various individuals who were kind enough to allow me to interview them: Mike Alexander, John Archer, Jenny Attala, Lenny Crooks, Eddie Dick, Murray Grigor, David Hayman, Paddy Higson, Steve McIntyre, Barbara McKissack, Penny Thompson. Various colleagues at the University of Exeter, including Lee Grieveson, Susan Hayward, Helen Taylor and Regenia Gagnier, read and made helpful comments on parts of this manuscript. I would also like to acknowledge the contributions made to this project at various stages by Judy Anderson, John Bartlett, Michael Begg, John Caughie, Ian Conrich, Pam Cook, Susan Dunlop, John Dupre, Victoria Evans, Lizzie Francke, Judith Higginbottom, Hester Higton, Ken Ingles, Nick James, Peter Jewell, Colin McArthur, Colin MacCabe, Seamus McGarvey, James Mackay, David Mackenzie, Scott Mackenzie, Ann Orr, John Orr, Nicola Pearson, David Sharp, David Sutton and Nick Thomas.

Special thanks must go to Dan MacRae and Eddie Dick, whose friendship and support not only provided much-needed inspiration but also a great deal of practical guidance. Their hospitality, and that of their respective partners, Liz Ingram and Linda Dick, also made my numerous research trips to Glasgow and Edinburgh extremely enjoyable.

Finally, as ever, I would like to express my love and gratitude to Rebecca Russell for putting up with the intrusion of this project from inception to completion with her characteristic patience and encouragement.

Introduction:
Some Key Issues in the Study of Scottish Cinema

The mid-1990s saw Scotland achieve an unprecedented profile in the realms of international cinema. This was sparked by the critical and commercial success of energetic and irreverent low-budget films like *Shallow Grave* and *Trainspotting* that served as a timely riposte to the British cinema's over-reliance on tasteful period films, many adapted from the 'English' literary canon. At the same time, Hollywood mounted its own celebration of Caledonia with the lavish historical epics *Rob Roy* and *Braveheart*, the latter film winning the Oscar for best picture in 1996. Suddenly, Scottish films were flavour of the month: Mel Gibson's celluloid portrayal of thirteenth-century Scots patriot William Wallace was co-opted as a powerful symbol by the Scottish National Party, while actors Ewan McGregor and Robert Carlyle found themselves in hot demand, heading an exciting new generation of young Scottish talent. At the same time, vital new sources of film finance materialised, creating the opportunity for a substantial increase in indigenous production and with it the first green shoots of an identifiable Scottish industry. This in turn created important opportunities for established film-makers like Bill Forsyth and Ken Loach (the acclaimed English director drawn to the vitality of Scottish screenwriting and new forms of indigenous financial support), while also announcing the emergence of distinctive new talents like Peter Mullan and Lynne Ramsay (whose respective debut films, *Orphans* and *Ratcatcher*, were two of the domestic cinematic highlights of 1999).

This book has been directly inspired by this upsurge in creativity and on the one hand is an attempt to document and analyse the emergence of this new Scottish cinema. At the same time it is important to locate these new developments within a broader historical framework. Until recently, the cinematic representation of Scotland had been largely an external creation, produced by and serving the commercial needs of a London-based British film industry, or occasionally Hollywood. The repertoire of images created by an emerging Scottish cinema represents both a challenge to and an extension of certain dominant cinematic projections of Scotland and the Scots dating back to the earliest days of the medium. Consequently, this is an opportune moment not only for a sustained engagement with the present, but also to reconsider the wider legacy of cinematic representations of Scotland, a rich terrain that has only just begun to be explored in any detail. With the exception of Norman Wilson's *Representing Scotland*,[1] a slim survey of mainly documentary production published in 1945, and Charles Oakley's *Fifty Years at the Pictures*,[2] a consideration primarily of Scottish exhibition published the following year, the major studies of the subject have all appeared in the last two decades. They include two collections of essays, *Scotch Reels* (1982)[3] and *From Limelight to Satellite* (1990),[4] edited by Colin McArthur and Eddie Dick respectively, and two idiosyncratic personal accounts: Forsyth Hardy's *Scotland in Film* (1990)[5] and David Bruce's *Scotland the Movie* (1996).[6]

Although inspired by very different intellectual preoccupations, *Scotch Reels* and *Scotland in Film* are both centrally concerned with the question of representation. McArthur and his colleagues draw heavily on the political and aesthetic concerns of Marxism and modernism, while Hardy's realist perspective betrays the influence of his mentor John Grierson, father of the British documentary.[7] On the other hand, both *From Limelight to Satellite* and *Scotland the Movie* are at least in part concerned with the economic and industrial contexts of the histories of moving-image production and consumption in Scotland. The former collection is described by its editor as a 'historical and contemporary mosaic of Scottish film', while Bruce's contribution encompasses a wealth of detail and insight accumulated over a long career at the centre of institutional film culture in Scotland,[8] despite being structured as an informal and highly fragmented gazetteer. In addition to these key critical and historical works, there have also been a small number of books on or by significant Scottish film-makers such as John Grierson, Alexander Mackendrick, Harry Watt, Stewart McAllister, Donald Alexander and Bill Douglas, and a handful of studies of exhibition, including individual works on the cinemas of Aberdeen, Glasgow and Edinburgh.[9]

Representing Scotland

Whatever the virtues of these major studies of Scottish cinema, the most influential critical and cultural analysis remains *Scotch Reels*. In attempting to map the field of Scottish film culture, the volume explores the negative influence of the discourses of Tartanry and Kailyard on cinematic representations of Scotland from the 1920s to the early 1980s. *Scotch Reels* constructs a detailed analysis of the continuities of these tropes from nineteenth-century literature and painting to cinema and television and various other forms of popular cultural transmission: postcards, whisky bottles, shortbread tins, tea towels and popular songs. The tartan myth in Scottish popular culture oscillates between the idea of the romantic and noble Highlander, associated with the Jacobite Rebellion of 1745 and the works of Sir Walter Scott, and what Cairns Craig describes as 'the parodic red-nosed, kilted, drunken, mean Scotsmen of music hall comedy and picture postcard jokes'.[10] While the Kailyard tradition has its origins in the late nineteenth-century novels of J.M. Barrie, Ian McLaren and S.R. Crockett and is described by Tom Nairn in the following manner:

> Kailyardism was the definition of Scotland as consisting wholly of small towns full of small-town 'characters' given to bucolic intrigue and wise sayings. At first the central figures were usually Ministers of the Kirk (as were most of the authors) but later on schoolteachers and doctors got into the act. Their housekeepers always have a shrewd insight into human nature. Offspring who leave for the big city frequently come to grief, and are glad to get home again (peching and hoasting to hide their feelings). In their different ways village cretins and ne'er-do-wells reinforce the essentially healthy *Weltanschauung* of the place.[11]

What unites Tartanry and Kailyard is the abdication of any engagement with the realities of the modern world. Rather than being directed towards transformation or transcendence of material conditions, the popular imagination seeks shelter in the retreat into a nostalgic mythic past.

The seminal critique of Tartanry and Kailyard in the context of the cinema is McArthur's essay 'Scotland and Cinema: The Iniquity of the Fathers', the central analysis around which all the other essays in *Scotch Reels* revolve. McArthur traces the influence of Tartanry and Kailyard (and hybrids of the two) from British silent productions such as *Bonnie Prince Charlie* (C.C. Calvert, 1923) and *Young Lochinvar* (W.P. Kellino, 1923); through the 'Hollywoodisation' of Scotland in the 1930s via films like *The Little Minister* (Richard Wallace, 1934),[12] *Bonnie Scotland* (James Horne, 1935) and *Wee Willie Winkie* (John Ford, 1937); to a number of post-war productions constituting 'the definitive modern statements of Tartanry and Kailyard in the cinema'.[13] The former comprises two historical costume dramas, *Bonnie Prince Charlie* (Anthony Kimmins, 1948) and *Rob Roy: The Highland Rogue* (Harold French, 1953), and Vincente Minnelli's definitive tartan fantasy *Brigadoon* (1954) which famously constructed its vision of the Highlands in the MGM studios in Culver City; while the modern version of the cinematic Kailyard is represented by a group of British productions shot largely on location in Scotland and including *Whisky Galore!* (Alexander Mackendrick, 1949), *Laxdale Hall* (John Eldridge, 1953), *The Maggie* (Mackendrick, 1954),[14] *Geordie* (Frank Launder, 1955) and *Rockets Galore* (Michael Relph, 1958). Each of these revolves around the dramatic intrusion of the modern world into small, rural Highland and Island communities. Modernity takes the form of unwelcome outsiders, representing the forces of the state, the law, big business and the city, who invariably gets their come-uppance at the hands of the wily locals. In addition to their relationship to the Kailyard tradition, the films are also aligned with what McArthur refers to as 'the Ealing ethos' (although only Mackendrick's two films were actually Ealing comedies):

> Central to this was a detestation of modernity as it related to the city and to the power of capital (though the films are by no stretch of the imagination pro-socialist; they are rather pro-feudal) and in particular to the power of central government bureaucracy. Set against these ills, the films construct a set of contrary humane values invested in a range of loveable rural eccentrics and non conformists. … These films … are in a very precise sense politically reactionary in that they restore and sanctify the quasi-feudal social structure of rural Scotland. Like so many other representations of Scotland and the Scots they are culturally reactionary as well in offering for endorsement and 'identification' a range of figures and situations which offer no guidance to the solution of the problems of the modern world which some of the films themselves pose.[15]

McArthur then turns his attention to potentially more *progressive* films which would seem on the face of things to be more directly engaged with the problems and contradictions of modern life. These include *Floodtide* (Frederick Wilson, 1949) and *The Brave Don't Cry* (Philip Leacock, 1952), features set against the industrial background of shipbuilding and coal mining respectively, and some of the documentaries made under the auspices of the Films of Scotland Committee from 1955 onwards. This group constitutes a third key discourse, that of 'Clydesidism', a version of Scotland associated primarily with working-class, masculine industrial labour. But, for McArthur, these works similarly fail to escape the taint of regressive discourses, eschewing any political analysis of the realities of class conflict or industrial relations by seeking refuge in human drama. Consequently, the ultimate indictment of the dominant traditions in the cinematic representation of Scotland and the Scots has been their total inadequacy in addressing 'the historical and contemporary reality of Scotland',[16] a charge McArthur also lays against the institutions comprising official Scottish film culture such as the Scottish Film Council and Films of Scotland. This failure stems from the absence of any engagement with the kind of radical and politically progressive analysis of the relationship between cinema and society achieved elsewhere:

> Scotland has produced no equivalents of Syberberg's, Bertoluccis's, Angelopoulous', Alvarez's and Mulloy's treatments of their respective national

histories, no equivalents of Godard's, Oshima's or Makavejev's anatomising of the sexual mores of the societies in which they live; no equivalents of the sustained reflection on the process of cinema evident in the work of Snow and Straub/Huillet; and – perhaps most damagingly of all – no equivalents of the accounts of women's experience to be found in the work of Akerman, Rainer and Wollen/Mulvey.[17]

Despite having a very different philosophical conception of the real to McArthur,[18] Forsyth Hardy makes a similar call for Scottish film-makers to search for 'a path through the myths to reality'.[19] He praises 'genuine efforts to achieve authentic and credible portrayal' of Scotland, even by English and American film-makers, contrasting this with that prime example of mythologisation, *Brigadoon*. It is in this spirit that his survey of cinematic representations of Scotland is subsequently constructed guided by his commitment to the virtues of documentary realism.

The Critique of *Scotch Reels*

The enduring virtue of McArthur's essay, and the *Scotch Reels* polemic as a whole, is that it provides an invaluable starting point to thinking systematically and critically about the dominant cinematic representations that have defined a certain national image. It has also sketched out the terrain on which subsequent commentaries have had to engage. Not surprisingly, McArthur's negative interpretation of particular film texts such as *Whisky Galore!* and *The Maggie* have been challenged,[20] while other writers have turned their attention to what they regard as more fundamental flaws in the analysis itself. The most perceptive and sophisticated critique has come from two of the original contributors to the *Scotch Reels* project. John Caughie, for example, has identified a tendency towards reductiveness at the level of both content and context.[21] On the one hand, those films that didn't fit the analysis were simply ignored, the glaring example cited by Caughie (and echoed elsewhere by Andrew Noble)[22] being Bill Douglas's autobiographical *Trilogy*,[23] but a similar case could be made with regard to various other important films such as *Edge of the World* (Michael Powell, 1937), *I Know Where I'm Going* (Michael Powell and Emeric Pressburger, 1945) and *The Brothers* (David MacDonald, 1947).[24] Caughie also suggests that the *Scotch Reels* analysis was also flawed by the deployment of a rather homogenous conception of the Kailyard tradition, blind to the anti-Kailyard discourse of the novels of John MacDougall Hay and George Douglas Brown.[25] These writers deployed the familiar tropes of the Kailyard but in a critical and oppositional way, revealing the repressive and negative underbelly of the small Scottish community. Caughie suggests this could be similarly applied to the films of Bill Douglas, and could equally provide a context for analysing *The Brothers*,

The Kidnappers (Philip Leacock, 1953) or even John Laurie's brief but memorably unsettling appearance as the jealous, patriarchal crofter in Hitchcock's *The Thirty-Nine Steps* (1935).[26]

Broadening the frame of analysis, Cairns Craig has subsequently argued that the kind of critique epitomised by *Scotch Reels* was actually based on the profound antipathy towards the kitsch and inauthentic nature of Scottish popular culture. For him, this negativity was an inevitability given the project's reliance on the categories of Marxism and modernism, stressing the universality of historical process:

> What the Scotch Myths theory wanted was to mock the Scottish past out of existence so that we could start over with a clean slate. It wanted Scotland to be in *real* history, not fake history, and real history, of course, was the one narrative of class operating everywhere the same; real history was the history of our incorporation into a modernity in which all advanced countries were identical with each other and all other places would eventually catch up and share the same identity. Real history, in other words, happened as though geography, and difference, and alternative pasts did not matter, as though we had become inheritors of one past (the development of capitalism; the development of socialism) which was everywhere the same and which was carrying us into a future of identically 'pluralist' societies.[27]

To subscribe to such processes of universality is, for Craig, to ultimately deny difference and to negate the need for a distinctive and unique Scottish cultural identity. And even if this perspective had some veracity in 1982, it has surely been eclipsed by the subsequent collapse of socialism and the resurgence of nationalism and issues of national identity as a defining, sometimes catastrophic, element of contemporary European experience.

Craig's assessment has found echoes elsewhere. Pam Cook, for example, also addresses the confinement of the *Scotch Reels* analysis to the realms of a debased popular culture, locating the project within a broader tendency of writings on national culture to regard the realm of the popular with deep suspicion, to effectively see it as a repository of regressive or reactionary ideologies.[28] This is why the popular is countered with an appeal towards forms of 'progressive' modernism. For Cook, such a strategy attests not only to the critic's cultural elitism but also a profound unease with his own national identity:

> This inability to confront their implication in popular expressions of national identity afflicts many writers on the left. In their desire to be pure, untainted by the slightest whiff of conservatism, they construct the popular as mediator of the ideologically impure. In so doing, they fail to come to terms with either

the complexity of the popular and its imaginative appeal, or their own investment in traditional forms and myths – what Alison Light in *Forever England* (1991) calls 'the Tory in us all'.[29]

Such analyses of culture invariably oppose romantic nostalgia with the desire to identify a more 'authentic' construction of national identity that will express reality rather than languid and regressive fantasy. But as Cook suggests, 'it is rarely considered that nostalgia might play a productive role in national identity, releasing the desire for social change or resistance'.[30] Cook's critique also raises the important issue of gender: the popular, the nostalgic, the inauthentic being closely associated with feminine forms of pleasure such as the romantic novel, soap opera, cinema melodrama, while the progressive, serious and high cultural associations of modernism have often been coded masculine. The gendering of Scottish cultural identity has also been noted by the sociologist David McCrone who suggests that the modernist project of giving voice to the distinctive and self-contained essence of a national culture relegated women to mere guardians of the moral and family values of the nation:

> It is, then, no coincidence that those identities diagnosed as archetypically
> Scottish by friend and foe alike – the Kailyard, Tartanry and Clydesidism –
> have little place for women. ... there is no analogous 'lass o' pairts'; the image
> of Tartanry is a male-military image (and kilts were not a female form of
> dress); and the Clydeside icon was a skilled, male worker who was man
> enough to 'care' for his womenfolk.[31]

At the root of the problem is the particular conception of the function and value of myth deployed in *Scotch Reels*. As Cairns Craig notes, this is a Marxist conception in which myth is serving to mask the real conditions of economic and class oppression. Consequently the only progressive response is for such myths to be 'unveiled, demystified, torn aside so that the real can stand forth and be recognised for what it is'.[32] Craig identifies an alternative and more positive conception, derived from Nietzsche, in which myth functions to redeem humanity from the dissipating affects of history. Rather than negating action, it is the creation of myths that make creative human action possible. Moreover, Craig argues that the 'great cultural outpouring of the 1980s and 1990s' has effectively moved Scotland from the Marxian moment, crystallised by the Scotch-myths position, to a Nietzschian moment marked by the construction of new myths about Scottish identity and history. The cultural renaissance alluded to by Craig has been seen by some cultural commentators as a direct response to the ill-fated referendum on Scottish devolution in 1979 – in which the majority vote in support of a Scottish parliament was undermined by the rule that 40 per cent of the

Scottish electorate had to be in favour – and the election of a new Tory administration representing, under the leadership of Margaret Thatcher, the insular
values and aspirations of Middle England. Angus Calder, for example, regards
the emergence of a new sense of cultural independence in Scotland in the light
of: 'an increasing sense of distance from the United Kingdom's south-eastern
metropolis which turned, during the Thatcher years into something not far from
contempt, and a corresponding urge to relate art, music and literature in Scotland to non-insular tendencies, to what had been going on in Europe, in the New
World and in the South (Third World).'[33]

As this book will, I hope, demonstrate, the cinema has also occupied an
important position in this cultural renaissance. But the value of Craig's reclamation of the value of myth also suggests alternative ways of thinking about the
history of representations of Scotland, particularly within such a popular mass
medium as the cinema. Rather than the uncompromising condemnation of
Scotch Reels, which, by virtue of its moment of inception, is more a reflection of
the radical political reaction to the dissatisfaction of the late 1970s than the 'carnivalesque activities of the 1980s which Scots improvised to defy the Thatcherite
threat to their country',[34] this history needs to be re-examined with a sensitivity
towards questions of inclusiveness, popularity, pleasure and the complex negotiation of cultural meaning. As Adrienne Scullion incisively puts it:

> The role of mythology, legend and fable, the Gothic, the supernatural and the
> unconscious within the development of the Scottish imagination is not a
> symptom of psychosis but a sophisticated engagement with the fantastic that
> other cultures might celebrate as magic realism.[35]

Screening Scotland: Outline of the Study

The historical analysis that comprises the first half of this book will reconsider
the major representational contours in the map of Scottish cinema inspired by
this more positive conception of the production and consumption of popular
culture. The first chapter will examine the centralisation of British film production and the consequences of this for representations of Scotland. Stressing
continuities within a history of intellectual and artistic emigration since the
eighteenth century, the contribution of key Scots to the development of a
London-based British cinema will also be considered. Having established this
essentially externalised perspective, I will then explore three major traditions
in the representation of Scotland that bear certain similarities to the familiar
tropes of Kailyard, Tartanry and Clydesidism but without embracing the profound negative connotations associated with them. The first addresses directly
the construction of Scotland as a peripheral and remote place far from the met-

ropolitan heart of British culture, an imaginary space in which a range of fantasies, desires, fears and anxieties have been projected. The second examines the cinematic contribution to the romantic legacy of Jacobitism, the dominant theme in the representation of Scottish history, looking beyond the negative associations of Tartanry to embrace concepts of cinematic spectacle and pleasure. While the third focuses on the very different set of concerns that informs the representation of urban Scotland as a site defined by industrial activity and working-class leisure – moving the analysis beyond the association of Scotland with a particular kind of geographical and social environment and providing a means of exploring the theme of social consensus and Scotland's patriotic incorporation with the Union.

The second half of the book charts the emergence of a very different kind of Scottish cinema, one that could gradually claim to be an increasingly independent or indigenous entity. The roots of this emergence are traced by way of a close consideration of the sponsored documentary in Scotland from the 1930s through to the 1980s, one area in which limited forms of state intervention allowed the establishment and nurturing of an indigenous film-making sector comprising a small number of independent production units. Alongside this strand of development is the equally significant history of Scottish television drama, and the gradual convergence of cinema and television in terms of production techniques and institutional structures. This major agent of this convergence has been Channel Four in its role both as the single most important funding body in British cinema and a national broadcaster established with a remit to address the cultural diversity of the United Kingdom. The final three chapters consider the emergence of the Scottish feature film in the 1980s and 1990s. The first concentrates on the issue of 'Art Cinema' during the 1980s, examining the inspirational work of a small number of distinctive writer/directors such as Bill Forsyth and Bill Douglas characterised by overtly personal concerns and an affinity with certain continental modes of cinema. The extension and consolidation of Scottish production in the 1990s is then charted in two different ways. First, the establishment of important new sources of funding for Scottish production is explored in detail in the attempt to identify the key components of a new indigenous infrastructure. This is followed by a detailed analysis of the numerous features produced during the latter half of the 1990s, the quantity of output even allowing a tentative discussion of the reworking of the dominant representational motifs in terms of a new intensified engagement with urban experience, a reworking of the peripheral and a resurrection of the historical. This breadth and depth of this productivity has not only positioned cinema at the forefront of the ongoing Scottish cultural revival, it also signifies for the first time the emergence of something laying claim to being a *bona fide* 'Scottish National Cinema'.

Notes

1   Norman Wilson, *Representing Scotland: A Film Survey*, (Edinburgh: Edinburgh Film Guild, 1945).

2   Charles Oakley, *Fifty Years at the Pictures* (Glasgow: Scottish Film Council, 1946).

3   Colin McArthur (ed.), *Scotch Reels: Scotland in Cinema and Television* (London: BFI, 1982).

4   Eddie Dick (ed.), *From Limelight to Satellite: A Scottish Film Book* (London: BFI/SFC, 1990).

5   Forsyth Hardy, *Scotland in Film* (Edinburgh: Edinburgh University Press, 1990).

6   David Bruce, *Scotland the Movie* (Edinburgh: Polygon/SFC, 1996).

7   Hardy's association with film culture in Scotland began in the late 1920s and encompasses the founding of the Edinburgh Film Guild, the magazine *Cinema Quarterly*, the Edinburgh International Film Festival (all with Norman Wilson) and the second Films of Scotland Committee. The promotion of the documentary film was an important aspect of all these initiatives.

8   Bruce was a protégé of Hardy, working as his assistant at Films of Scotland in the 1960s before subsequently becoming Director of the Scottish Film Council from 1986 to 1994.

9   See for example Janet McBain, *Pictures Past: Scottish Cinemas Remembered* (Edinburgh: Moorfoot, 1985), Michael Thompson, *Silver Screen in the Silver City* (Aberdeen: Aberdeen University Press, 1988), Maurice Lindsay and David Bruce, *Edinburgh: Past and Present* (London: Robert Hale, 1990), Peter Bruce, *100 Years of Glasgow's Amazing Cinemas* (Edinburgh: Polygon, 1996).

10 Cairns Craig, 'Myths Against History: Tartanry and Kailyard in 19th-Century Scottish Literature', in Colin McArthur (ed.), *Scotch Reels*, p. 10.

11 Tom Nairn, *The Break-Up of Britain*, 2nd expanded edn, (London: Verso, 1981) p. 158.

12 This was the fourth screen adaptation of Barrie's novel. Previous productions included a 1915 British version directed by Percy Nash for Neptune, and two Hollywood adaptations made in 1921 by Paramount and 1922 by Vitagraph.

13 Colin McArthur, 'Scotland and the Cinema: The Iniquity of the Fathers', *Scotch Reels*, p. 45.

14 For McArthur, *The Maggie* represents 'Scotland at its most self-lacerative', ibid., p. 47.

15 Ibid., pp. 47–9.

16 Ibid., p. 66.

17 Ibid., pp. 67–8.

18 During the 1970s McArthur wrote a regular film column for the socialist weekly *Tribune*. Consequently, his commitment to socialism and the potentially progressive qualities of cinema dominates (and indeed continues to dominate) his writings.

19 Forsyth Hardy, *Scotland in Film*, p. 5. The ghost of authenticity is difficult to lay as is demonstrated in Jeffrey Richards's recent essay on representations of Scotland. Richards begins with an unapologetic and spirited defence of the pleasures of the 'inauthentic' in popular cinema as represented by films like *Brigadoon* and *Whisky Galore!*. Yet when he later attempts to deal with films with which he has little sympathy, such as more contemporary productions marred by an over-dependence on graphic violence, he falls back on a more familiar style of critique, describing *Braveheart* as 'a contrived, one-dimensional and schematic distortion of the known facts of the life of ... William Wallace'. *Film and British National Identity: From Dickens to Dad's Army* (Manchester: Manchester University Press, 1998), p. 185.

20 For alternative readings of Mackendrick's films in particular, see John Brown, 'Land Beyond Brigadoon', *Sight and Sound*, Winter 1983/84, Charles Barr, *Ealing Studios* (London: Cameron & Tayleur/David & Charles, 1977), chapter on *Whisky Galore!* and Philip Kemp, *Lethal Innocence: The Cinema of Alexander Mackendrick* (London: Methuen, 1991), chapters 2 and 5.

21 John Caughie, 'Representing Scotland: New Questions for Scottish Cinema' in Eddie Dick (ed.), *From Limelight to Satellite*.

22 Andrew Noble, 'Bill Douglas's Trilogy' in Eddie Dick (ed.), *From Limelight to Satellite*.

23 *My Childhood* (1972), *My Ain Folk* (1973) and *My Way Home* (1978).

24 This point was also made by John Brown in a letter to *Cencrastus*, vol. 12, Spring 1983.

25 This anti-Kailyard tradition is epitomised by Brown's 1901 novel *The House with Green Shutters*, and Hay's 1914 work *Gillespie*. The former is described by literary scholar Roderick Watson as 'a howl of anger at the sentimentality of Thrums (a reference to the work of J.M. Barrie) and all its Kailyard inheritors', *The Literature of Scotland* (Basingstoke: Macmillan, 1984), p. 332.

26 As Tom Ryall notes, the sequence in which the hero Richard Hannay (Robert Donat) encounters the crofter and his downtrodden wife, sketched with equal depth and subtlety by Peggy Ashcroft, 'introduces a powerful current of sexual repression and cruelty which contrasts somewhat starkly with the tone of the rest of the film'. *Alfred Hitchcock and the British Cinema* (London: Athlone, 1986), p. 129.

27 Cairns Craig, 'Absences' in *Out of History: Narrative Paradigms in Scottish and British Culture* (Edinburgh: Polygon, 1996), p. 112.

28 Pam Cook, *Fashioning the Nation: Costume and Identity in British Cinema* (London: BFI, 1996).

29 Ibid., p. 24.

30 Ibid., p. 26.

31 David McCrone, *Understanding Scotland: The Sociology of a Stateless Nation* (London: Routledge, 1992), p. 190.

32 Cairns Craig, 'Posting to the Future' in *Out of History*, p. 219.

33 Angus Calder, 'Art for a New Scotland?' in *Revolving Culture: Notes from the Scottish Republic* (London: I.B. Tauris, 1994), p. 244.

34 Angus Calder, 'Introduction: Culture, Republic and Carnival' in *Revolving Culture*, p. 11.

35 Adrienne Scullion, 'Feminine Pleasures and Masculine Indignities: Gender and Community in Scottish Drama' in Christopher Whyte (ed.), *Gendering the Nation: Studies in Modern Scottish Literature* (Edinburgh: Edinburgh University Press, 1995), p. 201.

Part One

EXTERNAL CONSTRUCTIONS

Chapter One
Scotland and the British Cinema

Perhaps the major difficulty in examining or analysing the historical relationship between cinema and Scotland is the thorny question of what constitutes a 'Scottish film'? Since the very beginnings of the cinema a great many films have been made which feature Scottish subject-matter, Scottish locations, Scottish actors and even on occasion Scottish directors. But practically all of these have, by and large, been initiated, developed, financed and produced by individuals and companies based either in London or Los Angeles. In other words, from an *industrial* and *institutional* point of view 'Scottish' cinema is a construct subsumed within the history of the British cinema or of Hollywood. This is not to say that these films are somehow irrelevant or uninteresting; indeed they are informed by the discursive practices within which the dominant representations of Scotland and the Scots have been constructed. In her invaluable filmography comprising works whose content reflected some aspect of 'Scottishness', Janet McBain lists almost 350 titles released between 1898 and 1990.[1] This filmography charts the contours of the historical relationship between Scotland and film, beginning with a spate of early actuality, comedy and trick films featuring Highland dancers and hallucinating drunks before producers recognised the rich potential of Scottish history and literature as a source. By 1914 there had been no less than six productions based on the life of Mary Queen of Scots, five versions of *Macbeth* and several adaptations of the works of Sir Walter Scott, Robert Louis Stevenson and J.M. Barrie.[2] This process intensified as the longer narrative feature film emerged as the dominant cinematic form in the teens and 1920s and many of the films made from this point onwards will be examined in detail in the next three chapters of this book. But, first of all, I want to focus on the Scottish contribution to the formative development of cinema in Britain and the subsequent process of centralisation that came to define the British film industry.

The Early Development of the Cinema in Scotland
The development of the film industry in Britain involved the emergence of distinct but related spheres of activity: production, distribution and exhibition.

From the point of view of exhibition, the cinema established itself very rapidly in Scotland as a popular form of entertainment. The first public display of the Edison Kinetoscope recorded in Scotland was in Edinburgh on 24 December 1894 at H.E. Moss's Christmas Carnival, Waverley Market.[3] A major entrepreneur in the world of variety theatre, Moss was also instrumental in the first screening of projected moving pictures to a paying audience in Scotland. This event occurred on 13 April 1896 at his Empire Palace Theatre in Edinburgh, a mere six weeks after the first public demonstration of the Lumière *cinématographe* in London, on 28 February. In the very early days of the medium, the apparatus itself was the object of fascination and there is some confusion surrounding the Edinburgh event in terms of the actual device used to project the images. David Bruce notes that a report in the *Scotsman* of 14 April 1896 rather confusingly refers to both the 'Cinematographe' and Edison's Kinetoscope, but as the majority of the programme of films shown were by the British pioneers Robert Paul and Birt Acres it is more like that the projection equipment in question was in fact Acres's kineoptikon.[4] The *Scotsman* report noted insufficient brightness in the image, a flaw which is consistent with Acres's device. If this is the case, then the Scottish debut of the celebrated Lumière machine occurred in Glasgow on 16 May at the Ice Skating Palace in Sauchiehall Street. It was presented by Arthur Hubner, who, as Charles Oakley notes, subsequently became the first showman to present moving pictures in Scotland on a regular basis.[5] The Lumière cinématographe, under the management of Felicien Trewey who had brought the device to London, subsequently appeared in Edinburgh at the Empire Theatre for the first two weeks in June 1896, returning for subsequent bookings in July and September; while David Devant, owner of the Egyptian Hall in London's Piccadilly, toured the north-east of Scotland with Robert Paul's Theatrograph in October.[6]

The presentation of early film shows in music halls, vaudeville theatres and fairground travelling bioscopes gradually gave way to exhibition in purpose-built cinemas, which began to emerge from around 1909. According to Rachael Low, by 1917 there were 90 circuits in Britain operating 429 cinemas, and in three years this had increased to 157 circuits with 787 cinemas.[7] In each case, around 25 per cent of the cinemas were controlled by a small number of big circuits with ten or more halls. Cinema building in Scotland during this period was considerable and by 1920 four of the top twelve cinema circuits in Britain were Scottish owned and controlled.[8] This set a trend which was to continue with Scotland remaining an important sector of the British exhibition market. The historian Christopher Harvie identifies the cinema as a particularly important form of leisure for the Scottish population, noting that in 1950 Glaswegians attended the cinema on average 51 times a year and the Scots as a whole 36 times, compared with an English national average of 28 visits per annum.[9]

While the majority of equipment manufacturers and film-makers were based in London, important developments in cinematography were occurring elsewhere, particularly in Brighton and in Yorkshire, during the formative first decade of the new medium.[10] But by 1914 economic pressures had resulted in the greater concentration of film production in the south-east. Of the forty-seven production companies active in Britain during the 1906–14 period listed by Rachael Low, all but seven were located in and around London.[11] This pattern intensified in the 1920s as a more modern and highly capitalised industry began to emerge under the twin pressures of the 1927 Quota Act and the coming of sound. The distribution side of the industry had undergone a similar process of rationalisation in the 1920s, resulting in a comparatively small number of large rental companies with close links to the production sector, based mainly in Soho in the West End of London and resulting in the label 'Wardour Street' coming to signify the industry as a whole.

While Low makes no reference to Scottish film-making whatsoever, there were a small but significant number of isolated attempts to establish some kind of production north of the border during the early years of the new medium, particularly in the field of 'topical' or 'actuality' material. Some of these films were produced by English pioneers like Robert Paul who in August 1896 shot films depicting Glasgow street scenes and of the Gordon Highlanders leaving Maryhill Barracks, described in *The Era* as 'a stirring incident that never fails to elicit the heartiest applause'.[12] On 3 October 1896, Queen Victoria and her guests including Tsar Nicholas II of Russia, were filmed at Balmoral by J. & F. Downey of South Shields, the first moving pictures of British Royalty according to John Barnes. Other important productions included an 1897 Biograph film of the Gordon Highlanders made to capitalise on the regiment's recent military success on the Northwest Frontier. While in 1899 the Warwick Trading Company produced three major Scottish series: *On Royal Deeside*, *The gathering of the clans at Invercharron, Ardgay*, and an extraordinary 'phantom ride' depicting a journey from Dalmeny to Dunfermline via the Forth Road Bridge.[13]

But there was also important activity on the part of indigenous producers, who tended to also operate as touring exhibitors. One of the first such pioneers was William Walker, a bookseller and magic lanternist from Aberdeen, who in 1896, purchased a cinematograph machine and a selection of films to augment his lantern shows. A year later, he had begun to make his own films of local events which proved popular with audiences in the north-east. Walker was even granted permission to film Queen Victoria on 22 May 1897 and in the following October, he presented a programme of films at Balmoral, including scenes from the Diamond Jubilee procession in London as well as films shot locally in Aberdeen. Another important exhibitor/producer was the Glasgow-based J. Lizars, whose films were made available in London and who was also requested to present moving pictures at Balmoral. Other key figures include the Glasgow showmen William 'Prince' Bendon and George Green (whose family would become central to the development of cinema exhibition in Scotland), and the rather more obscure Gaylor from Hawick. Collectively, these pioneers established a basis for Scottish film production, instigating a small but tenacious tradition of indigenous non-fiction film-making. David Hutchison notes that certain cinema proprietors would also commission amateur and semi-professional film-makers to record important local events to help attract audiences. Green's company went one stage further in 1917, launching their own weekly newsreel, *Scottish Moving Picture News*, in line with the operations of London-based companies such as Topical Budget, Gaumont and Pathé. As Greens were also involved in cinema distribution, they could legitimately lay claim to being the first vertically integrated film company in Britain. The demand for sponsored film-making also led to the establishment of production companies such as Scottish Film Productions, formed in 1928 in Glasgow, which produced its own film magazine, *Things that Happen*, during the 1930s, and Campbell Harper Films, set up in Edinburgh in 1930.

By the mid-late teens, the narrative fiction film emerged as the pre-eminent form of cinematic entertainment, a process which is closely related to the concentration of production and distribution in a smaller number of companies, based mainly in London. The rare attempts to produce 'story films' in Scotland tend to be isolated 'one-off' affairs, and in most cases the resulting films have been lost.[14] Greens made one venture into fiction in 1916 with the two-reel comedy *His Highness* about which very little is known. More significant is a 1911 version of *Rob Roy* directed by Arthur Vivian for United Films with Glasgow stage actor John Clyde as the eponymous hero, and claimed by Janet McBain as the first British three-reel feature. The film was made on location in Aberfoyle and in a studio in Rouken Glen[15] on the outskirts of Glasgow that had been established by William Bendon's company for hire to Scottish producers. The studio was rather rudimentary, as David Cloy notes:

> Originally constructed as a tram depot, the building's power supply was still linked to the electrical current from the tramway power station, a linkage which resulted in lighting difficulties for the producers. Every time a tram passed on the main road outside the power to the studio was drained causing a 'fade out' and if two trams passed simultaneously, power was lost altogether![16]

In 1919 the Ace Film Producing Company made the feature *The Harp King* at the studio. Directed by Max Leder, this five-reel romance told the story of a farmer who wins the hand of the laird's daughter by his skilful playing of the harp. The film proved to be a great success in Glasgow but shortly afterwards Ace Films were bankrupt. As Patricia Warren notes in her history of British studios,[17] Rouken Glen later became the home of Broadway Cinema Productions whose output included the comedy feature *Football Daft* (*Fitba Daft*) (Victor W. Rowe, 1921) adapted from a music hall sketch about the misfortunes of a temperance observer who mistakenly drinks whisky.[18] As suggested by the title, the film also included exciting footage of a football match shot at Ibrox, the home of Glasgow Rangers. *Football Daft* gained a nationwide release and was extensively reviewed. Despite plans for further ventures, this was to be Broadway's last production and by 1924 the studio had closed. But like *Rob Roy* and *The Harp King*, no prints of *Football Daft* are known to have survived.

One early Scottish feature which has not been lost is *Mairi – the Romance of a Highland Maiden* (1912), a tale of smuggling and romance written, produced and shot on location at North Kessock by an Inverness photographer Andrew Patterson. A rather amateur effort featuring unconvincing performances, *Mairi* appears to have been a one-off production with Patterson returning to his portrait photography business. Elsewhere, the celebrated music hall entertainer Harry Lauder made his own intervention into film production in 1920 with two films, *All For the Sake of Mary* and *I Love a Lassie*, featuring himself and Effie Vallance. For whatever reason, neither was released commercially and Lauder's future involvement in cinema was to be as a performer only – most notably in two films directed by George Pearson for his London-based company Welsh–Pearson–Elder: *Huntingtower* (1927) and the part-talkie *Auld Lang Syne* (1929). The coming of sound, which necessitated the kind of major investment in new production facilities and equipment beyond the means of fly-by-night Scottish producers, curtailed the distribution of the 1928 production *The Immortals of Bonnie Scotland*. This was a reissue of two biographical films previously released in 1926 and directed by Maurice Sandground for the production company Scottish Film Academy: *The Life of Robert Burns* and *The Life of Sir Walter Scott*. As with most of the other efforts noted here, both films are also lost.

The Scottish Contribution to a 'British' National Cinema

The centralisation of the British film industry meant that subsequent Scottish contributions to the development of cinema were by individuals who had made the inevitable move to London. Such southward migration after the Union of 1707 had become increasingly common for ambitious Scots from the late eighteenth century onwards. Tom Nairn identifies a major wave of southern emigration by Scottish intellectuals during the nineteenth century, one of the consequences of which was the creation of a cultural void in Scotland that came to be filled by what Nairn calls a 'sub national culture', expressed through the regressive tropes of Tartanry and Kailyardism. At the same time the *émigré* Scots were to play a major role in the development of a distinctively British culture:

> Our former intelligentsia lost its cohesion and unitary function (its nature as an élite) and the individual members poured their formidable energies into the authentically 'organic community' centred on London. There, they played a very large part in formulating the new national and imperial culture-community. We must all be at times painfully aware of how England to this day languishes under the 'tradition' created by the Carlyle-Ruskin school of mystification, as well as the brilliant political inheritance nurtured by Keir Hardie and J. Ramsay MacDonald.[19]

The Scottish contribution to the construction and maintenance of a consciously 'British' national culture (as opposed to the idea that Scottish culture was subject to English hegemonic appropriation) is also noted by the historian Linda Colley[20] and literary scholar Robert Crawford, the latter arguing that 'in recent centuries much Scottish cultural energy has been directed towards the maintenance not simply of a Scottish but of a fully British ethos in which Scotland can play its part. Scott's novels, the *Encyclopaedia Britannica*, Sir John Reith's BBC – all of these are Scottish-rooted institutions geared to presenting Britishness that was significantly more than Englishness.'[21]

But while the impact of Scots on British politics and culture in general is clearly obvious, the role they played in the development of cinema has not been subject to the same level of critical attention. Indeed a quick trawl of the thousands of individuals associated with the British cinema during its heyday from the 1930 to the 1960s reveals relatively few high-profile Scots, the obvious examples being a handful of directors like Alexander Mackendrick, Harry Watt and David MacDonald, and stars such as Jack Buchanan, Will Fyffe, John Laurie, Finlay Currie, Deborah Kerr, Gordon Jackson, Ian Bannen and, the most famous of them all, Sean Connery.[22] But two Scots were to have, in very different ways, a major impact on how the cinema developed in Britain as a popular (and profitable) entertainment, and as a vital form of cultural expression.

The Father of the British Documentary

The major single influence behind the emergence and development of the documentary in Britain was John Grierson, a Scot from Stirlingshire. It was Grierson who established the documentary film unit at the Empire Marketing Board in 1929, who directed the first major British documentary, *Drifters*, in the same year, and who subsequently assembled a group of creative film-makers into one of the most celebrated 'movements' in British cinema history. The documentary

John Grierson, father of the British documentary

of the 1930s is closely associated with a social-democratic project that regarded cinema as the ideal form of mass communication and education in modern society. As practitioner, administrator and polemicist, Grierson did more than anyone else to shape this vision and the subsequent mission of the British documentarists. The genesis of Grierson's world view has been located by Ian Aitken in his intellectual formation at Glasgow University where he studied English and moral philosophy between 1919 and 1923: 'Grierson's epistemology, and aesthetic and political ideas, were primarily derived from a tradition of philosophical idealism which he encountered in Scotland prior to 1924. This tradition influenced Grierson's activities as a producer and administrator, and had a major influence on the development of the documentary film movement during the inter-war period.'[23]

Philosophy at Glasgow University during this period was dominated by neo-Kantian and Hegelian idealist traditions. The influence they exerted on the young Grierson informed his concept of society as an organic totality in which individuals and institutions were integrated at different levels. Conflict was the consequence of individuals and institutions failing to perceive their interdependency, an assertion which led Grierson to mistrust individualism while at the same time valorising the state as the agent in society offering the best means for promoting integration and constraining individualism. Hence his subsequent pursuit of state sponsorship for forms of film production which would in turn help to reinforce the very fabric of the state through the education of the population in the rights and responsibilities of citizenship. In addition to Glasgow, the other major centre of idealist philosophy during this period was Oxford, Balliol College in particular, and Aitken suggests that the combined field of influence served to link Grierson with Stephen Tallents, the Oxford graduate who would later employ him at the Empire Marketing Board (EMB), and several other individuals who would subsequently play major roles in establishing the public service and educational policies of the BBC.

Grierson's commitment to the use of symbolic expression to represent and foster an understanding of social interconnection dovetailed with an interest in the art of the film. This had been fostered both by his travels and studies in the United States between 1924 and 1927 and his involvement in the minority British film culture of late 1920s. For Grierson, the mission of the documentary should not be a didactic one, but rather it should strive to instil an understanding of social cohesion and process. As Aitken notes:

> Grierson defined the principal function of the documentary film as that of representing the inter-dependence and evolution of social relations in a dramatic and symbolic way. This function was, therefore, both sociological and aesthetic at the same time. It was sociological in that it involved the representation of interdependent social relations; and it was aesthetic in that it involved the use of imaginative and symbolic means to that end.[24]

Such a combination of the aesthetic and the sociological is for Aitken clearly identifiable in the British documentary from Grierson's own *Drifters* (which borrows heavily from the montage techniques of Eisenstein)[25] to *Song of Ceylon* and *Night Mail*.

But there are other influences on Grierson's formation beyond those of idealist philosophy. Forsyth Hardy notes that Grierson was a member of the Fabian Society and subsequently instrumental in forming the New University Labour Club in 1921.[26] This was a period of considerable political activism in Glasgow and Grierson himself later claimed as his 'masters' the great leaders of Scottish socialism including James Maxton, Keir Hardie, Bob Smillie and John Wheatley.[27] But despite Glasgow's association with hard-line radicalism symbolised by the term 'Red Clydeside', Aitken is at pains to point out that these figures were central to a tradition of moderate reformism, advocating an organic view of society and a parliamentary road to socialism which was inimical to the Marxist belief in class struggle and revolution.[28] Grierson also shared the religious elements of Hardie and the Catholic Wheatley's political philosophy. His own father was a schoolmaster, 'a dominie in the old tradition of Scottish education' as Forsyth Hardy puts it,[29] and Grierson was consequently raised in accordance with the traditions of Scottish Presbyterianism. The church and the school formed the backbone of a very particular form of popular democracy which was as repressive and authoritarian in its precepts as it was democratic in its forms. Religion was to play a more direct role in the young Grierson's life during his university years when he would occasionally preach sermons in churches around Glasgow. It is in these sermons, according to Hardy, that the germ of his subsequent vision of collective responsibility and social progress can be detected.

John Caughie directly links Grierson's formative years with those of another Scottish *émigré* who arguably played an even greater role in British cultural life during the inter-war period. John Reith, the first Director-General of the British Broadcasting Corporation, was the son of a Church of Scotland Minister in Glasgow. His personal influence on the development of the BBC, its relationship to the state and the role it assumed in the construction of a national culture has much in common with Grierson's vision of the social purpose of the documentary. Both men shared a concept of the relationship between the state and the public which stressed the ideas of 'independence' and 'public service'. They were also profoundly concerned with film and broadcasting as 'serious' cultural forms rather than frivolous entertainment. Again, for Caughie, the Presbyterian underpinning of such concepts has a significance beyond the merely symbolic:

> by the beginning of the twentieth century the Scottish presbytery was a system of local democracies quite at ease with the state, distinct from the tradition of English popular democracies which had been formed in organised conflict with the state for much of the nineteenth century. Reith and Grierson, quite different in most respects, shared a tradition which saw no contradiction between serving the people and serving the state.[30]

This 'British' perspective here is crucial in that Scottish Protestantism, particularly during the Edwardian period, was strongly supportive of the imperial project, ensuring that a distinctive Scottish cultural identity did not place any undue strain on the Union. As Graham Walker notes:

> [Presbyterianism] was a driving force behind an imperial identity which viewed the Empire as a means of showcasing and enhancing Scottish natural talents and virtues. Presbyterianism was central to a moral outlook which galvanised Scots to meet the challenges of empire building, missionary work, wealth creation and governance. Scotland's partnership with England in this

imperial mission did not, in the view of Scots, attenuate Scottish nationality; rather they considered their Scottishness to be complemented by wider British imperial identification.[31]

One of the central tenants shared by the Griersonian documentary movement and the Reithian idea of public service broadcasting, was the idea of a unified national culture, which places the two men firmly in the tradition of *émigré* intellectuals noted by Tom Nairn. Kathryn and Philip Dodd have also noted the extent to which a concern with the construction of a national culture pervades not only Grierson's work as a documentarian but also in his writings which are dominated by 'ideas of "citizenship", "national education" "the corporate nature of community life", and their centrality to any serious thinking about film'.[32] Grierson's reputation might have been called into question in recent years,[33] but he arguably remains the most high-profile Scottish figure in the history of British cinema.

John Maxwell and the Building of a British Film Industry

At the same time that the sponsored documentary began to make an impact in Britain, the mainstream commercial industry had also undergone a major process of transformation. Prompted by the Quota Act of 1927, which provided a level of protection for indigenous production, and followed by the conversion to sound in 1929–31, the industry was massively reorganised during this period. A key feature of this reorganisation was the building of modern studios and the emergence of vertical integration along the Hollywood model. This, it was hoped, would raise production values and help British cinema to compete with Hollywood, which had dominated British exhibition from the mid-1910s. One of the aims of the 1927 Act was to encourage the emergence of one or more vertically integrated film combines bringing together production, distribution and exhibition. Two such corporate entities did emerge: the Gaumont British Picture Corporation (GBPC) and the Associated British Picture Corporation, creating a duopoly which in various guises was to dominate the industry until the 1970s. Gaumont British was consolidated by the Ostrer brothers, Jewish merchant bankers who had helped finance an earlier management buy-out of the Gaumont production company. But it is the rise of GBPC's rival which is of interest here. As Alan Eyles notes:

Associated British Cinema and its sister companies in distribution and production were one of the unqualified success stories of the British Film industry in the Thirties, and of British business in general during a difficult decade. The Associated British group grew larger and larger, making profits and paying dividends every year, without any of the financial crises that

attended its major rival, the Gaumont-British Picture Corporation. … the
company owed its success principally to the drive, perseverance and financial
perspicacity of one man … a dour, tough, canny, fair-minded and honest
Scotsman named John Maxwell.[34]

Maxwell had first become involved in cinema via his legal firm, Maxwell,
Hodgson & Co, which, by 1912, had acquired a stake in several cinemas, beginning with the Prince's Cinema in Springburn, Glasgow.[35] In 1917 his interests
were merged into a single new company, Scottish Cinema and Variety Theatres
Ltd (SCVT) which by 1920 controlled twenty cinemas, the largest circuit in
Scotland and fourth biggest in Britain.[36] Maxwell continued to expand his
involvement in exhibition, registering Savoy Cinemas in London in 1924. But
he also moved into both distribution and production, becoming chairman of
the renting firm Wardour films in 1923 and two years later joining the board
of British National Pictures which had recently established studios in Boreham
Wood, Elstree. British National was founded by an American entrepreneur, J.D.
Williams, who had been instrumental in the development of the First National
combine in Hollywood. But in 1927 he was ousted by his board amidst allegations
of profligacy and replaced by Maxwell, whose plans, as Andrew Higson notes,
were almost identical to Williams's: to establish a major vertically integrated film

John Maxwell, an architect
of vertical integration in
the British Film Industry

company with international aspirations.[37] Maxwell subsequently registered a new company, British International Pictures, in April 1927, merging it with his existing interests in distribution and exhibition. But the empire was not yet fully built. In 1928 he acquired the distribution company First National Pathé in the attempt to gain access to the American market for his films, and in November of the same year Associated British Cinemas was registered as a public concern. Vertical integration was fully consolidated in 1933 with the formation of ABPC as a holding company to take over Maxwell's various interests which by now included BIP, British Instructional Films (which had a studio in Welwyn Garden City), Wardour Films, Pathé Pictures and ABC cinemas. The ABC chain began as an amalgamation of SCVT, Savoy and the four-site Favourite Cinema group, comprising a total of forty-three cinemas. Massive expansion followed in the 1930s by way of acquisitions and the building of new theatres with the result that by 1937 the company controlled a nationwide chain of 460 halls, compared to Gaumont's chain of 345 cinemas.[38]

Maxwell had built a company which was in various corporate reincarnations to remain one of the major forces in British production, distribution and exhibition for almost half a century. For a short period, Elstree was positioned at the epicentre of an invigorated production industry, as Rachael Low notes: 'By the end of the twenties [BIP] was the biggest and most successful producer in the country by far, and the most advanced example of vertical integration in the industry. It was led by the new type of businessman with ample finance, assured of distribution and sucking in talent from wherever it lay at home or abroad.'[39]

Among the film-makers under contract at the studio during this period were Alfred Hitchcock, the prodigy who had been signed from Gainsborough in 1927 and who was to direct eleven films at Elstree. BIP was also instrumental in importing top overseas talent to Britain from America and Continental Europe, including celebrated directors like E.A. Dupont, Arthur Robison and Henrik Galeen, top-class actors like Tallulah Bankhead, Lionel Barrymore, Syd Chaplin, Carl Brissom, Anny Ondra, Lars Hanson, Lya de Putti, Anna Mae Wong and Gilda Gray, and accomplished technicians including Charles Rosher, Werner Brandes, Theodor Sparkuhl, Rene Guissart and Alfred Junge. BIP was also a leading player in the British conversion to sound, setting up a temporary sound studio equipped with the RCA Phototone sound-on-film system in 1929. The first major production to include synchronised sound was Hitchcock's *Blackmail*, released in August of that year. But the expense of the conversion of sound was to have an impact on the ambitions of the company, which shifted its concerns from the production of big-budget prestige films in favour of a programme of comedies, crime films, musicals and operettas featuring popular performers like Stanley Lupino, Gene Gerrard and the Austrian tenor Richard Tauber. Maxwell ran a tight ship and the company continued to be profitable throughout the

1930s. But BIP productions were now rarely conducive to anything more than run-of-the-mill fare aimed at the home market. As Low concludes, the output of BIP during the 1930s was 'large and varied, and efficient management ensured that it operated at a profit … but with budgets cut to the bone the films did not compare well with the Hollywood films they imitated.'[40]

The verdict of film historians on John Maxwell has been rather non-committal. Low suggests there was 'little of the impresario about him' and the studio's history was 'strangely impersonal compared to the companies run by Michael Balcon, Basil Dean and Alexander Korda'.[41] Most of the other standard commentaries pass little or no judgement. His chief of production, Walter Mycroft, the former critic and founder member of the Film Society, seems to have been universally loathed and is often cited as one of the major reasons why Hitchcock left BIP in 1932. Yet Maxwell was clearly one of a small group of ambitious producers who helped to wrench the British cinema out of the doldrums and laid the foundations for the modern successful industry which in usually associated with Alexander Korda, J. Arthur Rank and Michael Balcon. Maxwell died on 2 October 1940 and an obituary in the 1941 *Kinematograph Year Book* suggested that his single great contribution to the British film industry was to have made it respectable in the eyes of the City, financial institutions having traditionally regarded cinema with deep suspicion.

Unlike Grierson, it is difficult to relate Maxwell's success to particular elements in his Scottish upbringing, although the association of his reputation for business acumen and financial prudence as characteristic of a particular kind of Scottish stereotype will not be lost on anyone. In this respect, Maxwell can be related to another 'canny' Scottish businessman who played an important, if less auspicious, role in the emerging British industry of the 1930s. Shepperton Studios, which, with Pinewood, remains one of the two major production facilities in Britain, was founded by Norman Loudon, a Campbeltown-born accountant. Loudon began producing flicker booklets in 1927, which featured frame-by-frame images of sportsmen and which when flicked produced the illusion of movement in exactly the same way as the popular pier-end mutoscope had done. By 1932 he had formed Sound City Film Producing and Recording Studios at Shepperton where he began making low-budget quota films. Like Maxwell, Loudon proved to be an efficient and capable manager and the studio prospered during the 1930s.[42] Shepperton was requisitioned by the government during the war, and a year after it reopened in 1945 was sold by Loudon to Alexander Korda whose association with big-budget international films helped to raise the studio's profile.

So, as in other areas of business and cultural life, Scots made a major contribution to the development to a *British* cinema which to all intents and purposes reflected a highly centralised metropolitan viewpoint. Grierson's documentary movement is firmly associated with the projection of a national culture rooted in a participative but essentially patrician form of bourgeois social democracy. Such a conception bound the nation together through the related ideas of citizenship and community, effectively overcoming the potentially divisive presence of class conflict or even (although this is less important in the context of the 1930s) forms of nationalist sentiment other than that fully supportive of the British state. Maxwell's project on the other hand was to build a successful business empire that also addressed the nation as a unified whole, this time as paying customers, principally through the largest nationwide cinema chain of its time – *Associated British Cinemas* – with sites from Aberdeen to Penzance.

A Colonised Cinema?

The implications of this chapter suggests that in cinematic terms Scotland was effectively colonised by a metropolitan British film industry. This invokes Craig Beveridge and Ronnie Turnbull's provocative analysis of what they refer to as the 'eclipse of Scottish culture', a process rooted in the profoundly negative representation of Scottish culture and history by Scottish intellectuals like Tom Nairn and Colin McArthur. Drawing on Frantz Fanon's colonial concept of 'Inferiorisation', Beveridge and Turnbull elaborate their account of the operation of metropolitan power over representations of Scotland:

> The strategy of inferiorisation is fully successful when the native internalises the estimation of local culture which is propagated, acknowledging the superiority of metropolitan ways. The imperial refrain which upholds the coloniser as the representative of civilisation, progress and universal human values, is then taken up by the *évolués*, those natives who try to escape their backwardness by desperate identification with the culture of the metropolis.[43]

Following such a perspective, the close association of *émigrés* like Grierson and Maxwell with the interests and development of a London-based film industry is evidence of their own collusion. Yet this is a rather problematic position to hold both in terms of the active participation of Scots in the creation of certain 'British' institutions bearing the influence of certain ideas and values that can be related to cultural formation of the individuals concerned. In this way, the culture of the metropolis is far more heterogeneous and cosmopolitan than Beveridge and Turnbull are prepared to acknowledge. Second, the representation of Scotland by the British cinema cannot be seen simply in terms of the operation of structures of superiority/inferiority. As I hope to demonstrate in the following chapters, the dominant representations of Scotland and the Scots embody a complex set of ideas that are as much about the fantasies, the desires and the anxieties of metropolitan culture, as they are about simply confirming the imposition of cultural power over the Celtic subaltern.

Notes

1   Janet McBain, 'Scotland in Feature Film: A Filmography' in Eddie Dick (ed.), *From Limelight to Satellite: A Scottish Film Book* (London: BFI/SFC, 1990), pp. 233–53.

2   British films in general have drawn heavily on novels, short stories and plays and in the Scottish case this was to be no different. In addition to Scott, Stevenson and Barrie other figures from the world of literature and drama who have provided fertile material for the cinematic imagination include John Buchan, Compton Mackenzie, Neil Gunn, James Bridie, George Blake, Muriel Spark, James Kennaway, William McIlvanney, John Byrne, Iain Banks and Irvine Welsh.

3   For a discussion of this event and the importance of H.E. Moss, see Adrienne Scullion, 'Geggies, Empires, Cinemas: The Scottish Experience of Early Film', *Picture House*, no. 21, Summer 1996.

4   David Bruce, *Scotland the Movie* (Edinburgh: Polygon, 1996), p. 96.

5   Charles Oakley, *Fifty Years at the Pictures* (Glasgow: Scottish Film Council, 1946).

6   These tours are discussed by John Barnes in *The Beginnings of the Cinema in England, 1894–1901*, Revised vol. 1 (Exeter: University of Exeter Press, 1999).

7   Rachael Low, *The History of the British Film 1918–1929* (London: Allen & Unwin, 1971), pp. 40–1.

8   Ibid., p. 41.

9   Christopher Harvie, *No Gods and Precious Few Heroes: Scotland 1914–1980* (London: Edward Arnold, 1981), p. 121.

10 John Barnes, *The Beginnings of the Cinema in England 1894–1901: Volume 2, 1897* (Exeter: University of Exeter Press, 1996). First published in 1983. The so-called 'Brighton School' included some of the most notable British pioneers, including George Albert Smith and James Williamson.

11 Rachael Low, *The History of the British Film 1906–1914* (London: Allen & Unwin, 1949). Appendix to Chapter III, Compiled by Baynham Honri, pp. 139–40. Of the exceptions, two companies were based in Brighton, one in Hastings, two in Manchester, and two in Yorkshire.

12 Quoted in John Barnes, *The Beginnings of the Cinema in England 1894–1901*, Revised vol. 1, p. 131.

13 The latter film was 650ft long and lasted for twelve minutes.

14 A list of these 'Lost but not Forgotten' films are noted by Janet McBain in *Scotland in Silent Cinema: A commemorative catalogue to accompany the Scottish Reels programme at the Pordenone Silent Film Festival, Italy 1998* (Glasgow: Scottish Screen, 1998), pp. 28–29.

15 Some commentaries refer to the location of the studio as Thornliebank, an alternative name for the district in question which lies to the south-west of Glasgow close to Barrhead.

16 David Cloy, 'Scottish Film Production in the Silent Period' in Janet McBain (ed.), *Scotland in Silent Cinema*, p. 7.

17 Patricia Warren, *British Film Studios: An Illustrated History* (London: B.T. Batsford, 1995).

18 The Rouken Glen comedies, featuring Dora Lindsay, are noted by Charles Oakley in his survey, *Fifty Years at the Pictures* (Glasgow: Scottish Film Council, 1946).

19 Tom Nairn, *The Break-Up of Britain*, expanded edn, (London: Verso, 1981), p. 125.

20 Linda Colley, *Britons: Forging the Nation 1707–1837* (Yale University Press, 1992), Chapter 3, 'Peripheries'.

21 Robert Crawford, 'Dedefining Scotland' in Susan Bassnett (ed.), *Studying British Culture: An Introduction* (London: Routledge, 1997).

22 Some Scottish *émigrés* looked further afield than London, finding their way to Hollywood. Several Scots who appeared in Hollywood films before 1920 are noted by David Bruce, among their number are two who also gained reputations as directors. In addition to acting in both films, Donald Crisp worked as an assistant director to D.W. Griffith on *Birth of a Nation* (1915) and *Broken Blossoms* (1919), and subsequently established himself as a director before returning to acting after the coming of sound. His major performances include those in *Mutiny on the Bounty* (Frank Lloyd, 1935) alongside Charles Laughton and Clark Gable, and in John Ford's *How Green Was My Valley* (1939) for which he won the Oscar for best supporting actor. Crisp also appeared in several films with a Scottish connection, including *Beside the Bonnie Briar Bush* (1921), which he also directed, *The Little Minister*, *Mary of Scotland* and *Greyfriars Bobby*. Frank Lloyd (director of the above-noted *Mutiny on the Bounty*) was also a Scot who made a major impact on Hollywood. Born in Glasgow, Lloyd arrived in Hollywood in 1914 and within a year had begun directing. He made over 100 films, the highlights including *The Divine Lady* (1929), *Cavalcade* (1932) – both of which won him Oscars for best direction, *Mutiny on the Bounty* (1935) and *Rulers of the Sea* (1939).

23 Ian Aitken, *Film and Reform: John Grierson and the Documentary Film Movement* (London: Routledge, 1990) p. 247. See also Ian Aitken, 'John Grierson, Idealism and the Inter-War Period', *Historical Journal of Film, Radio and Television*, vol. 9, no. 3, 1989.

24 Ian Aitken, *Film and Reform*, p. 252.

25 Grierson had literally taken the Soviet director's masterpiece *Battleship Potemkin* apart and put it back together again in America where he had been hired to prepare the English inter-titles for the film.

26 Forsyth Hardy, *John Grierson: A Documentary Biography* (London: Faber & Faber, 1979), p. 11.

27 See Grierson's 'Preface' to the 1952 edition of Paul Rotha, *Documentary Film* (London: Faber & Faber, 1952).

28 Indeed it was Hardie's ILP which commanded the greatest support and in the 1922 general election won ten of Glasgow's fifteen parliamentary seats.

29 Forsyth Hardy, *John Grierson: A Documentary Biography*, p. 11.

30 John Caughie, 'Broadcasting and Cinema: Converging Histories' in Charles Barr (ed.), *All Our Yesterdays: 90 Years of British Cinema* (London: BFI, 1986), pp. 192–93.

31 Graham Walker, 'Varieties of Scottish Protestant Identity' in T.M. Devine and R.J. Finlay (eds.), *Scotland in the 20th Century* (Edinburgh: Edinburgh University Press, 1996), pp. 250–1.

32 Kathryn Dodd and Philip Dodd, 'Engendering the Nation: British Documentary Film, 1930–1939' in Andrew Higson (ed.), *Dissolving Views: Key Writings on British Cinema* (London: Cassell, 1996), p. 39.

33 See for example Nicholas Pronay's introduction to the special edition of the *Historical Journal of Film, Radio and Television*, vol. 9, no. 3, 1989, dedicated to Grierson, and Brian Winston's book *Reclaiming the Real: The Documentary Film Revisited* (London: BFI, 1995).

34 Alan Eyles, *ABC: The First Name in Entertainment* (London: Cinema Theatre Association/BFI, 1993), p. 11.

35 David Bruce, *Scotland the Movie*, p. 162.

36 Based on figures in Rachael Low, *The History of the Cinema in Britain 1918–1929*, p. 41.

37 Andrew Higson, 'Polyglot Films for an International Market: E.A. Dupont, the British Film Industry, and the Idea of a European Cinema, 1926–1930, in Higson and Richard Maltby (eds), *'Film Europe' and 'Film America'* (Exeter: University of Exeter Press, 1999).

38 Figures from Alan Eyles, *ABC: The First Name in Entertainment*.

39 Rachael Low, *The History of the British Film 1918–192*, p. 185.

40 Rachael Low, *Film-Making in 1930s Britain* (London: Allen & Unwin, 1985), p. 126.

41 Ibid., p. 116.

42 While most of the more notable films connected with Shepperton were outside productions renting facilities, Sound City did produce at least one important director during this period, John Baxter, a pioneer of British realism and social commitment with films like *Doss House* (1933) and *Song of the Plough* (1933).

43 Craig Beveridge and Ronald Turnbull, *The Eclipse of Scottish Culture* (Edinburgh: Polygon, 1989), p. 6.

Chapter Two
The View from the Metropolis

The metropolitan basis of British cinema has had major implications for the way in which Scotland has been represented. Viewed from the centre, Scotland is a distant periphery far removed from the modern, urban and cosmopolitan social world inhabited by the kind of people involved in the creation of such images. Consequently, Scotland tends to be represented as a picturesque, wild and often empty landscape, a topography that in turn suggests certain themes, narrative situations and character trajectories. Central to this is the idea of remoteness – physical, social, moral – from metropolitan rules, conventions and certainties. Scotland is consequently a space in which a range of fantasies, desires and anxieties can be explored and expressed; alternatively an exotic backdrop for adventure and romance, or a sinister and oppressive locale beyond the pale of civilisation. Such a construction of Scotland as essentially 'other' finds echoes in the representation of the far-flung outposts of the Empire in British cinema, which also function as much to expose and examine the complex subjectivity of the coloniser as to celebrate or glorify imperialism.[1] The cinematic projection of Scotland also shares certain similarities with the depiction of other remote parts of the British Isles, including Cornwall, Dartmoor, the East Anglian Fens, Cumbria and North Wales.

Scotland and 'Otherness'

In 1935 two important films appeared that in different ways characterise the dominant external cinematic construction of Scotland. Alfred Hitchcock's adaptation of *The Thirty-Nine Steps* is described by Tom Ryall as 'a quintessentially Hitchcockian film',[2] the blend of suspense, romance and light comedy made it hugely popular with audiences both in Britain and, significantly, in the United States. As John Russell Taylor notes, this success proved to be the making of Hitch as a truly international figure, resulting in the first flood of offers for him to work in Hollywood.[3] The film also introduced the first of many Hitchcockian 'cool blondes', Madeleine Carroll paving the way for Ingrid Bergman, Grace Kelly, Kim Novak, Vera Miles, Janet Leigh and Tippi Hedren. *The Thirty-Nine Steps* begins and ends in London music halls but the bulk of the action features hero Richard Hannay (Robert Donat) on the run in Scotland, attempting to clear his name for a murder he did not commit, and to unmask a plot by foreign agents. The Scottish sequences include Hannay's famous escape from the police as his train crosses the Forth Bridge – such dramatic use of famous landmarks became a recurring element in Hitchcock's work – before the action moves to a characteristic Highland location near Killin on the edge of Rannoch Moor.[4] In these sequences, the Scottish landscape functions as an expansive and empty wilderness through which the fugitive alternatively pursues and is pursued. This familiar scenario is also a recurring feature in various novels and films set against the backdrop of the eighteenth-century Jacobite rebellions.

In *The Thirty-Nine Steps*, the landscape functions as a dramatic natural space within which the hunter and the hunted attempt to gain the upper hand. But it is also a place fundamentally beyond the certainties of the modern world. Writing about John Buchan's original novel, Cairn's Craig suggests that:

> The space of Scotland is the space in which the conflicts of the world can be brought into the open, since Scotland's space operates as a synecdoche of the wildness beyond the boundaries of imperial history. Scotland is a place where history is suspended – Hannay simply has to stay on the run for twenty days – and where space is dominant, allowing the conjunctions of these different spatial forces to be revealed.[5]

For Craig, the modern Scottish novel is marked by a negotiation between the progressive narrative of history and its other: 'between the map-maker's map and an "otherworld" where space has different dimensions'.[6] While Craig's concern is with indigenous cultural responses to modernity offered by the novel, the largely external construction of Scotland as space in British cinema appears to entail a similar negotiation between the rational concerns of modernity and progress and the possibilities associated with the realms of fantasy and irrationality. This construction of Scotland as fantasy space is epitomised by the Hollywood musical *Brigadoon* (1954). Shot entirely in the studio at MGM,[7] this famous tale of a mythical Highland village that comes to life for only one day in every century is praised by Colin McArthur for the way in which its vision of Scotland is revealed precisely as artifice: 'At one level it takes the Romantic representation of Scotland as a given, but at another level – that of the working through of the personal obsession of its director, Vincente Minnelli, with the question of illusion and reality – this representation is revealed as the dream *par excellence*, as a fiction created to escape from the urban horrors of the 20th century.'[8]

For McArthur, this self-reflexivity gives *Brigadoon* a progressive force that no

British feature dealing with Scotland possesses. However, what I hope to demonstrate in this chapter is that there is a vibrant tradition that is equally concerned with the possibilities of fantasy. Scotland is a place closely associated with the supernatural through a rich tradition of folklore, ballads and literature abounding with haunted castles, demonic practices, witches' curses and blind seers. This has inspired numerous features, most notably the various adaptations of Shakespeare's *Macbeth* with its heady brew of witches, ghosts, murder and treachery.[9] While Scotland's most famous indigenous 'monster', the prehistoric occupant of Loch Ness, has cropped up in various productions including *The Secret of the Loch* (Milton Rosmer, 1934), *The Private Life of Sherlock Holmes* (Billy Wilder, 1970) and the recent attempt to exploit the popularity of the post-*Jurassic Park* obsession with dinosaurs, *Loch Ness* (John Henderson, 1996). Scotland has also been the setting for a number of low-budget science fiction films dealing with alien visitation, including the deliciously kitsch *Devil Girl from Mars* (David MacDonald, 1954), *X the Unknown* (Leslie Norman, 1956) and *The Night of the Big Heat* (Terence Fisher, 1967).

But one of the most accomplished contributions to the tradition is a sophisticated comedy, *The Ghost Goes West* (1935), directed by the Frenchman René Clair and produced by Alexander Korda. The film's prologue introduces the historical feud between rival Scottish clans, the Glouries and the McLaggans, culminating in the death of Murdoch Glourie (Robert Donat), a womanising coward who is condemned to being an earth-bound ghost haunting Glourie Castle. The plot jumps forward 200 years to find the present destitute owner, Donald Glourie (also played by Donat), being pestered by his creditors. Salvation arrives in the shape of a rich American, Joe Martin, who buys the castle and ships it brick by brick back to his home in Florida. Martin regards the ghost as a bonus, earning him publicity and an advantage over his rival Ed Bigelow. The inevitable romance between Donald and Martin's daughter Peggy is complicated by the appearance of Murdoch's ghost, who Peggy takes to be Donald in fancy dress. All is resolved when Murdoch discovers that Bigelow is the last of the McLaggans, and making full use of all his ghostly powers to terrorise the American, he extracts the oath required to enable him to redeem himself and depart the earth forever.

But the real force of *The Ghost Goes West* lies in the sophisticated way in which it deals with the constructions of Scottishness. On the surface, the film abounds with familiar tropes of both Tartanry and Kailyard: from the magnificent Highland dress of the warring clans to the penny-pinching local tradesmen and suppliers who scuttle around Donald Glourie with their unpaid bills. But the fabricated and mutable nature of identity is constantly alluded to, from Martin's outlandish appropriation of his very own 'authentic' Scottish castle to the playful acknowledgement of Tartanry as masquerade. This is particularly effective in the scenes were Martin and Bigelow become Scotsmen by donning full Highland dress, and in the appearance of a band of black musicians in kilts playing a hybrid of Scottish and Caribbean music. The central opposition between Scotland and America, old and new, tradition and vulgar materialism, is similarly handled with considerable subtlety. The attack on modernity is confined to a gentle critique of American excess and it is significant that Donald Glourie remains in America to marry Peggy rather than returning to Scotland where he had clearly been hindered through his ties to the past. As a celebration of the pleasures of fantasy, masquerade and inauthenticity, *The Ghost Goes West* is not only an important precursor of *Brigadoon*, it is also representative of a particular cinematic construction of Scotland as significant as the dramatic and darker connotations of *The Thirty-Nine Steps*.

Islands of Desire

Another central trope in the cinema's engagement with Scotland is the literal and metaphorical figure of the 'island', a space in which remoteness or isolation is enhanced by virtue of its detachment from the mainland. In literature islands have had a wide range of utopic and dystopic associations, from Prospero's magical domain in *The Tempest*, through the imperial solitude of *Robinson Crusoe*'s island, to the descent into barbarism of *Lord of the Flies*, and, more recently, *The Beach*. Many of these ideas are equally relevant to cinematic representations of Scotland. A key individual in this respect is Michael Powell, one of the most innovative and visionary film-makers in British cinema history, who made three important features set on Scottish Islands: *Edge of the World* (1937), *The Spy in Black* (1939) and *I Know Where I'm Going* (1945).[10] According to Raymond Durgnat, Powell's attraction to the far-flung peripheries of the United Kingdom was just one aspect of a personal cinema inspired by a deep fondness for romantic mysticism:

> when the brilliant technician Powell leaves off, there begins a man who dabbles in mysticisms and romantic emotions of every kind: not only the 'Kiplingism' of his English officers and countryside, but in his fables for the Celtic fringe (*Edge of the World, I Know Where I'm Going, Gone to Earth*), in pagan spiritual forces repelling Christian nuns from Himalayan peaks in *Black Narcissus*, in the fate-time warp of *A Matter of Life and Death*, in the hothouse world of opera-ballet (*The Red Shoes, Tales of Hoffmann, Oh ... Rosalinda!!, Honeymoon*), in the hallucinated soul (*The Small Back Room, Peeping Tom*).[11]

Powell's romantic affinity for Scotland not only led him to identify with Burns, Scott, Stevenson and Buchan – 'all great tale spinners and subtle propagandists

for their mother country'.[12] He also attended a ceremony at Glenfinnan in 1945
to celebrate the 200th anniversary of the landing in Scotland of the Young Pretender, Charles Edward Stuart. Indeed, one of the projects Powell and his partner,
the Hungarian *émigré* Emeric Pressburger, failed to realise was a film of the Jacobite Rebellion of 1745.[13] But it was to be Powell's fascination with the elemental
power of landscape and environment to shape the lives of human beings, rather
than the Jacobite romanticism of Walter Scott, that ultimately guided his creative
engagement with Scotland. Of the three films noted above, *The Spy in Black* is
the least interesting in this respect, although it did mark Powell's first collaboration with Pressburger who had been hired by Alexander Korda to adapt J. Storer
Clouston's novel as a vehicle for the German star Conrad Veidt who plays Captain Hardt, a U-boat commander on a mission to blow up the British fleet based
at Scapa Flow. While the bulk of the film was shot in the studio at Denham, Powell was able to make a brief trip to Orkney for some establishing location shots,
the most effective being the images of the Old Man of Hoy, the 600-foot rock
pillar separated from the main island, which provide a suitably atmospheric
location for Hardt's secret night-time landing.

The island environment is much more central to *Edge of the World* and *I
Know Where I'm Going*, key works in the cinematic construction of Scotland

The elusive isle: Roger Livesay and Wendy Hillier in Powell and Pressburger's hymn to
Celtic mysticism, *I Know Where I'm Going*

during the 1930s and 1940s. Inspired by the famous evacuation of the Hebridean island of St Kilda in 1930, *Edge of the World* was shot largely on location on island of Foula in the Shetlands after permission to film on St Kilda had been denied by the Ministry of Defence. It tells the tale of two families, the Mansons and the Grays (headed by formidable patriarchs John Laurie and Finlay Currie respectively), set against the backdrop of a traditional way of life that is becoming ever more unsustainable. The two sons, Robbie Manson (Eric Berry) and Andrew Gray (Niall McGinnis), represent the different options facing the islanders: to leave and find work on the mainland as Robbie has done, or to stay and struggle, which is Andrew's view. Andrew also plans to marry Ruth Manson (Belle Chrystall), whose father Peter is equally determined to stay on the island despite his son. Robbie and Andrew decide to resolve their quarrel with a race to the cliff top, a challenge culminating in Robbie's tragic death. Forbidden to marry Ruth by her devastated father, Andrew reluctantly leaves the island only to discover that she has borne his child. When the baby has to be rushed to the mainland for an emergency operation, the decision is finally made to evacuate the island. Stubborn to the last, Peter Manson climbs the cliffs for a guillemot's egg. But his rope breaks and, like his son before him, he falls to his death, claimed by the landscape from which he and his ancestors had scraped their living. The main narrative is told in flashback; the prologue featuring an English tourist and his wife (played by Powell and his own future wife Frankie) taken to the now uninhabited island by a local guide who is subsequently revealed to be an older Andrew Gray.[14]

With the exception of a small number of close-ups and brief scenes (including the interior of the trawler during the storm and the doctor operating on the child) shot in the small Joe Rock studio at Elstree, *Edge of the World* was filmed almost entirely on location, a rarity for feature films during the period in question. The landscape of Foula consequently assumes a central presence throughout, from the opening shots of the towering cliffs, abandoned cottages and the predatory eagle, to the montage sequence conveying the wild elemental forces of a gathering storm. There is also a chilling image of the shadow of a cloud moving over the cliff face moments before Robbie Manson plunges to his death during the cliff race. Indeed, the two deaths can almost be understood as sacrificial offerings to an island whose name is translated as 'death' by Andrew in the prologue. This privileging of landscape led some commentators to compare *Edge of the World* to Robert Flaherty's documentary *Man of Aran* (1934)[15] and in 1945 Norman Wilson, former editor of *Cinema Quarterly*, and a champion of the documentary film, called *Edge of the World* 'the most important film about Scotland that has yet appeared'.[16] However, Powell strongly rejected any comparison with Flaherty, arguing that documentaries were the domain of 'disappointed film-makers or out-of-work poets'.[17] Yet Powell clearly sought a certain realism, recruiting several locals from the island to perform alongside the professional actors with the justification that 'Islanders have an inner strength and repose that other men and women do not have, and it shows in their faces. The smaller and more remote the island, the greater the individuality'.[18] *Edge of the World* also contains several brief scenes depicting the islanders' way of life – the sermon, the shearing of the sheep, the ceilidh – that would certainly not be out of place in a documentary of the period.

Ian Christie has usefully suggested that *Edge of the World* is actually poised between two different cinematic worlds, 'that of the romantic silent cinema which had originally seized Powell's imagination, and the anticipation of a future cinema based on location shooting. But it lay closer to the 1920s in spirit'.[19] The powerful use of superimpositions – Andrew's vision of the ghosts walking past, the close-up of Ruth's face superimposed on top of the sea, hinting at possible thoughts of suicide – recall the subjective techniques of silent cinema, while the centrality of montage to the construction of the film provides a link to both silent technique and the documentary. The shooting conditions on Foula were such that Powell returned with an enormous amount of footage, much of it silent. The task then became one of creating a coherent film through the editing down of this mass of material. The original editor, John Seabourne, took ill and after two months of struggling with the footage an experienced editor, Derek Twist, who had worked with Alfred Hitchcock among others, was brought in to finish the film. The subsequent foregrounding of montage also gave full reign to Powell's poetic sensibilities, particularly in the creative treatment of the island environment and its inhabitants.

In its mourning of the passing of a traditional way of life, *Edge of the World* shares an elegiac quality with the work of a number of important Scottish writers of the twentieth century such as Edwin Muir, Neil Gunn and George Mackay Brown.[20] In contrast Powell's other major Scottish film, *I Know Where I'm Going*, embodies an optimistic resolution of the central conflict between materialism and spirituality. This time the initial idea was Pressburger's, the project originally called 'The Misty Island' before being superseded by a title inspired by a popular Irish song which is also incorporated into the film. The central character of *I Know Where I'm Going* is Joan Webster (Wendy Hillier), a headstrong modern young woman who travels to the Hebridean Isle of Kiloran where she intends to marry her rich industrialist fiancé, Robert Bellinger. But Joan's carefully laid plans go awry when, stranded by the weather on Mull, she falls in love with the impoverished owner of Kiloran, the romantic Torquil McNeil (Roger Livesay). Jeffrey Richards suggests that the film strongly echoes various preoccupations of Powell and Pressburger's previous production, *A Canterbury Tale* (1944):

Both films hymn the rural beauties of Britain. Both chart the spiritual awakening of city-dwelling materialists. In both films, the travellers from the modern world are stranded in a thick fog, emerging into a community rooted in older, deeper values. As the fog clears, so do their misconceptions and muddles as they move to a realisation of life. Both invest in the local squire/laird an almost unearthly power, locating in him the source of ultimate wisdom.[21]

I Know Where I'm Going combines evocative and poetic location work on Mull (made all the more technically challenging by the fact that Livesay was unable to travel to Scotland, necessitating the use of a body double) with dark, brooding interiors. These are skilfully and subtly integrated, combining to suggest the power of an ancient and elemental force that works its spell on Joan, breaking down her resolve, exposing her inner fears and desires, and ultimately determining her fate. The uncanny environment begins to assert itself from the moment Joan arrives at the port of Erraig: the images of sky, sea, mist and Highland cattle, accompanied by the ethereal voices of the Glasgow Orpheus choir on the soundtrack, anticipating an altogether darker and more troubling fantasy space than *Brigadoon*. The heightened atmosphere is enhanced by the characters Joan subsequently encounters, particularly the sensuous and faintly predatory Torquil (the latter quality signified by his connection to the Major's eagle who is named after him), and the wild figure of Catriona Potts, whose memorable entrance with her hounds suggesting a Celtic Diana returning from the hunt. The elements, in the form of thick fog followed by a storm, not only prevent Joan from crossing to Kiloran for three consecutive days but also impinge on modern communications in other ways, the most amusing example being the phone box which is sighted next to a noisy waterfall. But the destructive power of nature is most forcefully conveyed by the deadly whirlpool of Corryvreckan which almost claims the lives of Joan, Torquil and the young boatsman Kenny.

While on a certain superficial level, *I Know Where I'm Going* would appear to retreat into mystical romanticism, the anti-materialist stance of the film is given a specific context by Kevin MacDonald who regards it as part of a nationwide disgust at black marketeers and war profiteers, the unseen character of Sir Robert Bellinger constructed as rather pompous and even unpatriotic.[22] This also chimes with the mood which ushered in the Atlee government with its programme of nationalisation and the heavy taxation of the rich. Joan's dilemma also involves much more than ditching ambition, self-determination and materialism for tradition, community and mysticism. Her problem is one of repressed emotion and desire, and the fear of the loss of control giving into desire entails. The effect the island environment has on her physical and emotional

Dangerous passions: Maxwell Reed and Patricia Roc in *The Brothers*

journey is anticipated during the sequence when she travels north by train from Manchester to Glasgow. In her sleeping compartment she dreams of her marriage, not to a flesh-and-blood individual but to Consolidated Chemical Industries. The images here of machinery and dynamic movement and power invoke a certain tradition of documentary which has its roots in the work of Vertov and Ruttmann; there is also the obvious pun on *Night Mail* (Harry Watt, 1935) with the rhythmical voice-over. The oppressive mechanical pounding gives way to a feeling of soothing calm when the border is crossed. But the image world changes to a kitsch landscape of tartan hills, like the black Highland band of *The Ghost Goes West* a signifier of the alternative pleasures and possibilities.

The question of desire is also central to *The Brothers* (1947), a film that also presents a rather darker vision of island remoteness, in this case an insular and superstitious community on the Isle of Skye at the turn of the century. Directed by Helensburgh-born David MacDonald and produced by Sydney Box, head of Gainsborough studios,[23] *The Brothers* also begins with an arrival: this time of Mary Lawson (Partricia Roc), a young orphan raised in a Glasgow convent who has been sent to work for widower Hector Macrae (Finlay Currie) and his two sons John (Duncan Macrae) and Fergus (Maxwell Reed). The disturbing presence of the young female in this all-male household immediately gives rise to a hotbed of barely repressed sexual tension. Rejecting the advances of the lascivious John, Mary is attracted to the handsome but rather bovine Fergus but, finding him unable through deference to patriarchal authority to show any signs of reciprocation, she seeks solace in the arms of Willie McFarish, a member of a rival family. The film abounds with tropes familiar from *The Edge of the World*: the harsh but beautiful landscape (dominated by the brooding Cuillin Hills plunging down to dark lochs), a hard-bitten community dominated by a harsh and repressive moral and religious code, and the clannish feud between rival families leading to a trial of strength which ends in tragedy (in this case the death of old Hector after the rowing contest).

But in true Gainsborough style, the enduring power of *The Brothers* lies in a combination of melodramatic excess, and the direct acknowledgement of female desire. The underlying cruelty of the islanders' existence is graphically represented early on in the film when an informer who has attempted to betray the Macraes to the authorities for distilling illicit whisky is tried and then put to death. The method of execution is both comically absurd and chilling: secured to floats, he bobs helplessly in the loch, a fish tied to his head. This acts as bait for a large sea bird which dive-bombs for the fish, cracking the poor victim's skull. Cruelty also informs the kind of expressions of desire which bubble to the surface: Willie McFarish's initial overtures to Mary culminate in an attempted rape; Fergus's attempts to flog Mary leading to steamy love scene on the beach; Fergus later being forced to cut off his own thumb which has become trapped in the mouth of a conger eel in a rock pool. A heady sado-masochistic brew familiar from many of the Gainsborough melodramas. Unable to have her, John persuades Fergus that Mary is the root of all evil, the cause of their father's death and of Fergus's symbolic castration. Fergus reluctantly agrees to deal with the problem, drowning Mary on a boating trip before taking his own life in remorse. But the plot is overheard by the local seer and the community takes its revenge on John, putting him to death in the traditional manner and bringing this exercise in Celtic *Grand Guignol* full circle.

Some interesting comparisons can be made between *The Brothers* and *I Know Where I'm Going*. Both foreground the issue of female desire, a force unleashed in part by the strange remote environment in which they find themselves. But the 'problem' this poses is worked through in rather different ways. At first the upright and headstrong Joan Webster represses her true feelings for the noble savage Torquil, but through the working of mystical forces she ultimately relents and finds happiness. In contrast, Mary Lawson is inexperienced and has no active control over her life, regarded by the men on the island as a problem, the root of all temptation. Yet she embodies the life-affirming virtues of vitality, spontaneity and practicality they conspicuously lack: letting down her hair, bathing naked and actively pursuing Willie McFarish when it appears that Fergus has no feelings for her. The Macraes are retarded by prejudice, superstition and sexual repression, forces that result not only in the cruel murder of Mary but ultimately in their own destruction. In setting of the film firmly in the past, *The Brothers* may not directly address the problems of modernity that inform *I Know Where I'm Going*. Yet Mary embodies the very progressive spirit of liberation and self-fulfilment that paved the way for modern women like Joan Webster who confronts and is transformed by a very different construction of the dialectic between modernity and tradition.

That Ealing Spirit

This conception of the cinematic construction Scotland as a liminal space within which fantasies can be played out, desires fulfilled, anxieties expressed, can offer a more productive engagement with some of the films condemned as the epitome of the modern cinematic Kailyard. The most important example is undoubtedly the 1949 Ealing studios production *Whisky Galore!*, directed by Alexander Mackendrick, a graduate of the Glasgow School of Art, and filmed entirely on location on the Hebridean island of Barra.[24] This was a consequence of the increase in British production in the wake of the notorious 1947 Dalton duty, a 75 per cent tax imposed on all luxury imports, including film, which led to an American embargo on distributing their films in Britain. Space was limited at Ealing and the only way an expanded production programme could be realised was to make a film outside the studio. *Whisky Galore!* was based on the novel by Compton Mackenzie, itself inspired by certain events which had occurred in 1941 when the cargo ship SS *Politician* ran aground in the channel between Eriskay and South Uist. The cargo included 22,000 cases of whisky, a considerable proportion of which were appropriated by the islanders. The fictional version of this story is set on the island of Todday and dramatises the rather forlorn attempts of the English captain of the Home Guard, Paul Waggett, to prevent the looting of the wreck, renamed the SS *Cabinet Minister*.

Whisky Galore! has been condemned for its association with the sentimental and reactionary 'Ealing ethos', a whimsical depiction of a world in which fair play, decency and native wit allow the small man to triumph over faceless, ruthless and corrupt forces of power. Yet this is challenged by Charles Barr in his pioneering study of the studio in which he regards the film as tangential to the prevailing character of Ealing comedy epitomised by the vision of screenwriter T.E.B. Clarke demonstrated in productions like *Passport to Pimlico* (Henry Cornelius, 1949) and *The Lavender Hill Mob* (Charles Crichton, 1951). Barr writes:

> if Clarke's comedy is daydream, Mackendrick's is *dream*, in the sense of a
> playing out, in compressed or symbolic forms, of conflicts as they in fact are
> ... [Clarke's] comedies celebrate the triumph of the innocent, the survival of
> the *un*fittest ... Mackendrick's show the survival of the fittest, with no

implication of things 'really' being otherwise. The island community does not represent an indulgent fantasy of escape from modern pressures ... it is a community in whose capacity for survival we can believe. It embodies an ancestral Celtic shrewdness and toughness, from which we should learn.[25]

Barr goes on to describe Mackendrick's vision as machiavellian in the way *Whisky Galore!* undermines the Ealing polarisation of nice, wholesome and harmless versus course, tough and brutal, replacing this with a clear-sighted and unsentimental analysis of how social behaviour is actually motivated. Barr's evocation of the operation of a dreamscape supports and reinforces the general argument of this chapter, allowing *Whisky Galore!* to be placed in the same tradition as the films discussed above.

Led by the wily old postmaster, Hamish Macroon (Wylie Watson), the islanders of Todday are not the backward-looking reactionaries of the Kailyard. Rather, the downfall of the Englishman Captain Waggett (Basil Radford), the commander of the island's Home Guard, is brought about through the arrogance of the white settler who makes no effort to understand the traditions and the language of the host community. Waggett cannot speak Gaelic, uses quaint Scottishisms without any sense of meaning or irony, and the map on his wall is of the English Channel. Worst of all, he completely fails to understand either the fundamental importance of whisky to the well-being and functioning of an

Whisky Galore!:
Constructing a set on the
Isle of Barra

island that has run out of its quota, or the depths of ingenuity and subterfuge which will be employed to obtain the precious cargo of the SS *Cabinet Minister*. Wagget is even happy to drink lemonade in the absence of any *uisgebeatha* (water of life). His alienation contrasts with the integration into the community of the other English character, Sgt Odd (ironically, played by a Scotsman, Bruce Seaton). Odd proposes to Peggy Macroon (Joan Greenwood) in Gaelic and is a competent dancer as is demonstrated at the *rèiteach* (the celebration marking his engagement to Peggy and that of her sister Catriona to the shy schoolteacher George Campbell, portrayed in typically gauche fashion by Gordon Jackson). He is also prepared to turn a blind eye while on watch over the wreck of the SS *Cabinet Minister*, and to allow the islanders to liberate a number of the cases of whisky before the boat sinks.

On a technical level Mackendrick encountered certain problems that recall Michael Powell's experience in making *Edge of the World*. The shoot was hampered by poor weather and consequently took much longer than planned, pushing the budget up from the planned £50,000 to £105,000 in the process. *Whisky Galore!* was also largely saved in the cutting room. Ealing studios boss Michael Balcon had considered cutting it down to sixty minutes for release as a second feature before being persuaded by Charles Crichton that he could considerably improve the film with re-editing. But the unusual production circumstances of *Whisky Galore!* also provided some significant virtues. The integration of professional actors with the local people of Barra is very successful (again echoes of *Edge of the World*), particularly in the three big set pieces. The opening prologue is constructed as a parody of a Griersonian documentary about the island and its inhabitants, featuring the image of numerous young children in descending age running out of a basic cottage over an authoritative commentary about how the islanders were happy people with simple pleasures. The first tasting of the whisky builds up into a montage of happy faces and a building crescendo of mouth music, culminating in the character of old Hector, apparently on death's door, coming back to life, the sunshine literally chasing away the gloom. And the montage depicting the disposal of the bottles of whisky in every conceivable place, leading up to the last shot of a bottle being placed in a cot and the baby back on top of it just as Waggett and the Excise men begin their raid. Each of these sequences is underpinned by a mischievous celebration of life, ingenuity and wit.

The considerable success of *Whisky Galore!* in Scotland, the United States and France made Mackendrick one of Ealing's top directors. In 1953 he returned to Scotland for his fourth feature, a project suggested by the tales of the old puffer boats that had similarly inspired Neil Gunn's *Para Handy* stories. *The Maggie* derives its title from the clapped-out vessel skippered by the lovable rogue MacTaggart (Alex Mackenzie) and his two-man-and-a-boy crew. By rather devious means they take charge of a cargo of luxury domestic items destined for the holiday home of Calvin B. Marshall (Paul Douglas), an American industrialist. The bulk of the narrative involves Marshall's various attempts to first of all retrieve his property from MacTaggart, and then, after giving in to the inevitable, trying to ensure than they arrive at the destination on time. Like Waggett, he ends up humiliated, the cargo sacrificed to the deep to save the puffer. Once again, locations are central to the drama, the bulk of the film being shot on Islay and the Argyllshire coast. The crew of the Maggie were also played by inexperienced actors, Alex Mackenzie being a part-time player from the Glasgow Citizens theatre, and Philip Kemp praises Mackendrick's skilful integration of professional and amateur actors whereby 'any disparity in acting styles comes across as a difference of character, not of technique'.[26] Mackenzie's low-key and somewhat perplexed performance in particular providing a very refreshingly different tone to that associated with British screen acting of the period.

The Maggie has been regarded in some quarters as a lesser achievement than Whisky Galore! Charles Barr considers the film to be 'the least satisfying of Mackendrick's quintet of Ealing films'[27] locating it within the decline of Ealing into a somewhat caricatured and ossified version of quaint reactionary nostalgia typified by The Titfield Thunderbolt (1953). Colin McArthur is even more damning, describing the film as 'the locus classicus of everything that is wrong with Scottish film culture'.[28] But other critics have defended The Maggie as much more complex and challenging, John Brown for example identifying 'a strong tendency towards allegory' and noting the distanciating irony in naming a character Calvin Marshall, combining overtones of Presbyterianism and American aid in a film set in a part of Scotland that is largely Catholic and which failed to reap much of the benefit of post-war economic investment.[29] Once again the construction of Scotland as a 'land beyond', facilitates the contemplation of more serious issues, albeit this time with a more direct relevance to Scotland itself. Despite the occasional lapses into sentimentality, particularly in some of the speeches given by young Dougie the cabin boy, The Maggie retains some of the anarchic charm of Whisky Galore!, particularly in MacTaggart's stubborn opposition to Marshall's demands. McArthur berates the film for the wilful perversity it demonstrates in allowing MacTaggart to triumph: 'In true Kailyard style, what is not achievable at the level of political struggle is attainable in the delirious Scots imagination.'[30] Yet surely the role of cinema is to provide a space for such oppositional fantasies, celebrating the power of the imagination to suggest alternatives.

Sentimental Visions

But this is not to suggest that all of the films attacked by Colin McArthur and others are equally worthy of critical recuperation. Indeed, the virtues of

Mackendrick's films are brought more sharply into focus when seen alongside a number of contemporary comedies boasting a similar narrative premise, range of characters and rural setting. An instructive example is provided by *Laxdale Hall* (1952), John Eldridge's adaptation of Eric Linklater's novel which begins with the five owners of motor vehicles in the isolated Highland community of Laxdale refusing to pay their road tax in protest at the poor condition of the road, causing a parliamentary commission led by Samuel Pettigrew MP (Raymond Huntley) to be dispatched to investigate the situation. Despite hailing from the community, Pettigrew rejects the pleas for a new road, presenting an alternative plan to move the entire community to a new industrial town to be built some 200 miles away. But he is forced to back down when he becomes unwittingly implicated in a poaching incident and is found drunk in a hearse containing the carcass of an illegally killed deer. The polarisation of the forces of repressive authority and machiavellian anarchy that provides *Whisky Galore!* with its narrative bite is diluted here by having the thoroughly Anglicised Laird of Laxdale Hall, General Mathieson (Ronald Squire), as leader of the local community rather than, say, the village shopkeeper, taxi driver and occasional poacher Roderick McLeod (Jameson Clark). In addition to being thoroughly hierarchical in a way that the islanders of Todday are resolutely not, the Laxdale community is depicted in warm but faintly ridiculous terms. The attempts to entertain their guests include a ridiculous performance of Shakespeare's *Macbeth* in the pouring rain which is abandoned half-way through when the cast, in period costume, are called to help catch a band of 'Spivs from Glasgow' who have been poaching Mathieson's salmon and deer. These unwelcome outsiders also serve to facilitate an understanding to be reached between the locals and the parliamentary commission, cemented by the rather predictable device of having two of the members fall in love with Mathieson and McLeod's respective daughters.

Even more instructive as a comparison with *Whisky Galore!* is *Rockets Galore* (Michael Relph, 1958) a direct sequel, scripted by Monja Danischewsky, a major initiator and producer of the original production. Once again the narrative concerns the interference of outsiders, this time the decision by the British government to use Todday for a new nuclear rocket site, a project that will necessitate the relocation of many islanders to the mainland. The military despatch the likeable Hugh Mander (Donald Sinden) to reconnoitre the situation, but matters are complicated when he falls in love with both the natural beauty of the island and with Janet Macleod (Jeannie Carson), daughter of the island rogue. When the islanders discover the plans for the rocket site they set about sabotaging the work being done by surveyors, going as far to destroy a test rocket that had gone off course and landed in a field. The government retaliate by sending in paratroops to occupy the island and supervise the eviction of the islanders. A desperate situation is finally resolved when Janet hits upon the idea of dyeing some of the seagulls pink, generating a national debate resulting in the decision to abandon the rocket site and designate the island a bird sanctuary. The deception is subsequently reinforced by a touch of divine intervention with the island Presbyterian minister and Catholic priest (one interesting change from the all-Protestant community in the film version of *Whisky Galore!* but more representative of the Catholic majority on Barra and in Compton Mackenzie's original novel) discovering some newly hatched pink gulls.

Shamelessly sentimental, *Rockets Galore* is a pale parody of its predecessor with even the inevitable ceilidh sequence an insipid affair compared with the rowdy joyous celebration of the first film. The emphasis throughout is on the natural beauty of an island threatened by modern science and technology, Reg Wyer's Technicolor cinematography consequently abounding with long lingering shots of the picturesque landscape. The island community is also far more crudely constructed, the inhabitants of Todday depicted as sentimental and superstitious, responding to the toppling of a large boulder that has remained perched precariously on a rock for centuries with a spontaneous lament accompanied by a lone piper. The militarisation process is primarily driven by the rocket scientist Dr Hamburger, a barely disguised Nazi modelled on the real-life Wernher Von Braun who also inspired the character of Dr Strangelove in Stanley Kubrick's 1964 film. His foreign fanaticism stands in stark contrast to the English Air Commodore, a decent chap who, like Mander, appreciates nature, being a bird watcher. In this way the establishment and the islanders are united in their xenophobic opposition to the threat posed by dangerous 'alien' ideas and impulses.

Herbert Wilcox's 1954 production, *Trouble in the Glen,* begins more promisingly with Orson Welles (playing the role of an Argentinean cattle rancher who has returned to his ancestral home in the Highlands) bemoaning everything he has found on his arrival in Scotland: the weather, the people, the roads, the fishing, the landscape. Forsyth Hardy suggests this offers 'a delightful antidote to some of the too, too polite films about Scotland'.[31] It also anticipates the possibility of a robust deconstruction of the kind of representation of Scotland that by the mid-1950s was decending into uninspired repetition and cliché. But *Trouble in the Glen* quickly degenerates into a blend of farce and sentimentality featuring a by now over-familiar generic repertoire including the outsider who falls in love with the laird's daughter, the conflict between the laird and his ungrateful tenants over a closed road on his estate, and a showdown between a band of tinkers (led by a rather miscast Victor McLaglen) and a group of drunken Glaswegian thugs recruited by the laird's unscrupulous factor. The American visitor is revealed as the real father of a young girl crippled with polio who thinks he is her uncle and refers to him as 'Sir Lancelot', and the convoluted resolution manages to combine the reopening of the road, the young girl taking her first steps and the marriage of the hero to the laird's daughter. The latter event providing the excuse for an inevitable climactic display of Tartanry, including a fully bedecked laird who had previously sworn that he would never wear the kilt.

Equally depressing are Frank Launder and Sidney Gilliat's two forays into the territory. Rather than conform to the familiar narrative trope of having an outsider come to the isolated community, these feature the adventures of a parochial Scot (in each case played by Bill Travers) venturing into the outside world in an essentially patronising and Kailyardic vision of the innocent abroad. In *Geordie* (1956) a gamekeeper's son, with the help of Henry Sampson's body-building course, grows from a stunted ten-year-old into a muscle-bound young man who goes on to win the hammer event for Britain at the 1956 Melbourne Olympic Games. Despite his brawn, Geordie McTaggart is a rather naïve and slow-witted character, unable to convey his love for childhood sweetheart Jean or to recognise the dangers when he is hit upon by the predatory Danish shot-putter Helga Svenson. Geordie is clearly out of his depth on the tour; he suffers from acute homesickness having never been away from home before – 'The furthest I've been before is Perth, and I dinna like Perth'. He is also stubborn, insisting on wearing his late father's Black Watch kilt during the games against the wishes of the British Olympic committee. This adds up to a rather cringing depiction of couthy insularity, a lack of curiosity or interest in the world outside the hills, glens and lochs of the Highlands. *The Bridal Path* (1959) constructs a similar story, in this case a lugubrious bachelor from the remote isle of Beag, Ewan McEwan, travels to the mainland in search of a wife, where he is mistaken for a white slave trader, then a notorious criminal while spending most of his time being pursued by rather hapless policemen and amorous women. Ewan's fellow islanders are stupid bigots, providing him with a list of unsuitable characteristics to aid his search for a bride, including Catholics, Campbells, English, Irish and Welsh women. In addition to the rather unimaginative plots and characteristics of the two films, Launder and Gilliat's visual representation of the Highlands and Islands epitomises the chocolate-box image of Scotland *par excellence*.

Coda: A Return to the Dark Side

By the end of the 1950s, the rich and complex cinematic construction of Scotland associated with *Edge of the World*, *I Know Where I'm Going*, *The Brothers* and *Whisky Galore!* had been eclipsed by a retreat into rather uninspired parody that more readily lends itself to the categories of the *Scotch Reels* critique. But the tradition had not yet fully exhausted itself, the return to a rather more sinister contemplation of the Celtic hinterland being signalled some year later by *The Wicker Man* (1973), the cult classic directed by Robin Hardy from a screenplay by Anthony Shaffer.[32] The film recounts the chilling tale of a police sergeant who travels to the Outer Hebrides to investigate the disappearance of a young girl. In the course of his investigations, he discovers that the islanders are engaged in forms of pagan worship and fertility rites that he finds both indecent and blasphemous. Suspecting initially that the missing girl has been murdered, he comes to the horrifying conclusion that she is to be used as a human sacrifice to appease the gods. Sergeant Howie (Edward Woodward) is himself a devout Christian and a virgin and in a chilling climax he finds himself lured into a trap set by the villagers whereby he is to be the sacrifice, burned alive in a huge wicker man on a cliff top overlooking the sea.

The most commonly seen version of the film opens with a deliberately misleading acknowledgement:

> *The Producer would like to thank the Lord Summerisle and the people of his island off the West Coast of Scotland for this privileged insight into their religious practices and for their generous co-operation in the making of this film.*

Despite the remote isolation of Summerisle as suggested by the credit sequence when Howie flies over an expanse of islands and water, *The Wicker Man* was mainly shot in the Scottish borders county of Wigtown.[33] The religious practices depicted are also subject to creative licence, comprising a pot-pourri of elements drawn from a variety of pagan rituals and including some very English motifs, such as the maypole, the Green Man and the figure of Mr Punch. But to criticise the film for its lack of authenticity is a pointless exercise. The enduring power of *The Wicker Man* lies in the way it successfully creates a powerful sense of unease as Sergeant Howie is lured into the islanders' trap. The soft-focus eroticism may be a little dated but the film still abounds with disturbing images challenging Howie's own strict Presbyterian code of morality. These include the sight of a young woman breast-feeding in a ruined church and the dream-like vision of numerous couples copulating on the grass outside the Green Man, shot in slow motion. The narrative is strongly driven by the central performances from Woodward and horror stalwart Christopher Lee as Lord Summerisle; while the community itself comprises a strange mix of ordinary-looking Scottish extras and exotic supporting players. These include the blond trio of Britt Ekland, Diane Cilento and Ingrid Pitt, making this one of the most bizarre depictions of a peripheral Scottish community in cinema history.[34] Its dark destructive powers echo back to *The Brothers*, while Philip Kemp has seen *The Wicker Man* as a reworking of *Whisky Galore* with Howie's meeting a similar (if more extreme) fate to Captain Waggett, another principled if rather arrogant figure who is also manipulated and outwitted in his attempt to impose his authority on the community. Whatever the connections, Hardy's film is a timely reminder of the way in which the remoteness of the Scottish environment functions as a space that is the 'otherside' to history, to paraphrase Cairns Craig,[35] providing a rich soil for the propagation of cinematic creativity and imagination.

Notes

1   Features like *The Four Feathers* (Zoltan Korda, 1939), *Black Narcissus* (Michael Powell and Emeric Pressburger, 1947), *Lawrence of Arabia* (David Lean, 1962) and *The Charge of the Light Brigade* (Tony Richardson, 1968) in different ways explore certain psychological and social problems at the heart of the imperial project.

2   Tom Ryall, *Alfred Hitchcock and the British Cinema*, (London: Athlone, 1996), p. 115.

3   John Russell Taylor, *Hitch: The Authorised Biography of Alfred Hitchcock* (London: Faber & Faber, 1978).

4   In the novel, the location is the rather less dramatic and remote border country of Galloway. See Christopher Harvie 'Decoding Buchan' in *Travelling Scot* (Glendaruel: Argyll Publishing, 1999), p. 91.

5   Cairns Craig, 'Narrative and the Space of the Nation' in *The Modern Scottish Novel: Narrative and the National Imagination* (Edinburgh: Edinburgh University Press, 1999), p. 238.

6   Ibid., p. 241.

7   In the spring of 1953, the producer Arthur Freed visited Scotland in order to scout possible locations for his planned screen version of the the hit Broadway musical written by Alan Jay Lerner and Frederick Loewe. He was taken on a major tour by Forsyth Hardy from Argyll to Aberdeenshire but in the end decided to shoot the film back in Hollywood, declaring that on his trip he couldn't find anything that looked like Scotland! Forsyth Hardy, *Scotland in Film* (Edinburgh: Edinburgh University Press, 1990), p. 1. The reality was that the unpredictable Scottish weather and the pressures from an MGM front office anxious to exercise tight financial over all new projects forced Freed and Minnelli to construct the magical village of Brigadoon and the surrounding landscape entirely in the studio.

8   Colin McArthur, 'Scotland and Cinema: The Iniquity of the Fathers' in McArthur (ed.), *Scotch Reels: Scotland in Cinema and Television* (London: BFI, 1982), p. 47. Stephen Harvey however criticises the film for not going far enough in this direction: 'the painted-scrim Scotland erected on Metro's stage 15 was too literal for wistful fancies, and less vivid than any one-reel travelogue. Once confined indoors, Minnelli ought to have indulged his bent for artifice, and transformed his *Brigadoon* from an approximation of a

Highland retreat to a refuge as intangible as dew, and seductive because it resembled no place on earth. Instead, George Gibson's diorama looks like the world's biggest *nature morte*; distant lochs glint like silver cardboard, unseen clouds cast static shadows on a flat sea of heather.' Stephen Harvey, *Directed by Vincente Minnelli* (New York: MOMA, 1989), p. 130.

9   Janet McBain's filmography in Eddie Dick (ed.) *From Limelight to Satellite: A Scottish Film Book* (London: BFI/SFC, 1990) lists five silent versions of *Macbeth* in addition to the 1948 production by Orson Welles and the lurid 1971 version directed by Roman Polanski. Since then, there has also been a more recent 1997 addition by Cromwell Productions.

10 Powell also directed *Red Ensign* (1934), concerning a Clydeside shipbuilder. Compared to the films considered here, this was a minor production, somewhat removed from the kind of cinema with which Powell is associated. It is considered in Chapter Four alongside other representations of Urban Industrial Scotland.

11 Raymond Durgnat, 'Michael Powell' in Ian Christie (ed.), *Powell, Pressburger and Others* (London: BFI, 1978), pp. 66–7. Originally published in *Movie*, no. 14, 1965.

12 Michael Powell, *A Life in Movies* (London: Heinemann, 1986), p. 540.

13 Powell and Pressburger did get as far as writing and shooting a single sequence of *The White Cockade* with David Niven and Pamela Brown as Bonnie Prince Charlie and Flora MacDonald. The casting proved to be prophetic: Niven was cast soon afterwards as the Young Pretender in Alexander Korda's 1948 production *Bonnie Prince Charlie*.

14 Cairns Craig has suggested that such a motif is central to cinematic representations of Scotland in which the narrative trajectory is driven by that of the outsider, while the indigenous characters (the Scots) are necessarily fixed as peripheral or other: 'Visitors From the Stars', *Cencrastus*, no. 11, New Year 1983.

15 The other near contemporary production to which *Edge of the World* has been compared is *Turn of the Tide* (Norman Walker, 1935), a feature set in a Yorkshire fishing community that Ian Christie suggests was the only model in British cinema at the time for the kind of film Powell wanted to make: Ian Christie, 'Introduction: Returning to the Edge of the World' in Michael Powell, *Edge of the World: The Making of a Film* (London: Faber & Faber, 1990).

16 Norman Wilson, *Representing Scotland: A Film Survey* (Edinburgh: Edinburgh Film Guild, 1945), p. 10.

17 Michael Powell, *A Life in Movies*, p. 241.

18 Ibid., p. 255.

19 Ian Christie, 'Introduction: Returning to the Edge of the World' in Michael Powell, *Edge of the World* p. xiii

20 Roderick Watson refers to this as an edenic or mythopoeic vision of Scotland in his essay 'Maps of Desire: Scottish Literature in the 20th Century' in T.M. Devine and R.J. Finlay (eds), *Scotland in the 20th Century* (Edinburgh: Edinburgh University Press, 1996), p. 288.

21 Jeffrey Richards, *Films and British National Identity: From Dickens to Dad's Army* (Manchester: Manchester University Press, 1998), p. 200.

22 Kevin MacDonald, *Emeric Pressburger: The Life and Death of a Screenwriter* (London: Faber & Faber, 1994).

23 MacDonald made several films for Box at Gainsborough, including *Good Time Girl* (1947), *Snowbound* (1948), *Christopher Columbus* (1949) and *The Bad Lord Byron* (1949).

24 Colin McArthur, 'Scotland and Cinema: The Iniquity of the Fathers', *Scotch Reels*, p. 47. John Brown actually coins the phrase 'the *Whisky Galore* syndrome' to refer to his conception of the contemporary Kailyard tradition. 'Land Beyond Brigadoon', *Sight and Sound*, Winter 1983/84.

25 Charles Barr, *Ealing Studios* (London: Cameron & Tayleur/David & Charles, 1977), pp. 117–18.

26 Philip Kemp, *Lethal Innocence: The Cinema of Alexander Mackendrick* (London: Methuen, 1991), p. 93.

27 Charles Barr, *Ealing Studios*, p. 167

28 Colin McArthur, 'The Maggie', *Cencrastus*, no. 12, Spring 1983.

29 John Brown, 'Land Beyond Brigadoon', *Sight and Sound*, Winter 1983/84.

30 Colin McArthur, 'Scotland and Cinema: The Iniquity of the Fathers' in *Scotch Reels*, pp. 47–8.

31 Forsyth Hardy, *Scotland in Film*, p. 96.

32 Ian Conrich discusses these different versions in an unpublished paper, 'The Wicker Man, A View to Pleasure'. These include an 86-minute version, the most commonly available film print, an 89-minute version screened on British TV and a 100-minute version available on an American video release.

33 See David Bruce, *Scotland the Movie* (Edinburgh: Polygon, 1996), p. 244.

34 Philip Kemp, *Lethal Innocence: The Cinema of Alexander Mackendrick*, pp. 39–40.

35 Cairns Craig, 'Narrative and the Space of the Nation' in *The Modern Scottish Novel*.

Chapter Three
The Jacobite Legacy

With the exception of *The Brothers*, the cinematic representation of Scotland explored in the previous chapter is located in the present. But it should come as no surprise to learn that the construction of a Scottish past is equally dependent on the construction of mythic projections rooted in fantasy, romance and the power of the imagination. While encompassing a range of subjects and historical periods, including various versions of *Macbeth* and dramatic accounts of the life of Mary Queen of Scots,[1] the dominant historical vision of Scotland in the cinema is primarily associated with the Jacobite rebellions of 1715 and 1745. This resistance to incorporation into the newly unified British state had already inspired a potent mythical construction of Scottish identity propagated by the nineteenth-century novels of Sir Walter Scott and Robert Louis Stevenson, which in were to provide rich material for numerous filmic adaptations. Central to this romantic tradition is the image of the Highlander as a kind of 'noble savage', a heroic individual prepared to fight and die for clan and country in the name of justice and liberty. In this struggle, he is pitted against external forces of oppression, personified by brutal and ruthless agents of the Hanoverian British state, who threaten his freedom and his way of life. The action invariably takes place against a picturesque backdrop of untamed Highland wilderness reflecting the honour, nobility and defiance of those who have inhabited this land for centuries. Moreover, such a construction of the Highlands is placed in dialectical relation to a 'cultivated' Lowlands associated with acquiescence in the Union.

The cinematic appropriation of the Jacobite romance also drew upon certain pre-existing pictorial traditions of representation including the paintings of Sir Edwin Landseer, best known for *The Monarch of the Glen*, his much-reproduced painting of a majestic stag against a typical Highland backdrop, and Skeoch Cummings, whose influence on subsequent cinematic representations is explored by Murray Grigor in his photo-essay 'From Scott-Land to Disney Land'.[2] This visual tradition is frequently tarred with the regressive brush of Tartanry and associated with the gradual incorporation of what were former symbols of rebellion by the British establishment from the late eighteenth century onwards.[3] Peter Womack has examined the emergence of what he terms 'the Highland Picturesque', one aesthetic element within a broader colonial discourse of cultivation or 'improvement' of the Highlands that occurred in the aftermath of the crushing of the 1745 Rebellion.[4] While Trevor Pringle has noted the contribution of painters like Landseer to 'the emergence of a Victorian Highland Myth ... in which the contingent and historical are lost in an image of tranquil natural order'.[5] For commentators like Womack and Pringle, such representations served to conceal the real political, economic and social tensions affecting the Highlands and the massive reorganisation and transformation wrought by capitalism, leading to wholesale clearance of the indigenous population either to the rapidly expanding towns and cities or into permanent exile. Such an argument clearly invokes the *Scotch Myths* critique, with popular representation serving to extend and revitalise a reactionary tradition of representation in which historical truth is concealed by romanticised fabrication.

But, as we have already seen, there are problems associated with such a concept of mythologisation. While the historical incorporation of the Highlands into the modern British state was certainly assisted by certain representational strategies, the function of such representations cannot be simply reduced to the ideological needs of the British capitalism and imperialism. The critique of Walter Scott's romantic 'fabrication' of Scottish history for example has been challenged by Cairns Craig who identifies a recurring device in his fiction by which geography functions as an equivalent to history: 'to cross the Highland boundary is effectively to step back into the past',[6] a past that is fundamentally dominated by the imagination. Craig regards this not as a retreat from reality into romance, but rather as a challenge to 'the confining truth, to the limits of the "historical" and the "real"'.[7] His defence of Scott against the charge of being anti-historical is founded on the idea of a counter-historical tradition that confronts the absences and blind spots of historical consciousness: 'Counter-history is the inevitable product of a history that, by claiming to be the only inevitability in human life, leaves so much out of history.'[8] As we have already seen, the representation of Scotland as a wilderness in cinematic fictions has facilitated a similar opportunity for the imagination of alternative worlds, emotions and possibilities. It is in this context that I will now examine the cinema's contribution to the depiction of Scottish history.

The Jacobite Romance and Silent Cinema

The literary construction of eighteenth-century Scottish history associated primarily with Scott and Stevenson proved irresistible to film-makers on both sides of the Atlantic from an early point in the history of the medium. American film adaptations began appearing as early as 1909 with productions of *Lochinvar* and

The Bride of Lammermoor, followed soon afterwards by versions of *The Lady of the Lake* (1912), *Rob Roy* (1913) and a 1917 five-reel version of *Kidnapped*. The fledgling British film industry responded with the 1911 Scottish production of *Rob Roy* (the only indigenous contribution to the tradition) and several productions made by London-based companies including a 1914 adaptation of *The Heart of Midlothian* by the Hepworth company and a 1915 Gaumont version of *Lochinvar*. More substantial British features began to appear in the early 1920s, a crucial moment in the industry marked by a concerted attempt to raise production values in the attempt to resist the almost total domination of Hollywood product in the British domestic market. Among the major productions that can be viewed in the light of this strategy are a trio of British films that effectively established the Jacobite romance as a potent cinematic spectacle. *Rob Roy* (W.P. Kellino, 1922) and *Bonnie Prince Charlie* (C.C. Calvert, 1923) were both produced by the Gaumont company, while *Young Lochinvar* (Kellino, 1923) was made by Stoll, a particularly prolific British producer during the period operating out of studios in Cricklewood. All three features are characterised by a mix of action, romance and picturesque settings and some of the major British stars of the period – including Ivor Novello and Gladys Cooper who play the Young Pretender and Flora MacDonald respectively in *Bonnie Prince Charlie* and Owen Nares as the eponymous romantic hero of *Young Lochinvar*.

The use of locations is particularly significant in these productions, establishing a cinematic topography that looks back to a pre-existing pictorial tradition in painting but also anticipates subsequent filmic contributions to the genre. The incorporation of dramatic landscape and scenery also served to enhance their novelty and appeal given that, as Rachael Low points out, interior sets constructed in British studios during this period still tended to be rather flimsy and unimaginative.[9] Extensive use of the Trossachs is made in *Rob Roy* while, according to Low, *Bonnie Prince Charlie* featured the staging of a battle scene shot on Culloden Moor with 12,000 extras.[10] *Rob Roy* sets the prevailing tone, opening with an image of a Highland landscape accompanied by the title 'The Banks and Braes of Bonnie Scotland'. This is followed by a montage of mountains and lochs, vividly constructing the magnificent backdrop against which its narrative will subsequently unfold. *Young Lochinvar* begins in almost identical fashion, although this time the accompanying titles testify to the bravery of the clans: 'wrapped in the immortal tartans of their line, their battle cry echoes through the mists of time – SCOTLAND FOR EVER'. Yet the actual conflict within the film is *between* the clans, involving a vague sense of opposition between the Highlands and Lowlands. There is no identified common enemy and no sense of a cohesive Scottish identity, other than in the shared uniform of white shirts, kilts, bonnets and rather ludicrous shaggy wigs.

Political divisions between Scotland and England, or between the Highlands and the British government, are similarly played down in *Rob Roy*. There is feuding between the MacGregors and a band of gypsies, but the major narrative conflict is between Rob and the Duke of Montrose and involves an affair of the heart. When Helen Campbell decides to elope with Rob, the jealous and treacherous Montrose plots his revenge, resulting in the MacGregors being burnt out of their homes and driven off their land to seek shelter in a secluded cave. (Which coincidentally had once provided sanctuary for none other than Robert the Bruce!) The narrative then jumps ten years: Montrose has built a fortress on the ruins of Rob's old settlement at Inversnaid and old rivalries are reignited by a breathless series of events culminating in a major battle and the victory of the MacGregors being signalled by Montrose's flag being replaced with a tartan one! Despite heavy-handed symbolism and a convoluted plot structure, *Rob Roy* displays a sense of dynamism rare in the British cinema of the period. The battle scenes are full of action, fast-paced and exciting, while the burning of the MacGregor cottages is staged in an equally dramatic manner.[11] There is little camera movement, but momentum is maintained by the combination of movement within the frame, frequent cutting between long shots and medium close-ups and the occasional use of parallel editing. Moreover, the numerous flashbacks provide a further level of narrative sophistication and interest.

Young Lochinvar is equally impressive, being described by Low as 'one of the most spectacular and visually pleasing films made in Britain during the period in question'.[12] Once again, the reliance is on a heady and rather complicated brew of romance and skulduggery. Attempts to resolve the bitter feuding between rival clans involves the marrying of children from opposing clans. One such marriage has been arranged between Young Lochinvar and Cecilia, the daughter of Johnson of Lockwood. But meanwhile Lochinvar has fallen for Helen, the daughter of another rival chieftain, Graeme of Netherby, a problem compounded by the fact that Johnson's conniving son Alick is also in love with Helen, who, for good measure, is pledged to yet another character, the Lowlander Musgrave. In the subsequent twists and turns of the plot, our hero is imprisoned, escapes, survives an attempt on his life by Alick, arrives in the nick of time to stop Helen's marriage to Musgrave and carries her back to his castle where they are immediately married before Graeme's men storm the castle. But the inevitable massacre is averted when Musgrave graciously accepts his loss, giving Lochinvar and Helen his blessing. Throughout, the melodrama is lightened by the comic antics of Lochinvar's rather grotesque servants, the rough but loyal Jamie the Ox and the simple-minded Brookie the Whistler. And while the landscape ultimately plays a less dramatic role than in *Rob Roy*, certain key sequences are shot on location to enhance the spectacle, including Young Lochinvar's pledge to Helen by the tranquil lochside and his fight with

Alick, culminating in the villain being thrown down a hill to his death. As befits a romantic melodrama the elements also play a major part in the proceedings, Lochinvar's meeting with Helen being brought about by a thunderstorm. The darker side of nature is also alluded to when Alick is first introduced, a face of a fox dissolving into a close-up of his cunning features. Not only is his countenance strikingly similar to Olivier's celebrated screen personification of Richard III in his 1955 adaptation of Shakespeare's play, but the technique of conveying essential character information through the use of a symbolic image anticipates Sergei Eisenstein's celebrated use of the device in his first film *Strike* (1924).

Colour, Spectacle and Exoticism

After this initial flurry of activity, the cinema's engagement with Jacobitism became less prolific, the continuity of the tradition marked by the odd Hollywood production such as the 1927 Lillian Gish vehicle *Annie Laurie*, directed by John S. Robertson for MGM, and the 1938 20th Century-Fox version of *Kidnapped* directed by Alfred L. Werker and starring Freddie Bartholomew and Warner Baxter in the roles of David Balfour and the Jacobite fugitive Alan Breck respectively. Only loosely based on Stevenson's original novel, the latter production also eschews the usual vision of Scotland as open wilderness in favour of a rather claustrophobic studio-bound look which is most effective in the 'House of Shaws' sequences. Then in the late 1940s and early 1950s a vivid new wave of productions appeared, distinguished by the addition of Technicolor and serving to re-establish the Jacobite romance as cinematic spectacle. Various experimental colour processes had been tried out in film-making from the earliest days of the medium when prints were painstakingly hand-painted frame by frame. But it was not until the 1930s when the American Technicolor Company introduced a fully satisfactory and sustainable colour system that could replicate the full range of the visible spectrum. Initially used for Disney cartoons, the first live-action feature in three-strip Technicolor was the 1935 historical costume drama *Becky Sharp*, directed by Rouben Mamoulian. As Ed Buscombe points out, the use of Technicolor was initially restricted to non realistic genres such as animation, musicals, Westerns, costume romances, fantasies and comedies. Rather than serving realism, colour was used to signify luxury or spectacle: 'Whether employed in the Western to enhance the beauties of nature, in the costume drama to portray the sumptuousness of the Orient or the Old South, or in musicals to render the dazzle and glamour of showbiz, colour serves to embody a world other than our own which, for the price of a ticket, we may enter.'[13]

Buscombe's discussion is restricted to Hollywood but there are certain similarities in the way colour was introduced and used in Britain. In the British imagination exotic spectacle had a close association with images of the Empire and its attendant themes of travel and exploration, glorious conquest and imperial rule. Such themes readily leant themselves to the Technicolor treatment and, consequently, of the eight colour features made in Britain between 1937 and 1940, six have obvious imperial connections.[14] British Technicolor was also promoted by a series of travelogue films, *World Windows*, shot in Italy, Palestine, Lebanon and India, powerfully demonstrating the process's ability to display exotic landscapes, buildings, costumes and people in vibrant terms. It consequently wasn't long before the spectacle of Tartanry received the Technicolor treatment. The empire drama *The Drum* (Zoltan Korda, 1938) features a Scottish regiment stationed on the Indian North-West frontier and the film's display of tartan is clearly linked to the projection of British imperial might, the army marching in and out of frontier settlements accompanied by pipes and drums. Social rituals are given a similar touch: in one scene the pipers march ceremoniously around the table in the officers' mess, culminating in a toast to the King-Emperor in Gaelic from the lead piper; while in another a dance band is dressed in a combination of tartan kilts and plaid with blood-red tunics, an appropriate visual signifier of the Scottish–British relationship in the imperial project.[15]

Technicolor for feature production was heavily restricted during the World War II, and consequently a fuller expression of the romantic spectacle of Tartanry had to wait until after the conflict had ended. The full-blown Jacobite romance finally received the Technicolor treatment in Alexander Korda's 1948 production *Bonnie Prince Charlie* featuring David Niven as the Young Pretender. The film has taken its place in British cinema history as a monumental failure both critically and commercially, and alongside the unfinished epic *I, Claudius*, it was to be one of the major regrets of Korda's career.[16] The project had been initially developed by producer Ted Black with Leslie Arliss as his intended director. But when Black suddenly died, Korda was forced to take over direct responsibility for the production. Niven had been loaned to Korda by Samuel Goldwyn and was a reluctant participant: '*Bonnie Prince Charlie* was one of those huge florid extravaganzas that reek of disaster from the start. There was never a completed screenplay and never at any time during the eight months we were shooting were the writers more than two days ahead of the actors.'[17]

In addition to script problems, there were three subsequent changes of director. Arliss was replaced by Robert Stevenson, then Korda himself took over the reins before passing the job on to Anthony Kimmins. There also seems to have been an obsession with authentic detail on the production regardless of either expense or effect in the final film.[18] The press book for the world première of the film in Edinburgh makes a great play of this, stating that 'No film has ever had such an authentically defined Scottish background as *Bonnie Prince Charlie*. Stress is placed on the contribution of various Scottish experts in assisting with the historical references and the design of the costumes, including the special weaving of accurate period tartans for the principal players.'[19] But characteristically, Korda was more interested in producing a popular film rather than obsessing over questions of authenticity, creating further tensions on the set.[20] Judy Campbell, who played the role of Clementina Walkinshaw, recalls 'a running battle between the historians who'd been brought in as advisers and the producers who kept demanding more ringlets and cleavage because Margaret Lockwood and *The Wicked Lady* had been such a success'.[21]

On a superficial narrative level, *Bonnie Prince Charlie* is structured in two distinct halves charting the rise and fall of the 1745 Jacobite rebellion. Beginning in the exiled Jacobite court in Rome, the first section depicts the uprising from the landing of the Young Pretender for the very first time in Scotland; the gathering of the clans and the raising of the standard at Glenfinnan and the subsequent campaign against the government forces which takes in the triumphant march of the Highland army through Edinburgh to Holyrood Palace; the unlikely victory over Cope's superior forces at Prestonpans; the progress south to Derby and the subsequent retreat culminating in the debacle of Culloden. The second section concentrates on the fugitive prince's attempts to evade capture by the ruthless Captain Ferguson, the famous role played in this by Flora MacDonald (Margaret Leighton) including his escape to Skye dressed as an Irish maid called Betty Burke, and ending with his final return into exile. Despite this narrative simplicity, the negative effects of the chaotic and fragmented production process can be frequently discerned on screen. Niven's rather uninspired portrayal of the prince as a naïve idealist is insufficiently complex to carry the weight of the narrative and this is exacerbated by a overall lack of tension or excitement to justify the 136 minutes of screen time. The visual texture is also highly uneven, the arbitrary cutting between real locations and exteriors clearly created in the studio creating a very jarring effect.

This is unfortunate because there are some very powerful and effective sequences creating a sense of display and spectacle. *Bonnie Prince Charlie* was photographed by a very experienced team including Robert Krasker, who supervised the studio work at Shepperton, and Osmond Borrodaile, one of the most accomplished specialists in location photography.[22] The locations are a return to the dominant representational tradition with Scotland depicted from the outset as a romantic land of lochs and mountains, heather and thistles. But this time Highland pictorialism is rendered via a vibrant Technicolor palate of greens, blues, purples and browns. The spectacle of Tartanry is considerably enhanced by the use of colour: the scene when the Clan chieftains first meet the prince onboard his ship is a blaze of red, green and yellow tartans, while Charlie himself is presented as an exquisitely dressed, golden-haired dandy. But even this moment is eclipsed by the dramatic arrival of the clans at Glenfinnan, hordes of wild fighting men rallying from all directions to pledge their allegiance to the Young Pretender. Colour is also put to effective use in the later scenes in which government dragoons pursue the royal fugitive, their vivid red tunics a symbol of oppression forcefully imposing itself on the more muted and natural hues of the natural environment. The use of studio artifice is occasionally very atmospheric, particularly in the aftermath of Culloden which begins with a group shot of forlorn old men, women and children huddled on a hillside, before panning away to the image of a blood-tainted stream and then revealing the carnage of the battlefield strewn with corpses.

The Jacobite heroes in the film are presented as rather noble figures and include the distinguished figure of Tullibardine (Finlay Currie) a surrogate father-figure to Charlie who, having successfully seen his protégé enter Edinburgh in triumph, dies peacefully in his sleep; and Jack Hawkins's bluff pragmatist Lord George Murray, the head of the Jacobite army. The experienced Murray provides a rugged contrast to the rather passive prince, with Hawkins dominating the scenes he shares with Niven. Margaret Leighton's Flora MacDonald assumes a similarly active role in the latter section of the film, further undermining the presence of the central character. While there is a reliance on certain Highland grotesques – the prince's faithful servants Donald of Eriskay (Morland Graham) and the seer, blind Jamie (John Laurie), reminiscent of Young Lochinvar's rather ridiculous companions – the casting of the main villains of the piece is much more novel and interesting. From the king, 'German Geordie', to the villainous Captain Ferguson (the Hungarian actor Charles Goldner) who barks orders with a strong accent in a manner reminiscent of a Gestapo officer, the Hanoverians are clearly coded as Teutonic gangsters, a negative depiction which clearly would have carried a great deal of resonance in 1948.

Before long, Hollywood was also picking up on this renewed cinematic engagement with Jacobitism. During the years following the end of the Second World War the major Hollywood studios faced restrictions on how much of their earnings could be repatriated from European markets. In the case of Britain, the 1948 Anglo-American film agreement allowed US companies to withdraw $17 million annually, leaving $40 million blocked in British bank accounts. The solution to this problem of 'blocked funds' was to reinvest in productions made in these countries, a phenomenon referred to by Thomas Guback as 'Runaway Production'.[23] This strategy had the added bonus of allowing what were ostensibly American productions to qualify as 'British' and so be eligible for the subsidy provided by the Eady levy scheme implemented in 1950 to encourage indigenous producers. Other factors also influenced the kind of subjects the Hollywood studios were drawn to during the period in question. Sue Harper notes that in the mid-1940s the British Film Producers' Association adopted a new policy on the purchasing of rights to fiction in line with the practice of the Motion Picture Association of America, a system of registration of novels by writers who had been dead for more than 50 years, and once a company had registered an interest in a novel other studios were legally barred from competing for the property.[24] This meant that British producers no longer had an open call on the British literary heritage, including what Harper refers to as 'the most "cinematic" novels of Scott, Dickens and Robert Louis Stevenson',[25] allowing Hollywood access to this rich source of material.

The subsequent flurry of historical adaptations included two distinct cycles of American-funded production in Britain. Pandro S. Bermann's production unit based at the new MGM British studios in Elstree embarked on a series of colourful medieval adventures including *Ivanhoe* (1952) and *The Adventures of Quentin Durward* (1955), both adapted somewhat appropriately from novels by Walter Scott. Scott was also the source for one of the major films in the second category of historical costume films, the reinvigoration of the Jacobite Romance. *Rob Roy – The Highland Rogue* was directed in 1953 by Harold French for Walt Disney. Blocked funds had led directly to a spate of live action features made in Britain by a studio associated primarily with animation. Beginning with *Treasure Island* (Byron Haskin, 1950) this also included *The Story of Robin Hood and His Merrie Men* (Ken Annakin, 1952), *The Sword and the Rose* (Ken Annakin, 1952) and *Rob Roy*. Warner Bros. got in on the act with *Captain Horatio Hornblower RN* (Raoul Walsh, 1951) and the 1953 adaptation of Stevenson's *The Master of Ballantrae*, starring Errol Flynn and directed by William Keighley. These American productions were to prove much more successful than Korda's Jacobite adventure, Sue Harper suggesting the following reasons:

> Korda had used the 1745 rebellion as a symbol of failure, and his misjudgements resulted in a disaster. American producers, on the other hand, used Bonnie Prince Charlie and the 'Glorious '45' for a double purpose. Firstly, they deployed the romantic Scottish rebellion against British rationality as a sort of 'prequel' of the American War of Independence, and were thus able to incorporate the rebellion into a debate about individualism versus legitimacy. Secondly, the fights and kilts afforded endless opportunities for masculine display.[26]

Certainly the contrast between Niven's excessively groomed, golden-haired and effete Charles Edward Stewart and both Richard Todd's virile and muscular depiction of Rob Roy MacGregor and Errol Flynn's swashbuckling James

Durie could not have been greater. The latter characters are presented as traditional Hollywood goal-oriented heroes, generally dominating proceedings and driving the action. This new emphasis on the masculinity of the Jacobite hero not only signifies a shift from the more overtly feminine contemplation of Scotland in films like *I Know Where I'm Going* and *The Brothers* – although the construction of the active male body as spectacle was clearly aimed as much at female as male spectators – it also anticipates the much more recent celebrations of raw Celtic physicality epitomised by the 1995 versions of *Rob Roy* and *Braveheart* featuring Liam Neeson and Mel Gibson respectively.

Rob Roy – the Highland Rogue also benefits from a taut and fast-paced narrative, eschewing historical accuracy in favour of action and romance. Set in the aftermath of the 1715 rebellion it replays the familiar tale of Rob Roy MacGregor and his struggle for liberty for his clan, robbed of their land and their name as punishment for continued resistance to the British state. The forces of oppression this time are not coded as continental but rather are personified by the dandified and rather devious Marquis of Montrose (Michael Gough) and his ruthless henchman Kilearn (Geoffrey Keen), the active agents of a repressive British government led by the Prime Minister Walpole. More sympathetic to Rob's cause is the pragmatic Duke of Argyll (James Robertson Justice), who, despite his loyalties to King George, is also at pains to assert his credentials as

Screen incarnations of
Scotland's most famous
outlaw, Rob Roy McGregor:
from highland warrior
(opposite), *Rob Roy* (David
Hawthorne, 1922) …
to romantic beekcake (left),
Rob Roy – the Highland Rogue
(Richard Todd, 1953)

a Scottish patriot. This sets Argyll against the ambitious Montrose who replaces him as Secretary of State for Scotland with Walpole's support. The Hanovarian monarch is also depicted in a favourable light, holding views distinct from those of his Prime Minister and intrigued by Rob's fame, inspired by the publication of a pamphlet 'The Highland Rogue' (based on an actual publication which appeared in London in 1723 and which helped to create the romantic myth later embellished by Scott).[27]

Once again dramatic spectacle is foregrounded, with the opening battle sequence setting the tone. This also presents an extreme contrast between the primitive wildness of the MacGregors, many of them half-naked waving rather archaic-looking claymores and shields, and the government dragoons, at this point still commanded by Argyll, who are well drilled, armed with modern rifles and artillery and supported by cavalry. The later siege of the garrison at Inversnaid fort is also effectively mounted, with the Highlanders advancing on the fort through the cover of the mist. Richard Todd's[28] robust noble savage, sporting dyed red hair and beard, is subsequently civilised through the donning of his best plaid, kilt and sporran, all set off by a crisp white shirt, a sartorial elegance which is never less than totally masculine. His mastery is slightly undercut by the rather clumsy manner in which he attempts to woo Helen Mary (Glynis Johns), a steadfast and shrewd female presence augmented by that of Rob's redoubtable mother Lady Glengyle (Jean Taylor Smith), who is, through being a Campbell, kin to the Duke of Argyll. Helen Mary is a more rational character than Rob, demonstrating an understanding of the political manoeuvring required to outwit Montrose and achieve a workable settlement for the MacGregors. This is all embellished with a surfeit of Scotticisms: from the picturesque scenery (a return to the Trossachs) of lochs, mountains and Highland cows, to the obligatory Highland dancing, pipe and fiddle, and traditional mouth music at Rob's wedding. Helen Mary's father Hamish McPherson (Finlay Currie) also serves to provide comic relief with his exaggerated tales of heroics at the battle of Killicrankie and his rather ridiculous piping.

If *Rob Roy*'s appeal to Hollywood lay in its associations with the American struggle for independence and liberty from the British in the eighteenth century, then that of *The Master of Ballantrae* can be related much more directly to generic expectation. Loosely based on the novel by Stevenson, the film takes the form of the kind of international swashbuckling adventure associated with its star Errol Flynn. Although set in the immediate aftermath of the '45 – the opening voice-over enunciated in a North American drawl – and concerning the adventures of the Jacobite fugitive James Durie, at least a third of the story takes place overseas. This narrative detour features piracy on the high seas, flamboyant buccaneers from France and Spain, and a suitably exotic interlude on a Caribbean island (filmed at Palermo on Sicily), recalling earlier Flynn vehicles including *Captain Blood* (Michael Curtiz, 1935) and *The Sea Hawk* (Michael Curtiz, 1940). *The Master of Ballantrae* also provides several opportunities for Flynn to show off his characteristic duelling prowess, the most spectacular being the energetic display on the upper deck of the pirate ship between Durie and the rapier-wielding French dandy. Flynn's characteristic womanising is also to the fore, juggling his affections between his intended wife, the Lady Alison (Beatrice Campbell) and the more earthy, raven-haired wench Jessie (Yvonne Furneaux). In contrast, the 1745 rebellion is conveyed in economical fashion by way of several shots from Korda's *Bonnie Prince Charlie*, including the raising of the standard at Glenfinnan, the march into Edinburgh and the battle scenes at Prestonpans and Culloden. The Highland topography is constructed in an equally precise fashion via footage shot at Dornie, Ballachulish and Glencoe, with Eilean Donan castle near the Kyle of Lochalsh standing in for Ballantrae. *The Master of Ballatrae* is also distinguished by some fine studio photography by Jack Cardiff, particularly in the low-key interior sequences and in the dramatic escape in the fog when Jamie and Burke take to the high seas.

Colour was also used to breathe new life into Stevenson's other major Jacobite novel, *Kidnapped*, previously filmed in Hollywood in 1938. This classic adventure story was resurrected in a 1959 Disney production directed by Robert Stevenson and featuring James MacArthur as the young David Balfour, cheated out of his inheritance by his miserly and scheming Uncle Ebenezer (John Laurie), and Peter Finch as the renegade Jacobite Alan Breck Stewart. Balfour is a supporter of King George, but fate brings the two together and they are forced to flee across Highland terrain from the red coats. Along the way, they meet various Highland 'types' including a stingy Duncan Macrae, a steadfast Finlay Currie and Peter O'Toole as the unlikely son of Rob Roy MacGregor with whom Breck engages in a piping duel. While Stevenson emphasises the familiar aspects of the Highland romance, the subsequent 1971 version of *Kidnapped*, directed by Delbert Mann and starring (a rather miscast) Michael Caine as Alan Breck, shifts the focus to the context of the '45 rebellion. The film opens on a Culloden moor strewn with corpses, wounded Highlanders being indiscriminately bayoneted by government troops and the Duke of Cumberland ordering the pacification of the Highlands. This is subsequently enacted by way of brutal executions, the burning of crofts, and prisoners being marched to Edinburgh castle to await trial. But while the barbarism of government policy is emphasised, the Jacobite cause is also questioned by various rebels who criticise the Young Pretender for his lack of understanding of Scotland and poor leadership leading up to the debacle of Culloden. This culminates in even the idealistic Breck realising that the 'grand restoration' is a lost cause and the film ends with his surrender to the garrison at Edinburgh Castle, an honourable act that will save his innocent kinsman James Stewart from being executed for a murder Breck has committed.

The 1971 version of *Kidnapped* relies on a more muted and naturalistic colour scheme than its predecessors. This aesthetic approach, coupled with the historical revisionism of the film, may have been indirectly influenced by the 1964 BBC television film *Culloden,* by writer-director Peter Watkins. This film presents a radically different interpretation of the battle and its aftermath to the popular myth, revealing an ill-prepared and poorly led Highland army thrown into a conflict that in some senses was a 'civil war' pitting Lowlander against Highlander and in some cases even members of the same family.[29] The brutal savagery of Cumberland's army in the bloody aftermath of the battle is also clearly shown as the beginning of the systematic destruction of traditional Highland life. *Culloden* is shot in a *faux* newsreel style on 16mm black and white film, with hand-held cameras in the thick of the action throughout. There are also mock interviews with many of the participants, including the leaders of both armies and ordinary soldiers and an authoritative voice-over also carefully explains developments as they unfold as well as providing a critical commentary on the iniquities of the clan system, the composition of opposing armies and their comparative weaponry. This formally self-reflexive approach to the

Rebellion as reportage: Peter
Watkins's innovative BBC
film, *Culloden*

representation of the battle and its aftermath creates a very different kind of
spectacle, negating the romantic tradition by focusing on the violence and barbarism of warfare, the pain, suffering and confusion of the ordinary soldier and
the duplicity, arrogance and cowardice of their leaders, particularly on the Jacobite side. With historian John Prebble credited as an advisor, Watkins's *Culloden*
has been seen as providing a corrective to the overblown failure of *Bonnie Prince
Charlie*, using *cinéma vérité* technique to allude to the realities of eighteenth-
century warfare. Yet in drawing attention to the material process of the
film-making process, Watkins reveals his own work as a construct, an interpretation of events rather than unmediated reality. Consequently, his film should
perhaps be regarded more as an interesting and valuable contribution to the
genre, motivated by a particular political and aesthetic project, rather than a
negation of a proceeding tradition of false representation.

The Technicolor productions of the 1940s and 1950s remain the cinematic
pinnacle of the Jacobite romance, a vision in which Scottish history is constructed as flamboyant fantasy. The films discussed above foreground romantic
heroism and wild untamed landscape as exotic spectacle in much the same way
as Technicolor representations of the British Empire had done from the late

1930s onwards. But this time the colourful tartan-clad 'natives' are the heroes, fighting for justice and honour against the red-coated agents of external oppression. The introduction of colour also reconstituted the cinema's engagement with Jacobitism in terms of enhanced spectacle. And while this may be criticised for recycling the reactionary tropes of an invented tradition – George IV's celebrated visit to Edinburgh in 1822, dressed in kilt and pink tights, would seem ready-made for Technicolor – such a critique ignores the positive pleasures associated with overt display. Pleasures that also serve to link the Jacobite romance to other generic traditions such as the period melodrama, the medieval romance and the swashbuckler. The central importance of costume to the Jacobite romance allows these films to be related to the critically derided but highly popular 1940s Gainsborough melodrama. The transgressive pleasures associated with this cycle have been discussed by Pam Cook in terms of an emphasis on: 'the visual codes of costume and decor, whose decorative excess creates a feminised world in which spectacular display predominates, captivating the eye and luring it away from the concerns of narrative and dialogue.'[30]

Despite the greater emphasis on men rather than women, the Jacobite romance can also be coded as feminine, with the flamboyant kilted male heroes constructed in terms of overt spectacle and display. Cook also celebrates the inauthenticity of costume melodrama and the emphasis it places on masquerade, facilitating a productive exploration of identity precisely through the crossing of boundaries that dressing-up entails. Such a consideration also finds resonance in the cinematic representation of the trappings of Tartanry, and the diffuse but important link between this and the donning of the kilt by countless Scots and non-Scots alike in various social contexts. The pleasures and meanings attached to this act of dressing-up are far too rich and complex to be reduced to some reactionary acquiescence in the perpetration of a pernicious myth.

Beyond *Culloden*: Post-Clearance Communities

The longer-term consequences of the failure of the '45 rebellion, including the depopulation of the Highlands and mass emigration, have inspired surprisingly few feature films. There are two worth noting here, both of which perhaps significantly eschew the possibilities of Technicolor for a more sober and naturalistic monochrome. Clarence Elder's 1947 adaptation of Neil Gunn's novel *The Silver Darlings* is concerned with the development of the fishing industry in Caithness during the early nineteenth century. The film opens with familiar images of the empty Highland landscape but this time the emptiness is related to social upheaval rather than natural splendour, the clearances having forced those who remain to seek other forms of subsistence such as fishing, a rather more dangerous occupation than crofting. When a young crofter is press-ganged by the Royal Navy, his wife and child are forced to leave home and are befriended by a fisherman, Roddy Sinclair (Clifford Evans). Twelve years later the herring industry has thrived and young Fin, against his mother's wishes, joins Roddy's crew. A faithful wife, Katrine finally learns of her husband's death at sea and consents to marry Roddy who has been in love with her since their first meeting. Their union is bitterly opposed by Fin, creating a conflict that is resolved when Fin saves Roddy from almost certain death when his boat is caught up in a terrible storm and dashed against the rocks. Despite the fascinating historical backdrop, *The Silver Darlings* is a rather staid production, weakened by a general lack of narrative tension and some truly awful acting. And while Francis Carver's photography does at times capture a sense of the ruggedness of the environment and the devastating power of the seas, this is a long way from the poetic elementalism epitomised by *Edge of the World*. The political critique offered at the beginning of the film is quickly dropped, shifting emphasis away from issues of exploitation and towards the courage and industriousness of those hardy souls whose quest for 'the silver darlings' made the north-east of Scotland 'the herring mistress of the world'. In its celebration of masculine endeavour and the Scottish fishing industry, *The Silver Darlings* echoes the sentiments of Grierson's 1929 documentary *Drifters*.

A very different kind of social engagement is offered by *The Kidnappers* (Philip Leacock, 1953), an intimate depiction of a Scottish settlement in Nova Scotia in the early 1900s. It concerns the experiences of two young orphans, 8-year-old Harry (Jon Whiteley) and 5-year-old Davie (Vincent Winter), who have come to live with their grandparents. Jim Mackenzie (Duncan Macrae) is a hard-bitten Presbyterian, bitter at the loss of his son, killed fighting in the Boer war, for which he blames his Dutch neighbours. When the children are denied the dog they crave for a pet, Harry finds an abandoned child and decides to keep it in a secret hiding-place in the woods. It transpires that the child belongs to the Hooft family, the neighbours with whom Jim Mackenzie is engaged in a dispute over land. Davie reveals where the baby is hidden and Harry is charged with kidnapping and tried by the local Justice of the Peace. In the process, Jim is confronted with the realisation that his stubbornness and pride have contributed to the situation and he sets out to repair the damage he has caused both within his family and the community at large. *The Kidnappers* is distinguished by a simplicity of narrative and some strong performances particularly by Duncan Macrae as a man struggling to reconcile his devout Calvinism with his equally sincere humanity. The two children are equally effective, their naïve questions a constant probing of the hard shell of their grandparents' way of life. They carry much of the drama, yet there is never recourse to the kind of mawkish cuteness usually associated with children. The

Confronting the new world, Duncan Macrae and Vincent Winter in *The Kidnappers*

mise en scène is similarly low key, with director Leacock and his cinematographer Eric Cross making extensive but almost incidental use of the locations in Glen Affrick, Invernesshire (standing in for Canada) rather than reverting to the kind of overt pictorialism central to the dominant representation of the Jacobite romance.

A Scottish Heritage Film?

Fundamentally inspired by the mythic vision propagated by the novels of Scott and Stevenson, the cinematic projection of Scottish history is dominated by the romance, the images, tropes and symbols of eighteenth-century Jacobitism. Consequently, such images have played a vital role in the subsequent construction of the idea of Scottish heritage in the 1980s and 1990s as David McCrone *et al.* have demonstrated.[31] The concept of heritage has also been important within the historical analysis of British cinema, with a distinct genre or sub-genre labelled 'the heritage film' being identified and examined by a number of commentators, including Andrew Higson who writes: 'One central representational strategy of the heritage film is the reproduction of literary texts, artefacts and landscapes which already have a privileged status within the accepted definition of national heritage. Another central strategy is the reconstruction of a historical moment which is assumed to be of national significance.'[32]

Higson considers the heritage film to be primarily concerned with a projection of 'Englishness' rather than 'Britishness', associating it with a pastoral world epitomised by films such as *Comin' Thro' the Rye* (Cecil Hepworth, 1924) to the more recent adaptations of literary classics such as *A Room with a View* (James Ivory, 1986), *Howards End* (Ivory, 1992) and *Sense and Sensibility* (Ang Lee, 1996). Yet his definition above equally fits the construction and status of the Jacobite romance within the Scottish context. The heritage film has also constituted a terrain of spirited debate and argument in recent years. Initially attacked as an embodiment of Thatcherite values and part of a wider process of the commodification of history by the heritage industry, it has also been defended as a mode of cinema sensitive to questions of female identity, desire and transgression in ways that serve to link some examples of the heritage film to Gainsborough melodrama.[33] A similar debate can be constructed around the cinema's engagement with Scottish history which, as I have attempted to demonstrate, constitutes a full-blown celebration of myth, fantasy and overt display, rather than any concerted attempt to resurrect or engage with historical reality. Yet by revelling in the popular spectacle of inauthenticity these mythical constructions of Scotland, particularly as vibrant Technicolor dreamscape, directly engage a wide range of audience pleasures, emotions and fantasies. The associations of such pleasures with escapism, the popular and the domain of the feminine constitute an alternative aesthetic to that epitomised by the documentary-realist tradition in which Scottish identity is rooted in the masculine 'reality' of industrial labour. The Jacobite romance also retains a political resonance in certain quarters, preserving a kernel of radical opposition to Unionist incorporation. As Beveridge and Turnbull remind us: 'In the survival of Jacobitism was sustained a powerful expression of Scottish identity, a symbol of ideas and aspirations which though once defeated, cannot be forgotten or erased.'[34]

Notes

1   The most important being the Hollywood feature *Mary of Scotland* (John Ford, 1936), with Katherine Hepburn, and the British production *Mary Queen of Scots* (Charles Jarrott, 1971), starring Vanessa Redgrave and Glenda Jackson as Mary and Elizabeth I.

2   Murray Grigor, 'From Scott-Land to Disneyland', in Colin McArthur (ed.), *Scotch Reels: Scotland in Cinema and Television* (London: BFI, 1982). *Brigadoon* has had such a significance in terms of twentieth-century constructions of Tartanry that some commentators have identified prevailing discourses concerning the myth and reality of Scotland as 'Brigadoonery' and 'anti-Brigadoonery' respectively: see David McCrone, Angela Morris and

Richard Kiely, *Scotland the Brand: The Making of Scottish Heritage* (Edinburgh: Edinburgh University Press, 1995), p. 49.

3 For a representative overview of the complex history of Tartanry, see David McCrone, *Understanding Scotland: The Sociology of a Stateless Nation* (London: Routledge, 1992), pp. 180–4.

4 Peter Womack, *Improvement and Romance: Constructing the Myth of the Highlands* (London: Macmillan, 1989).

5 Trevor R. Pringle, 'The Privation of History: Landseer, Victoria and the Highland Myth' in Denis Cosgrove and Stephen Daniels (eds), *The Iconography of Landscape* (Cambridge: Cambridge University Press, 1988), p. 143.

6 Cairns Craig, *Out of History: Narrative Paradigms in Scottish and British Culture* (Edinburgh: Polygon, 1996), p. 70.

7 Ibid., p. 81.

8 Ibid., p. 81.

9 Rachael Low, *The History of the British Film, 1918–1929* (London: Allen & Unwin, 1971), p. 127.

10 I cannot verify this as a viewing print of the film is unavailable. In her autobiography, Gladys Cooper recalls that some of the film was shot on the Isle of Arran: *Gladys Cooper* (London: Hutchison, 1931).

11 In this Kellino is well served by his cinematographers, A. St Aubyn Brown and Basil Emmott. The latter also photographed *Young Lochinvar* and in a very different production context, John Grierson's ground-breaking documentary *Drifters* (1929), and is described by Rachael Low as 'one of the best British cameramen of the twenties'. *The History of the British Film, 1918–1929*, p. 128.

12 Ibid., p. 244.

13 Edward Buscombe, 'Sound and Colour' in Bill Nichols (ed.), *Movies and Methods: Volume 2* (Berkeley: University of California Press, 1985), p. 90. Originally published in *Jump Cut*, no. 17, 1977.

14 *The Drum* (Zoltan Korda, 1938) and *The Four Feathers* (Zoltan Korda, 1939) are boy's own tales of heroism and the putting-down of insurrections in the outpost of the British Empire. *Sixty Glorious Years* (Herbert Wilcox, 1938) is a biopic of Queen Victoria, culminating in the imperial pomp of her Diamond Jubilee on 1897. *The Mikado* (Victor Scherzinger, 1939), an adaptation of Gilbert and Sullivan's operetta is, like *The Thief of Bagdad* (Ludwig Berger/Michael Powell/Tim Whelan, 1940), an Oriental fantasy. Even *Wings of the Morning* (Harold Schuster, 1937) can be seen in relation to a colonial context in its reliance on the lush green Irish landscapes, which had been until relatively recently part of the British Empire. Although the two remaining films, *The Divorce of Lady X* (Tim Whelan, 1938) and *Over the Moon* (Thornton Freedland, 1940), were largely studio-based light comedy

vehicles for Merle Oberon, the latter does incorporate travelogue scenes shot in the south of France, the Alps and in Italy.

15 There are also two sequences in which 'traditional' cultural expression is showcased in the form of an almost tribal rendition of the 'Bonnie Banks of Loch Lomond' and the sword dance as a reciprocal form of 'native' entertainment.

16 See Michael Korda, *Charmed Lives: A Family Romance* (New York: Random House, 1979).

17 David Niven, *The Moon's a Balloon* (London: Book Club Associates/Hamish Hamilton, 1972), p. 249.

18 There are parallels here with other British historical films of the period, including the similarly big-budget Gainsborough productions *Christopher Columbus* (1948) and *The Bad Lord Byron* (1949), both directed by David MacDonald.

19 *Bonnie Prince Charlie*, Souvenir Programme for the World Première on 26 October 1948, the Regal Cinema, Edinburgh, p. 7.

20 The tension between cinematic construction and historical authenticity was also to mar later films made by Gainsborough, the studio responsible for *The Wicked Lady*. *Christopher Columbus* (1948) and *The Bad Lord Byron* (1949) have much in common with *Bonnie Prince Charlie*, being similarly overburdened by detail and lacking either narrative drive or expressive *mise en scène*.

21 Sheridan Morley, *The Other Side of the Moon: The Life of David Niven* (London: Weidenfeld & Nicolson, 1985), p. 158.

22 Borrodaile's work for Korda on the imperial epics *The Drum* (1938) and *The Four Feathers* (1939) had given these productions a pictorial grandeur which was rare in British cinema of the period.

23 Thomas Guback, 'Hollywood's International Market' in Tino Balio (ed.), *The American Film Industry*, revised edn (Madison: University of Wisconsin Press, 1985).

24 Sue Harper, 'Bonnie Prince Charlie Revisited: British Costume Films in the 1950s' in Robert Murphy (ed.), *The British Cinema Book* (London: BFI, 1997).

25 Ibid., p. 134.

26 Ibid., p. 138.

27 Peter Womack notes that this pamphlet portrayed Rob as an almost animal-like figure covered in red hair, but also someone forced to be an outlaw through injustice. Peter Womack, *Improvement and Romance* (see note 4).

28 Despite being from Northern Ireland, Todd was to play a Scot on three memorable occasions beginning with *The Hasty Heart* (Vincent Sherman, 1949), a portrait in the kind of stubborn adherence to principle and

understated emotion associated with the Scottish character. This was followed soon afterwards by a double role in *Flesh and Blood* (Anthony Kimmins, 1951), adapted from James Bridie's play *The Sleeping Clergyman*, and *Rob Roy – the Highland Rogue*.

29 The production subsequently received limited theatrical distribution by the BFI in 1979.

30 Pam Cook, *Fashioning the Nation: Costume and Identity in British Cinema* (London: BFI, 1996), p. 77.

31 David McCrone, Angela Morris and Richard Kiely, *Scotland the Brand.* Especially Chapter 3.

32 Andrew Higson, *Waving the Flag: Constructing a National Cinema in Britain* (Oxford: Clarendon Press, 1995), p. 27.

33 See for example Andrew Higson, 'Re-Presenting the National Past: Nostalgia and Pastiche in the Heritage Film' in Lester Friedman (ed.), *British Cinema and Thatcherism* (London: UCL Press, 1993) and the collection John Corner and Sylvia Harvey (eds), *Enterprise and Heritage: Cross Currents of National Culture* (London: Routledge, 1991). A defence of the heritage film has been suggested by Claire Monk's article 'Sexuality and the Heritage', *Sight and Sound,* October 1995 and reinforced by many of the arguments in Pam Cook's *Fashioning the Nation.*

34 Craig Beveridge and Ronnie Turnbull, *Scotland After Enlightenment* (Edinburgh: Polygon, 1997), p. 79. For a sustained positive evaluation of the Jacobite tradition, see also Murray Pittock, *The Invention of Scotland: The Stuart Myth and Scottish Identity, 1638 to the Present* (London: Routledge, 1991).

Chapter Four
An Urban Alternative

The films examined in the previous two chapters share a common denominator in terms of their depiction of Scotland as essentially rural. Despite this dominant cinematic projection as remote wilderness, Scotland, was by 1911, the most urbanised country in the world after England.[1] By 1951, two-thirds of the population lived in towns of over 5,000, and 42 per cent in towns of over 50,000 inhabitants.[2] The depiction of urban Scotland in cinema has two major strands. The image of the historical city tends to be associated with a rather Gothic vision of Edinburgh where under the surface of bourgeois respectability there lurks a dark and macabre world of terror and criminality. Such a dualistic image also corresponds to the contrasting physical environments that distinguish the Scottish capital, from the grandeur, openness and order of the Georgian new town to the grimy and narrow closes and winds that characterise the old town. The contemporary Scottish city on the other hand tends to be synonymous with Glasgow and is defined by industrial activity,[3] shipbuilding in particular. The representation of Scotland as a site of modern industrial production not only provides a significant contrast to the kind of anti-modern projections examined in previous chapters; as we shall see, it also provides a means of relating images of Scotland to more contemporary British national concerns.

A Tale of Two Cities

We have already seen the considerable influence of Robert Louis Stevenson on the cinematic depiction of Scottish history, but he is also a key figure in other contexts. In a classic study of the British horror film, David Pirie makes a convincing link between this popular tradition of domestic cinema and the English Gothic novel.[4] But what Pirie fails to acknowledge is the Scottish contribution to the tradition, a contribution primarily associated with Stevenson whose 'engagement with the world of the imagination was a strange marriage of moral and supernatural forces', as Roderick Watson notes.[5] In common with many other nineteenth-century writers Stevenson was fascinated by the romantic idea of the double, or *doppelgänger*.[6] The notion of duality has a particular resonance in the Scottish cultural imagination and collective psyche, echoed in the deep historical division between Highland and Lowland society and since the Union of 1707 in the so-called Caledonian anti-syzygy, the 'personality split between the Scottish heart and the British head'. The role of the dominant forms of Scottish religion since the Reformation is also important in this respect with John Herdman noting the significance of 'the schematic polarities of Calvinist theology'[7] in the Scottish awareness of duality. James Hogg's celebrated literary contemplation of dualism, *The Private Memoirs and Confessions of a Justified Sinner* (1824), is particularly concerned with the excesses of the Calvinist doctrine and the sharply overdefined opposition between good and evil. Hogg's writing in turn was to prove a major influence on Stevenson, whose own intellectual formation was marked by a strict Presbyterian upbringing in Victorian Edinburgh.

Stevenson experimented with the double theme in the short story 'Markeim' and the Jacobite novel *The Master of Ballantrae* (1889). But he is also responsible for creating one of the most enduring formulations of duality, *The Strange Case of Dr Jekyll and Mr Hyde*, first published in 1886. While set in Victorian London, the tale was inspired by the historical figure of Deacon Brodie, a respectable Edinburgh cabinet-maker by day who infamously lived a double life and was hanged in 1788 for his part in a robbery of the Excise building. It consequently also draws heavily on the topography of the Edinburgh old town, Brodie's nocturnal haunts, as various literary critics have noted.[8] The novella has proved a rich inspiration for film-makers, with numerous adaptations from as early as 1908.[9] While Stevenson's Edinburgh has been largely absent from this cinematic tradition – the celebrated 1931 Paramount version of *Doctor Jekyll and Mr. Hyde* draws more upon the visual iconography of 1920s German expressionism, for example – some Edinburgh old-town locations were integrated into the fog-bound studio sets of Stephen Frears's *Mary Reilly* (1996), itself based on the reworking of the original tale by Valerie Martin, from the point of view of a maid in the Jekyll household.

The cinema's engagement with Edinburgh itself embodies a certain duality. On the one hand, there has been a tendency to construct the Scottish capital as essentially a bourgeois city of art, culture and beautiful architecture. This is reflected in a variety of films from the light-hearted musicals *Happy Go Lovely* (Bruce Humberstone, 1951) and *Let's Be Happy* (Henry Levin, 1957), the black comedy *Battle of the Sexes* (Charles Crichton, 1959), to Ronald Neame's adaptation of Muriel Spark's novel *The Prime of Miss Jean Brodie* (1969). A contrast is provided by a dark alternative Edinburgh, a vision inspired jointly by Stevenson and the real activities of the notorious resurrectionists Burke and Hare. During the early part of the nineteenth century, due to religious and legal prohibitions, cadavers required for dissection by the Edinburgh medical school were in short supply. In 1828, over a nine-month period two Irish migrants, William Burke and William Hare, murdered sixteen people and sold the bodies to the anatomist Dr Robert Knox. Hare turned King's evidence and escaped the gallows but Burke was executed and his body consigned to the dissecting table. These events inspired Stevenson's short story *The Body Snatcher*, a dark tale concerning the grisly activities of two fictional medical assistants of Knox, Fettes and MacFarlane, which culminates in a moment of sublime horror during a nocturnal coach ride through the wind and rain when the stolen corpse of an old woman is transformed into the body of a man murdered by MacFarlane.

The Body Snatcher was adapted for the screen in 1945 by Hollywood producer Val Lewton who had made his reputation with a series of atmospheric low-budget horror films for RKO. Directed by Robert Wise, the film makes many alterations to the original, considerably expanding the role of the cabman Gray, MacFarlane's tormentor, to provide a memorable role for Hollywood's premier horror star Boris Karloff. Also cast in a minor part is that other stalwart of cinematic terror, Bela Lugosi, making a final screen appearance opposite his great rival. The low-key photography and claustrophobic sets combine to produce a dark and atmospheric recreation of the Edinburgh old town of 1831, establishing an enduring element of the cinematic iconography of the Scottish capital. The period detail is also impressive, particularly given the budgetary constraints, the topography combining location shots of some key Edinburgh landmarks, including the castle from the esplanade and Holyrood House, with studio recreations of the cramped old-town streets, the imposing arches of the Cowgate and the melancholic graveyard of Greyfriars. The first act of grave robbing depicted in the film involves the murder of a faithful dog, bludgeoned by the ghostly shadow of a figure subsequently revealed as Gray, the implied reference to *Greyfriars Bobby*, subsequently brought to the screen in saccharine style by Disney in 1961,[10] providing an added element of the macabre.

The first British film inspired by the Edinburgh resurrectionists, *The Greed of William Hart* (Oswald Mitchell, 1948), featured Tod Slaughter, star of numerous poverty-row British horrors of the 1930s and 1940s. Although clearly a dramatisation of the Burke and Hare story, the villains here are renamed Moore and Hart (portrayed with much melodramatic eye- and hand-rolling by Henry Oscar and Slaughter respectively), Dennis Gifford noting that the British censor's objection to any direct references to the real-life murderers necessitated the re-dubbing of new names throughout the film.[11] Other details remained unchanged however, including the characters of 'Daft' Jamie Wilson, the mentally impaired youth, and the prostitute Mary Patterson who both became victims of Burke and Hare. The budgetary limitations of *The Greed of William*

Hart are far more obvious than *The Body Snatcher*, the action being restricted to a limited number of cramped sets and shot largely in medium and close shots. The lighting and editing is equally crude, if functional, and the acting reminiscent of the excesses of pantomime, pitting the honest but stiff naval doctor Hugh Alston against the cardboard villainies of Moore and Hart and the fanaticism of his former teacher Dr Cox.

John Gilling, the writer and assistant director of *The Greed of William Hart*, was to revisit the same territory in his considerably more accomplished 1959 production *The Flesh and the Fiends*. Shot in anamorphic Dylascope, the film successfully opens out beyond the spatial and dramatic limitations of Mitchell's earlier production to create the definitive cinema version of Burke and Hare. The protagonists are portrayed with considerably more skill by George Rose as the slow-witted Burke, and Donald Pleasence as the manipulative and vicious Hare. Moments of laconic wit are juxtaposed with chilling brutality: Burke smothering their first victim with his bare hands, egged on by Hare who dances a maniacal jig with his hands over his face. Equally unsettling are Hare's assault on the prostitute Mary Patterson (Billie Whitelaw), marked by a close-up of his leering, ecstatic expression as he chokes the life out of her; and the death of 'daft Jamie' in the pigpen at Tanner's close, his horrible screams merging with those of the swine. After such brutality, the capture of the villains is fittingly dramatic,

The darker side of Edinburgh: Burke and Hare accost a victim in *The Flesh and the Fiends*

hunted down through the dark streets by a torch-wielding mob in a sequence clearly inspired by the pursuit of Bill Sykes in David Lean's adaptation of *Oliver Twist* (1948). Having turned King's evidence, Hare is turned loose by the police and immediately attacked by a couple of men who thrust a flaming torch in his face, leaving him horribly mutilated and blinded. This act of retribution symbolically links Hare to the blind beggar who appears in the scene when the resurrectionists 'abduct' Aggie, the first of their victims, and then again just before Hare is himself attacked. It also connects him with Knox, who has a bad left eye, and who is for much of the film blind to the wider implications of his ruthless need for fresh 'subjects'.

Knox stands at the centre of the drama in *The Flesh and the Fiends*. As portrayed by Peter Cushing – who had achieved a major breakthrough two years earlier in *The Curse of Frankenstein*, the Hammer production that heralded the British horror revival – Knox embodies a similar ruthless and cold scientific rationality to that of Cushing's Baron Frankenstein. He is indirectly to blame for Burke and Hare's actions and this is brought home in his cavalier and arrogant dealings with the members of the medical faculty. In the end, he is confronted with the demon he has become in the encounter with a child who fears that he might sell her to the evil Dr Knox, allowing the film to close with his exoneration by the medical council and a return to a packed and appreciative lecture theatre.

The Edinburgh of *The Flesh and the Fiends* embodies a stark contrast between the bourgeois gentility of the medical professionals and the squalor of the streets and taverns, the point of interaction between the two worlds being the trading of specimens by the resurrectionists. The incompatibility of the different social spheres is also underlined by the ill-fated relationship between Mary and Chris Jackson, one of Knox's students who is given a job assisting the delivery of specimens. Jackson is unable to tame Mary's wild ways and he ends up dead like her, stabbed in the back by Hare. The dark underbelly of the city echoes *The Body Snatcher* in its shadowy streets, enclosed closes and misty graveyards, the castle towering above on its volcanic rock. While far from lavish, John Elphick's sets convey a scale appropriate for Gilling's widescreen compositions, avoiding the sense of constraint occasionally perceptible in Hammer productions of the period. Eschewing Hammer's lurid use of colour, the black and white palate of *The Flesh and the Fiends* adds not only to the atmosphere of the piece, but is appropriate to the moral dimensions of a film in which the progressive clarity of modern science becomes entwined with the pernicious and shadowy degradation of evil.

Subsequent versions of the Burke and Hare story chart a rapid decline in cinematic imagination. The 1971 feature, *Burke and Hare*, directed by Vernon Sewell for United Artists concentrates on the more salacious aspects of the case in line with the increase in sexual explicitness in the horror film during this period. While the resurrectionists, played this time by Derren Nesbitt and Glynn Edwards, are in David Pirie's words, 'reduced from the memorable psychotic fiends of Gilling's film to a pair of garrulous Irish comedians'.[12] Equally mediocre is *The Doctor and the Devils* (1985), adapted by Ronald Harwood from a script by Dylan Thomas.[13] Ostensibly an attempt to foreground the moral dilemmas confronted by Timothy Dalton's surgeon, the film suffers badly from rather leaden direction by horror veteran Freddie Francis, with a potentially strong cast, including Jonathan Pryce and Stephen Rea as the resurrectionists, badly wasted in the process. The sense of place is also rather vague and erratic. The story begins and ends on the very distinctive terrain of Salisbury Crags in Holyrood Park, while Edinburgh is a nondescript place populated largely by cockney stereotypes, including Twiggy as a suitably chirpy prostitute.

Echoes of the Scottish city as dualistic site of light and dark, respectability and criminality, science and superstition can also be discerned in certain productions from outside the horror genre. David Lean's glossy production *Madeleine* (1950), based on the celebrated case of Madeleine Smith, the daughter of a Glasgow architect who in the 1850s was tried for the crime of poisoning her lover, is one such example. Featuring Ann Todd in the title role, the film is an atmospheric portrait of the seedy underbelly of Victorian Glasgow bourgeois society. While *Flesh and Blood* (Anthony Kimmins, 1951), an adaptation of James Bridie's stage play *The Sleeping Clergyman* depicting three generations of a Glasgow family, combines a melancholy obsession with heredity with familiar macabre themes of madness, blackmail, murder and suicide. The first episode, depicting the feverish attempts of a terminally ill scientist (Richard Todd) to prove the existence of bacteria before he dies, resurrects the struggle of light in the form of scientific progress against a darkness symbolised by the gloomy tenement attic in which Cameron lives and works and his encroaching death.

Industry, Patriotism and Social Consensus

A much more familiar cinematic image of Glasgow is that of the modern industrial city, providing another potent way in which the Scottish experience has been narrativised. As Ian Aitken notes, by the late nineteenth century, the Clyde economy had become 'the engine room of the British Empire', producing 60 per cent of the ships that were so vital to maintaining the commercial value of the colonies.[14] This is echoed by Michael Moss and John Hume who suggest that 'the ships and machinery turned out by the yards and engineering works of West-Central Scotland during the late nineteenth century formed a tangible expression of the imperial idea.'[15] Shipbuilding was to remain a matter of great cultural pride in the west of Scotland, and the epithet 'Clyde-built' became as applicable to a particular kind of hard-living, hard-drinking, working-class masculinity immortalised in numerous novels, plays and films. The idea of 'Clydesidism' is defined by John Caughie as 'the mythology of the Scottish twentieth century, the discourse which seems currently most potent, and not yet universally acknowledged as mythology'.[16] Such a close cultural identification with heavy industry and masculinised labour was to be considerably affected by the eclipse in Britain as a world power, and the economic cycles of boom and depression that marked the twentieth century. And as 'real' productive industrial labour has historically given way to an economy based on consumption, so this has marked a shift which can be characterised in gendered terms as a move towards a more feminised mode. As Caughie points out, Scottish urban masculinity has come to be associated more with violence and criminality rather than hard work and 'rough' leisure pursuits. The implications of this in terms of the generation of anxiety and conflict around gender issues are consequently identifiable in some of the films I will examine in the remainder of this chapter.

Within the domain of cinematic representations of urban Scotland, the image of shipbuilding has proved to be the most emblematic, particularly during the 1930s and 1940s when the uneven fortunes of the Clydeside yards provided the backdrop for a number of features. Since the 1880s, the Clyde had consistently provided one-third of the total British output before international demand for shipping began to stagnate in the 1920s. By the early 1930s output had fallen to less than 10 per cent of the 1913 record output of over three-quarters of a million tons built and launched on Clydeside.[17] There was a subsequent recovery, aided by high-profile passenger-line orders – the symbolic moment being the resumption in 1934 of work on the abandoned *Cunarder* (subsequently the *Queen Mary*) which had lain idle at Clydebank for three years – and ultimately by rearmament. Christopher Harvie has related the tragic failure of the Scottish shipbuilding industry in the post-war period to grasp new possibilities for development and modernisation directly to the organisation and structure of the industry on Clydeside which had traditionally comprised relatively small family-owned firms.[18] The intimate nature of this organisation, however, provided a useful device for film-makers who set about dramatising industrial activity in terms of the goals, desires, frustrations and ultimate achievements of individual characters.

A familiar narrative trajectory revolves around the figure of the shipbuilder as steadfast hero who has to overcome economic or personal adversity to achieve his goals and aspirations, which are significantly also in the interests of the workforce, of the shipbuilding industry, of the community and ultimately of the nation. *Red Ensign* (Michael Powell, 1934), for example, tells the story of

David Barr (Leslie Banks), a shipbuilder struggling to survive in the midst of economic depression. His solution is a revolutionary cost-effective design, but he has to face and overcome a series of obstacles including opposition from his board, industrial sabotage, blackmail and imprisonment before winning the day. In contrast to his devious rival Manning, who registers his ships under a foreign flag and sails them with foreign crews, Barr's economic interests are carefully elided to a steadfast patriotism. Shipbuilding is a patriotic endeavour with the Red Ensign the proud emblem of the British merchant fleet. Despite being largely studio bound and over-reliant on dialogue, *Red Ensign* features some powerful images of the Clydeside yards lying idle (including an aerial shot of the skeleton of the abandoned *Cunarder*) and in full production once the men have gone back to work.[19]

While the drama of *Red Ensign* is largely confined to boardroom struggles, the sympathies of *Shipyard Sally* (Monty Banks, 1939) are much more those of the workforce and of the community at large. With typically steadfast determination, unshakeable good humour and songs 'our Gracie' both personifies and defends the values of the working-class community, in much the same way as she does in her other films, including *Sally in Our Alley* (Maurice Elvey, 1931), *Sing As We Go* (Basil Dean, 1934), and *Queen of Hearts* (Monty Banks, 1936). This time she plays Sally Fitzgerald, a big-hearted Lancashire music hall singer duped by her unscrupulous father (Sidney Howard) into acquiring a pub, the Bonnie Brig, in Clydebank. Despite being a 'foreigner' she quickly and rather effortlessly wins over the locals with renditions of 'Grandfather's Bagpipes' and 'Annie Laurie'. And when the men are laid off due to a slump in demand for ships, it is Sally who travels to London to present a petition on their behalf to Lord Randall, the head of a government committee considering new subsidies for the shipbuild-ing industry. After some rather typical high jinks – including a memorable masquerade as a man to gain access to the male bastion of the Argyll Club in the hope of seeing Randall – Sally ultimately succeeds in her task and leads the men back to work with a rendition of 'Land of Hope and Glory'.[20] The association of shipbuilding with patriotic duty is reinforced by the use of newsreel footage of the *Queen Mary* being launched in the presence of the Royal Family, a sequence culminating in the image of the Union Jack flying triumphantly.

Jeffrey Richards has suggested that over the course of her career Gracie Fields's association with a particular class was transformed into a national sym-bol which served to reaffirm national consensus: 'Gracie's role as mediator between and reconciler of capital and labour could not have been more clearly demonstrated than it is by *Shipyard Sally*'.[21] The construction of Clydebank firmly within a 'British' perspective has interesting political ramifications in this context. Scotland is implicated as a fully paid-up member of the British national community; indeed, within the terms of the film, to be anything other would be unpatriotic. It is interesting to consider that the 1937 comedy *Storm in a Teacup*, directed by Victor Saville and Ian Dalrymple, presents Scottish nationalism in a very poor light. A young reporter, Frank Burdon (Rex Harrison) arrives in the provincial Scottish port of Bailie to work on the local newspaper. The local provost (Cecil Parker) is an arrogant, hypocritical, authoritarian bully and is exposed as such by Burdon over his refusal to do anything about a dog who is to be destroyed because his owner refuses to buy a licence. But significantly the provost is also standing for parliament as a member for the Caledonian League, a party campaigning for an Independent Scotland.

More complex and interesting representations of shipbuilding and working-class life on Clydeside are offered by *The Shipbuilders* (John Baxter, 1943). Adapted by George Blake from his 1935 novel, the film follows the fortunes of a wealthy shipbuilder Leslie Pagan (Clive Brook) and an ordinary riveter Danny Shields (Morland Graham) over a period of twelve years, beginning in 1931 with Pagan's yard facing closure as a direct consequence of the slump in world trade. After the inevitable shutdown, the narrative branches out along two very different tracks, charting the subsequent experience of boss and worker respectively. The minor branch (in terms of screen time) follows the benevolent Pagan as he searches desperately for new orders and lobbies politicians for assistance. This provides the film with a political and economic overview, firmly rooted in an uncritical acceptance of *laissez-faire* capitalism which is only displaced by the necessities of war. Danny Shields, on the other hand, faces unemployment and an acute loss of pride, having been robbed of his identity as a skilled craftsman. This hardship is compounded by severe domestic strife. First, Danny's eldest son Peter becomes involved in criminal activity and then gets his girlfriend pregnant before he is found a job in the navy with Pagan's help; to make matters worse, his disgruntled wife Agnes walks out on the family to take a job in Greenock, leaving Danny to look after their younger son Billy. While Blake's novel had featured a rather downbeat ending, the film uses the onset of war to provide a means to resurrect the industry, and with it the fortunes of both Leslie Pagan and Danny Shields, culminating in a reaffirmation of the national importance of shipbuilding and a restoration of purpose on the part of the protagonists.

Once again, the official discourse informing *The Shipbuilders* is overtly British rather than Scottish. The opening voice-over, which accompanies the images of the yards with their towering cranes and the great hulks under construction, informs the viewer of the historic importance of shipbuilding and ships to Britain and its important role in the world. The film ends with the same voice-over calling for a recognition of the importance and the nobility of loyal patriotic craftsmen like Danny Shields who only wanted the opportunity to serve their country by constructing the ships that in turn allowed Britain to build an Empire and preserve the freedom of the world. These words are accompanied by the now familiar image of a ship being launched by Royalty, this time George VI and Queen Elizabeth. As in *Red Ensign*, the good ship-builder is differentiated from the bad in terms of the alignment of economic activity and patriotism. During the slump, Pagan's arch rival Baird remains in business by selling machine tools and scrap to Germany, Italy and Japan. This leads Pagan to the realisation that the German and Japanese naval strength is being built up and the dire consequences this will entail if Britain does not follow suit. Direct links are made with the wisdom of Churchill (in contrast to the wrong-headedness of Chamberlain and his policy of appeasement) as Pagan attempts to persuades the politicians, accompanied by starkly contrasting images of Nazi rearmament and parades juxtaposed with a complacent Britain enjoying funfairs. Soon afterwards, it is announced that Pagan's yard is to reopen with an order for four destroyers.

In its overt erasure of class conflict, Baxter's film can also be seen as an affirmation of the consensus tradition in wartime British cinema. While the extent of this tradition has been recently questioned by some critics,[22] there is clearly an attempt by certain films of the period to project an idealised national community pulling together in the face of adversity to fight a common enemy, thereby minimising potentially fractious social divisions wrought by class, gender and ethnicity.[23] *The Shipbuilders* attempts to overcome class division by way of an appeal to the transcendent value of shipbuilding as a patriotic duty. Leslie Pagan is a version of the paternalistic country squire, a shipbuilder first and a boss second, who not only is prepared to buy his men a drink in the pub but whose friendship towards Danny extends to keeping a job for him after the other men have been laid off, and hiring a defence council for Peter Shields when the latter ends up in court on a murder charge. Pagan is also prepared to serve the community in wartime in his role as an air raid warden, sharing a cup of tea with people whose tenement has just been bombed. The war also provides a convenient means of resolving other conflicts: Danny's wife returns on learning that their old tenement has been bombed, while the Navy succeeds in making Peter Shields a son his father can be proud of. We learn he is serving alongside Pagan's son John, reaffirming the social consensus in the next generation, and when Peter is tragically killed in action it becomes clear that he died a hero, sacrificing his own life to save those of his comrades. The stoic Danny refuses the offer of taking the day off, preferring to 'get back to the job'.

Despite the rather crude nature of the film's ideological project, *The Ship-builders* is a fascinating portrayal of working-class life and domestic conflict.[24] Particularly interesting is the ways in which gender rather subtly comes to replace class as the site of social tension within the film, opening up cracks in the veneer of social consensus in the process. Within the rather cramped domestic environment, Danny is clearly portrayed in a much more sympathetic light than his wife, his unrelenting optimism and spirit contrasting with her scepticism and complaint. The importance of working-class leisure also figures strongly, but again this is contemplated within a gendered discourse, serving to further accentuate the differences between Danny and Agnes. He inhabits the homosocial world of the pub, the betting shop and the football match (the film features footage of an international at Hampden park attended by both Shields and Pagan – a further signifier of their bond), while she prefers the feminised spaces of the cinema and the dance hall. It is significant that in the one scene when Danny reluctantly accompanies his wife to a dance he is offered a job by his spivish brother-in-law Jim who is marked out by his flash suit and cockney accent. The division is echoed in the two Shields children: the younger son Billy is also a football fan and ultimately follows his father into shipbuilding, while the feckless Peter finally gets a job working as an usher at the Scala cinema, an occupation clearly regarded by Danny as unsuitable for a man.

Peter Shields's brush with the law also highlights briefly another axis of social tension. He is involved with a street gang who are collectively tried for the murder of a bookie's runner who has been slashed – a reference to the moral panic surrounding the Glasgow razor gangs that also inspired the novel *No Mean City* by A. McArthur and H. Kingsley Long which appeared in 1937. The gang leader is a swarthy Italian called Tinelli and it is significant that he is identified as the main perpetrator of the offence, a bad influence on the other four (Anglo-Celtic) members who are consequently acquitted. The Italian presence in Scotland has been a highly significant one in the twentieth century, Irene Maver noting that at the turn of the century there were some 3,000 Italians in Glasgow, comprising the third largest Italian community in the United Kingdom after London and Manchester.[25] These families tended to work in the catering trade and by the inter-war period almost every Scottish town had at least one Italian-run ice cream parlour or fish and chip shop. But they were also a source of social tension, including an upsurge in anti-Italian sentiment when Italy entered the war in 1940, leading to violent incidents in many cities.[26] The negative representation of Tinelli in *The Shipbuilders* should be seen in relation to this prevailing anti-Italian mood during wartime.

Released four years after the end of the war, *Floodtide* (Frederick Wilson, 1949) depicts an equally idealised version of Clydeside shipbuilding.[27] Co-written by George Blake, the narrative is structured around the rise of an ambitious young farmer's son, Davie Shields (Gordon Jackson), who realises his ambition to become a successful shipbuilder, winning the heart of the shipyard owner's daughter into the bargain. Mirroring broader ideological shifts in British cinema that occurred in the mid-1940s, the wartime vision of patriotic social consensus has been replaced with a greater stress on individualism, albeit one

Domestic tensions on Clydeside: Elizabeth Sellars, Jimmy Logan and Rhona Anderson in *Floodtide*

with a peculiarly Scottish resonance. Davie's 'lad o' pairts' trajectory provides an idealised way out of the class polarities of *The Shipbuilders,* more appropriate to the aspirations of the post-war Britain under Clement Attlee's Labour government. The film also embraces the pleasures of modern urban living with gusto. Davie leaves behind his dour Calvinist father, who scorns the city as 'a Sodom and Gomorrah, all noise, hammers and temptation', and finds employment in a shipyard with the help of his uncle Joe. He moves in with fellow riveter Tim Brogan (Jimmy Logan), a quick-witted, stylish and savvy urbanite who introduces Davie to the excitement of *both* the pub *and* the dance hall, dispelling the traditional–modern, masculine–feminine dichotomy applied to leisure in *The Shipbuilders.* Davie's professional and social rise is meteoric, culminating in the production of his own ship featuring a revolutionary new design, an achievement that also makes him more eligible in the eyes of Anstruther's daughter Mary (Rhona Anderson). But Davie's communitarian instincts remain largely intact, remaining good friends with Tim and being prepared to stand up a social engagement at the Anstruthers' in order to attend his friend's engagement party. This almost turns to disaster when Judy (Elizabeth Sellars), a former flame, turns up and attempts to win Davie back when he is drunk. But all is resolved when Davie, liberated from the clutches of Judy by Tim and Mary, redeems himself by bravely rescuing his newly built ship threatened by the floodtide.

Like *The Shipbuilders, Floodtide* is open to criticism in terms of the uncritical way in which it depicts industrial relations and class conflict, indeed Colin McArthur has attacked the film on the grounds that its celebration of the people of Glasgow is at the expense of any real analysis of their economic or political situation.[28] The representation of the industrial process is once again clearly rendered in wholeheartedly consensualist terms with everyone from the board room to the shop floor working together for the greater glory of shipbuilding. This also serves to overcome any potential disruption posed by class and articulated through Davie's dilemma in maintaining links with Tim despite his new status, and the rather melodramatic intrusion of the bad working-class girl, Judy, who threatens Davie's future happiness with Mary. But, more interesting is the way in which the texture of working-class Glasgow life is represented on-screen. The image of yards dominated by the great hulking ships is already familiar, but the shots of the grey tenamented streets, and the vibrancy of the Barrowland dance hall evince a fresh naturalism more usually associated in British cinema with the films of the 'kitchen sink' that appeared a decade later. The character of Tim Brogan is also significant in this context. Unlike Davie, he is content with his lot as a riveter and is depicted as someone whose working life does not wholly define his identity. A sharp dresser, accomplished dancer and piano player, Tim exudes a working-class confidence, energy and expressivity that allows him to excels in the world of leisure rather than of work. And as we have seen, the former is a sphere of (feminised) consumption rather than (masculinised) production, making Tim Brogan a rather different and more progressive image of working-class masculinity than Danny Shields of *The Shipbuilders*.

Ten years before *Floodtide* was produced, Hollywood had also tackled the subject of Clydeside shipbuilding. *Rulers of the Sea* (1939) was directed by the Scottish-born Frank Lloyd for Paramount and a brief consideration of this film helps to demonstrate some of peculiarly 'British' characteristics of the productions considered so far. *Rulers of the Sea* is primarily a tale of heroism, driven by the ambition of an old inventor, John Shaw (played by Scottish music hall star Will Fyffe), to build a steam-powered ship to cross the Atlantic. The only people who believe in him are his devoted daughter Grace (Margaret Lockwood) and Davie Gillespie (Douglas Fairbanks Jnr.), an experienced sailor who has resigned in protest at the risks being taken by merchants desperate to reduce transportation times for their cargoes. Shaw's obsession constantly keeps him from gaining promotion at the foundry where he works and he is consequently prone to black despair and drinking binges. Finally, Davie obtains backing from a London trader and the new company of Shaw & Gillespie is formed. But now they have a rival in the shape of the Great Western Company who are also building a steam ship and the race is on to perfect a new vessel. Unlike all of the British films discussed, *Rulers of the Sea* is deliberately distanced from any recognisable national, social or industrial community. The early nineteenth-century Greenock functions purely as a backdrop. The motivations that drive the narrative are those of classical Hollywood. Shaw is the inventor whose life is dedicated to achieving his goal whatever ridicule and hardship this might bring upon him and his family. His determination to succeed also ends in his death, but only after his ship has successfully arrived in New York fulfilling his destiny. Gillespie, on the other hand, is the selfless moral hero who inevitably gets the girl. Personal ambition and individual achievement stands in here for the greater glory of the British Empire and the patriotic vocation of the shipbuilder. At one point, a toast is proposed to 'Anglo-American co-operation', and the final image of the *Queen Mary* sailing the Atlantic is a reminder of the present-day outcome of such pioneering endeavour. For in the end it is the heroic taming of the Atlantic ocean, and the implications this has for British–American relations, rather than the building of ships and communities, that lies at the heart of *Rulers of the Sea*.

Beyond the Shipyards

While the 'shipbuilding' subjects share an orthodox aesthetic approach with regard to the construction of their narratives around recognisable goal-oriented heroes and heroines, there are examples of films which eschew this in favour of a multi-character approach. Particularly significant are two productions built around an ensemble of actors from the leading Scottish independent theatre companies. *The Gorbals Story* (1949) was an adaptation of Robert McLeish's extremely successful play written in 1946 for the radical Glasgow Unity theatre group. Established in the early 1940s, the group established a reputation as a politically engaged company which would in turn inspire later similar initiatives such as John McGrath's 7:84 Scotland company set up in the early 1970s.[29] In addition to the performance of works by writers with broadly socialist sympathies, such as Ibsen, Maxim Gorky, Sean O'Casey and Clifford Odets, Glasgow Unity also provided a platform for new Scottish playwrights and plays, including *The Gorbals Story* which proved to be the company's biggest success. After a run in London's West End, a film version was adapted and directed by David MacKane at Merton Park studios in London featuring a cast of Unity theatre players.[30]

The narrative of *The Gorbals Story* centres around Johnny Martin (Russell Hunter), a successful artist living in a comfortable West End apartment, who recalls his formative experiences living is an overcrowded tenement slum in the Gorbals. From the outset, Glasgow is depicted as comprising very different realities, the thriving bourgeois city of 'well-stocked shops, large and spacious stores, big hotels, comfortable restaurants, clean theatres, luxurious cinemas' and, on the other side of the Clyde, 'a Glasgow of grey skies, grey buildings, depression, frustration'. Johnny's narrative presents a series of vignettes of working-class domestic life set against a struggle against poverty, unemployment and an acute shortage of decent housing.[31] The film adopts a multi-character ensemble approach and we are quickly introduced to a range of individuals who live in the same tenement as Johnny, including the maternal figure of Peggy Anderson (Betty Henderson), the work-shy Wullie Mutrie (Howard Connell), his devoted but long-suffering wife Jean (Marjorie Thompson), Hector (Roddy McMillan), a likeable rogue who is constantly tempting Wullie to the pub, Magdalene (Sybil Thompson) who agrees to marry the Indian peddler Ahmed (Lothar Lewinsohn), and the tragic Francie Potter (Carl Williamson) whose wife dies in childbirth. Johnny is in love with Nora Reilly (Isobel Campbell), but he is humiliated by Nora's drunken bully of a father Peter (Jack Stewart) who threatens Johnny with violence if he has anything to do with his daughter. This leads to a descent into self-pity and drunkenness. Johnny is rejected by a girl at a dance hall, is slapped by another woman in the pub and culminates in his coming home and making an almost oedipal pass at Peggy as a thunderstorm rages outside. This final humiliation causes Johnny to leave the tenement, setting him on a path towards his eventual success as an artist.

The low-budget, studio-bound production, coupled with the non-linear episodic narrative and the multi-character structure of *The Gorbals Story*, gives the film an immediate affinity with early television drama. The sequences are staged in an overtly theatrical manner with a strong reliance on dialogue and a visual style that is functional, favouring long takes which preserve a sense of ensemble performance, continuity and flow for actors unaccustomed to performing for the camera. The budget clearly impinges on the ability of the film to open out the drama. The main set is the communal kitchen of the tenement, the exteriors are all set at night and obviously studio-bound, and there are no locations – indeed the only images of the 'real' Glasgow we see are the montage of shots of the city centre, the University and Kelvingrove Park which accompany Johnny's opening monologue. The events that befall him during his night of drunkenness and degradation, and the complex emotions which he feels, are largely recounted in voice-over. The accompanying images are impressionistic at best: a brief encounter with a woman at the dance hall (a single long shot), a montage of blurred images signifying drunkenness. All of these serve to restrict the film's effectiveness in cinematic terms despite the obvious freshness of the subject-matter and narrative construction. John Hill criticises the way in which the drama is ultimately de-contextualised, both in terms of the confinement of the characters to the tenement and the romantic strategy by which Johnny is allowed to escape from poverty:

In effect, then, what seems to happen in the film is the production of an ideology of individual self-achievement (in the form of that most 'individual' of creatures: the 'artist') set against a message of collective passivity whereby the working-class characters can only exist as the failed bearers of a socially and historically de-contextualised poverty, hunger, frustration, depression.[32]

For Hill, an aesthetic strategy like naturalism is ultimately unable to engage with or reveal the complexity of the political and social context that creates and maintains the kind of endless cycle of poverty and squalor within which the characters of *The Gorbals Story* are trapped. Yet, at the same time, the film clearly marks an important beginning in terms of a more indigenous engagement with contemporary urban Scottish experience, anticipating the subsequent emergence of a vibrant strain of Scottish television drama in the 1970s.

Another production that attempts to convey Scottish working-class life in overtly collective terms is *The Brave Don't Cry* (Philip Leacock, 1952). Based on the real near-disaster that had occurred at the Knockshinnock coal mine in Ayrshire when over 100 men were trapped underground, the film belongs very much in the tradition of G.W. Pabst's *Kameradschaft* (1931), and to a lesser extent Carol Reed's adaptation of A.J. Cronin's novel *The Stars Look Down* (1939). *The Brave Don't Cry* has a major concern with the strong bonds of the mining community, a community portrayed by members of the Glasgow Citizens' Theatre Company including Andrew Keir, Fulton Mackay, Archie Duncan, Jameson Clark, Meg Buchanan and Jean Anderson. Founded by James Bridie in 1943, the Citizens' had done much to nurture Scottish acting and writing talent which in time also came to be reflected in both cinema and television. In aesthetic terms, *The Brave Don't Cry* is an exercise in low-key naturalism, albeit with considerably higher production values than *The Gorbals Story*. The rescue effort to save the trapped men is led by John Cameron (John Gregson), a former miner who is now a member of the management, the operation a race against the clock with only sixteen hours to get the men out before their air supply is exhausted. The mounting tension is effectively conveyed by way of the continual cutting back and forward between the miners trapped underground and their worried relatives at the pit head. Initially, the male space of the workplace is clearly differentiated from the images of feminised working-class domesticity with the by now familiar iconography of kitchen sinks and ironing boards, but this division breaks down as the entire village is mobilised by the disaster underground. The most impressive sequences are those at the pit head in the opening section of the film before the water-logged earth collapses, trapping the back shift. The grey dreichness and the scarred industrial landscape conjures up an extremely unromantic but familiar environment, while the naturalism of the drama is heightened by the lack of any non-diegetic music.

The back shift trapped underground: *The Brave Don't Cry*, a Group 3 production directed by Philip Leacock

The Brave Don't Cry was made under the auspices of Group 3, a company under the chairmanship of Michael Balcon which had been set up in 1951 to divert a modest part of the public funding made available to the British film industry through the National Film Finance Corporation towards providing feature film experience for technicians untried in the field. Balcon appointed John Grierson as executive producer, the first time the father of British documentary had been directly involved in the production of 'story films' as Forsyth Hardy points out,[33] and John Baxter as production controller. Twenty-five films were produced under the auspices of Group 3 between 1951 and 1955 with Grierson acting as executive producer on ten of these. His influence can clearly be discerned in terms of the number of technicians from the field of documentary who became involved in Group 3 productions, including Philip Leacock and Arthur Grant, director and cinematographer respectively of *The Brave Don't Cry*. The film itself can be regarded as a rare exercise in British neo-realism featuring an appropriate subject close to Grierson's heart, and it proved to be one of Group 3's rare critical and commercial successes, opening the 1952 Edinburgh Film Festival. A further two Scottish subjects were made by Group 3, both of which are rather unexpectedly whimsical comedies. *You're Only Young Twice* (Terry Bishop, 1952), an adaptation of James Bridie's play *What Say*

They?, is set within the bourgeois environment of Glasgow University and consequently projects a very different image of the city to that of the shipyards. While the Kailyard-inspired *Laxdale Hall* (John Eldridge, 1952) has already been considered in Chapter Two of this book.

The urban and industrial representations of Scotland discussed above are clearly limited in terms of their ability to analyse and give articulation to the lived political and economic realities of Scottish cities and industries. Yet at the same time they serve to pose interesting questions concerning Scotland's identity within the context of the Union, and the emerging anxieties around gender relations in a rapidly changing world. Unlike the representational traditions examined in the previous two chapters and the first part of the present chapter, the engagement with contemporary urban Scotland has been less overtly concerned with the projection of fantasy or the contemplation of difference in the construction of space, place and history. As we have seen, contemporary representations of urban industrial activities such as shipbuilding have functioned as a way of locating Scotland within a British identity marked by economic activity, community and patriotism. As such, this vision of Scotland is a long way from the geographical and temporal dislocations associated with *I Know Where I'm Going, The Brothers* or the Jacobite romance. Yet, at the same time, these are not simply celebrations of social consensus; issue of conflict and crisis inevitably bubble to the surface particularly around the issue of gender. While the discourse of Clydesidism is essentially associated with a masculine experience, women are not exempt from the cinematic representation of this world. In some films, such as *Shipyard Sally* and *The Gorbals Story*, they occupy a position at the heart of the community; while in *The Shipbuilders* and *Floodtide* the relationship between men and women is clearly addressed as a potential site of tension and anxiety. This is one element of the way in which these films in particular provide an insight into the complex and changing social relationships at the heart of urban Scottish life between men and women, factory and home, work and leisure. In presenting such a dynamic vision of Scottish working-class urban life, these productions served to establish an alternative representational tradition that would be subsequently revitalised by television drama in the 1970s, in turn paving the way for a vibrant new wave of socially engaged cinema in the 1980s and 1990s.

Notes

1   Richard Roger, 'Urbanisation in Twentieth Century Scotland' in T.M. Devine and R.J. Finlay (eds), *Scotland in the 20th Century* (Edinburgh: Edinburgh University Press, 1996), p. 124.

2   Figures quoted by T.C. Smout, *A Century of the Scottish People 1830–1950* (London: Collins, 1986), p. 32.

3   The title of S.G. Checkland's historical study of Glasgow is derived from the
    Javanese Upas tree, believed to have the power to destroy other growths for a
    radius of fifteen miles, in a symbolic allusion with the position of the heavy
    industries in the Glasgow economy. S.G. Checkland, *The Upas Tree: Glasgow
    1875–1975* (Glasgow: University of Glasgow Press, 1976).

4   David Pirie, *A Heritage of Horror: The English Gothic Cinema 1946–1972*
    (London: Gordon Fraser, 1973).

5   Roderick Watson, 'Introduction' to Robert Louis Stevenson, *Shorter Scottish
    Fiction* (Edinburgh: Canongate Classics, 1995), p. vii.

6   As a literary theme the double has been ascribed particular significance by
    various scholars, including Karl Miller who notes that 'the double stands at
    the start of that cultivation of uncertainty by which the literature of the
    modern world has come to be distinguished, and has yet to be expelled from
    it.' Karl Miller, *Doubles: Studies in Literary History* (Oxford: Oxford University
    Press, 1985), p. viii. While the theme of duality can be discerned in the work
    of Hoffmann, Poe, Dostoevsky, Wilde, it also takes a particular Scottish form
    in the writing of James Hogg and Stevenson.

7   John Herdman, *The Double in Nineteenth Century Fiction* (London:
    Macmillan, 1990), p. 16.

8   For example, see David Daiches' 'Stevenson and Scotland' in Jenni Calder
    (ed.), *Stevenson and Victorian Scotland* (Edinburgh: Edinburgh University
    Press, 1981), p. 17, or Roderick Watson's 'Introduction' to the Stevenson
    collection *Shorter Scottish Fiction*.

9   Despite appearing a decade before the official birth of cinema, S.S. Prawer
    notes that the novella contains elements of a cinematic imagination rendering
    it particularly amenable to adaptation. S.S. Prawer, *Caligari's Children: The
    Film as Tale of Terror* (Oxford: Oxford University Press, 1980), p. 90.

10 *Greyfriars Bobby* (Don Chaffey, 1961) featured veteran Scottish actor Donald
    Crisp as the supervisor at Greyfriars churchyard who looks after the Skye
    terrier in its vigil over its master's grave.

11 Dennis Gifford, *A Pictorial History of Horror Movies* (London: Hamlyn,
    1973), p. 204.

12 David Pirie, review of *Burke and Hare*, *Monthly Film Bulletin*, vol. 39, no. 457,
    February 1972, p. 28.

13 Thomas had been originally commissioned to write a screenplay about Knox,
    Burke and Hare in the 1940s and the use of the pseudonyms Fallon and
    Bloom, and the unlikely Dr Rock, are hangovers from the censorship
    conventions of that period.

14 Ian Aitken, *Film and Reform: John Grierson and the Documentary Film
    Movement* (London: Routledge, 1990), Chapter 1.

15 Michael S. Moss and John R. Hume, *Workshop of the British Empire:*

Engineering and Shipbuilding in the West of Scotland (London: Heinemann, 1977), p. 3.

16 John Caughie, 'Representing Scotland: New Questions for Scottish Cinema' in Eddie Dick (ed.), *From Limelight to Satellite: A Scottish Film Book* (London: BFI/SFC, 1990), p. 16.

17 Anthony Slaven notes that the worst period for Clyde shipbuilding was in 1932 and 1933 when a mere 9 per cent and 7 per cent of the 1913 output was achieved. By 1933 seven Clydeside yards had closed down, two were in mothballs and a further three were working under restricted quotas. See Slaven, *The Development of the West of Scotland 1750–1960* (London: Routledge & Kegan Paul, 1975).

18 Christopher Harvie, *No Gods and Precious Few Heroes: Scotland 1914–1980* (London: Edward Arnold, 1981), p. 56. By the early 1960s, unable to compete with more modern and efficient yards in Germany, Sweden and Japan, the Clyde had relinquished its position as a world leader in the industry that had made its name.

19 Powell's distance from the documentary realist tradition is well documented. The inclusion of certain industrial documentary techniques in *Red Ensign* seems to be motivated by the economic conveying of narrative information rather than as a form of subtle send-up. However, he does include a minor character called Grierson who is introduced as 'the finest riveter on the Clyde'.

20 Her earlier send-off at Glasgow Central station was accompanied by the song 'Wish Me Luck as You Wave Me Goodbye' which, as Rachel Low points out, was to rank as one of Field's most successful numbers alongside 'Sing as We Go' and 'Smile When You Say Goodbye'. See Low, *Film Making in 1930s Britain* (London: Allen & Unwin, 1935).

21 Jeffrey Richards, *The Age of the Dream Palace: Cinema and Society in Britain 1930–39* (London: Routledge & Kegan Paul, 1984), p. 188.

22 See for example Pam Cook, 'Breaking in Consensus' in *Fashioning the Nation* (London: BFI, 1996).

23 This tradition includes films like *In Which We Serve* (Noel Coward and David Lean, 1943), *Millions Like Us* (Frank Launder and Sidney Gilliat, 1943) and *The Way Ahead* (Carol Reed, 1944).

24 John Baxter's interest in both the effects of the harsh social realities of modern industrial Britain and the indomitable spirit of working people in the face of adversity had been evident in his earlier work, including his 1941 adaptation of *Love on the Dole*. A similar spirit infuses *The Shipbuilders*, causing Forsyth Hardy to praise the warm and honest representation of Glasgow life in the film. Forsyth Hardy, *Scotland in Film* (Edinburgh: Edinburgh University Press, 1990), p. 64.

25 Irene Maver, 'The Catholic Community' in T.M. Devine and R.J. Finlay (eds), *Scotland in the 20th Century* (Edinburgh: Edinburgh University Press, 1996).

26 Callum Brown has also pointed out that the early part of the century witnessed a major moral panic in Scotland around ice cream parlours which became regarded as sites of delinquency and immorality. See Brown, 'Popular Culture and the Continuing Struggle for Rational Recreation' in Devine and Finlay (eds).

27 *Floodtide* is also interesting on a production level. It was one of four features made by Donald Wilson at Pinewood to test the viability of a new production system called Independent Frame, devised as a means of reducing costs and increasing the speed of the production process. The system involved a major emphasis on pre-planning and preparation, including a major utilisation of still and moving back projection plates in conjunction with prefabricated sets mounted on floats and action scenes shot on location, with doubles which reduced the amount of time-leading players had to be engaged on any particular production. Ultimately, the experiment failed, due mainly to the inflexibility of the system, particular on the set. But the technical standard of the BP systems was extremely high and *Floodtide* stands up against other examples of process shots from the period. Most of the background scenes of the yard, for example, are plates, but they rarely distract from the foreground action. For an analysis of the process and its use on *Floodtide*, see Julian Poole, 'Independent Frame', *Sight and Sound*, Spring 1980, pp. 109–10.

28 Colin McArthur, 'Scotland and Cinema: The Iniquity of the Fathers' in McArthur (ed.), *Scotch Reels: Scotland in Cinema and Television* (London: BFI, 1982).

29 See Linda McKenney, 'The People's Story 7:84 Scotland', in Randall Stevenson and Gavin Wallace (eds), *Scottish Theatre Since the Seventies* (Edinburgh: Edinburgh University Press, 1996).

30 John Hill notes that the film was well received by the trade but failed to gain general release and consequently disappeared from sight. John Hill, ' "Scotland doesna mean much tae Gesca": Some Notes on *The Gorbals Story*' in Colin McArthur (ed.), *Scotch Reels*.

31 Christopher Harvie notes that a survey conducted in 1935/6 revealed that almost a quarter of all Scottish homes were officially overcrowded, compared to less than 4 per cent in England. *No Gods and Precious Few Heroes*.

32 John Hill, ' "Scotland doesna mean much tae Gesca": Some Notes on *The Gorbals Story*' in Colin McArthur (ed.), *Scotch Reels*, pp. 109–10.

33 Forsyth Hardy, *John Grierson: A Documentary Biography*, (London: Faber & Faber, 1979), p. 180.

Part Two

THE MAKING OF A NATIONAL CINEMA

Chapter Five
Scotland and the Documentary

The Griersonian Documentary and Scottish Film Culture

The documentary occupies a position of particular significance in the historical relationship between Scotland and the cinema, particularly in terms of the sustenance of indigenous film production. The significance of actuality, topical and magazine films made by Scottish exhibitors from the 1910s onwards has already been noted, as has the influence of certain aspects of John Grierson's cultural formation as a Scot on the subsequent project of the British documentary movement of the 1930s. Despite his association with the nurturing and projection of a British national culture, Grierson nevertheless retained a strong attachment to the land of his birth and to his own identity as a Scot. This was to have implications for the selection of subject-matter for the documentaries made by the film units he ran, first at the Empire Marketing Board from 1929 to 1933 and then the General Post Office, Grierson's friend and biographer, Forsyth Hardy, argues that he 'ensured that whenever possible the cameras looked northwards'[1]. Beginning with Grierson's own film *Drifters* (1929), this connection includes productions like *O'er Hill and Dale* (Basil Wright, 1930), *Upstream* (Arthur Elton, 1930), *Granton Trawler* (John Grierson and Edgar Anstey, 1934), *Night Mail* (Harry Watt and Basil Wright, 1936), *North of the Border* (Maurice Harvey, 1938), *Mony a Pickle* (1938), *The Tocher* (Lotte Reiniger, 1938) and *North Sea* (Harry Watt, 1938). The documentary movement was also a sector in which several other Scots in addition to Grierson were to feature prominently including Harry Watt, Stewart McAllister, Donald Alexander, Norman McLaren and Grierson's own siblings Marion and Ruby.

The documentary also played a significant role in the development of an indigenous film culture in Scotland. In 1932 the journal *Cinema Quarterly* was founded out of the activities of the Edinburgh Film Guild and under the editorship of Norman Wilson quickly established itself as a major contribution to the kind of intellectual appreciation of international cinema associated with the film society movement and the journal *Close Up*.[2] Wilson and his colleague Forsyth Hardy were highly supportive of Grierson and consequently he and several other leading documentary film-makers became regular contributors to *Cinema Quarterly*, cementing its reputation as a critical mouthpiece for the British documentary movement. Grierson expounded his 'Principles of Documentary' in the early issues while Paul Rotha and Basil Wright contributed various articles and reviews. Wilson and Hardy were also instrumental in establishing the Edinburgh International Film Festival in 1947. Initially called the International Festival of Documentary Films, the event was dedicated to a wide range of international realist film-making[3] and provided an important forum for debate and discussion in the form of public lectures by leading practitioners like Grierson, Rotha and Wright. Writing about the Festival in 1948, Grierson suggested that the location of such a pro-documentary event in Scotland was no accident: 'Edinburgh has served the documentary idea from its inception with more continuity, more common sense, more constructive effort in film societies, film clubs, cinema quarterlies, and what not, and more of the stuff that it takes when it comes to the critical punches than any other city.'[4]

Despite the fact that the thinkers associated with the documentary movement tended to champion an indigenous film culture that was resolutely British, *Cinema Quarterly* did publish the occasional article by figures closely involved in the Scottish literary renaissance of the inter-war period, including Hugh MacDiarmid and Lewis Grassic Gibbon. While the latter simply used his contribution to celebrate the pleasures of going to his local cinema and to argue for the medium's superiority to theatre,[5] MacDiarmid's exploration of a potentially fruitful relationship between film and poetry includes a meditation on the close link between the local and the universal that clearly has (unacknowledged) implications for a productive cinematic engagement with the particularities of Scottish culture.[6] This is consistent with the poet's contention, inspired by writers like James Joyce, that literature could be both rooted in a specific culture while still having universal significance. As Roderick Wilson notes, 'the local need not be parochial, and MacDiarmid stressed the point by insisting that true internationalism could not even exist without small nations.'[7]

But by and large the Griersonian documentary's engagement with Scotland tended to embrace an avowedly unionist perspective consistent with a project of 'national projection' and its emphasis on images of British society, industry, cities, the countryside, the British people and the national character. Rather than being a 'Scottish' film as such, *Drifters* is more accurately a depiction of a British industrial process involving fishermen living and working out of ports on the eastern seaboard from the Shetland Isles to East Anglia. While production began in and around Lerwick – the sequences featuring the fishing 'community' at the start of the film, the shots of seabirds, the fish market, and the reconstructed interiors of life on the trawler were all filmed in the Shetlands – the dramatic catch and the storm sequences were shot on a trawler operating out of Lowest-

The herring fleet sets out from port in John Grierson's classic documentary *Drifters*

oft. Moreover, the underwater sequences featuring 'destroyers of the deep' (dog-fish and conger eels) and herring shoals were filmed in a tank at the Marine Biological Research Station in Plymouth. The degree of manipulation involved in the production of this 'documentary' extended to shoals of tiny roach doubling for herring, it being impossible to keep herring alive in tanks.

Ian Aitken suggests that certain features of *Drifters* set a pattern for subsequent documentaries made by the EMB Film Unit. These included an interest in the working practices of a particular industry, a fascination with the integral role of modern technology in this process and a celebration of the homosocial world of the masculine professional group, coupled with a very mild anti-capitalist sentiment towards the way in which market forces serve to commodify this otherwise heroic labour process.[8] As a silent production, *Drifters* relies heavily on poetic imagery and the techniques of montage to drive both the simple narrative forward and convey in aesthetic terms the dynamism of the industrial process (the hauling of nets and pumping of pistons) and the wild environment (the swelling seas and crashing waves). Grierson alludes to the wider significance of his approach to film construction in the following way: 'The life of a national cinema is in this massing of detail, in this massing of all the rhythmic energies that contribute to the blazing fact of the matter. Men and the energies of men, things and the function of things, horizons and the poetics of horizons: these are the essential materials.'[9]

The highly masculine images conveyed by this quote is instructive. Kathryn and Philip Dodd argue that the Griersonian documentary was effectively engaged in a re-gendering of the nation, 'the making of a new, masculine post-imperial national identity in opposition to the feminization of that national identity between the wars'.[10] The crisis in identity is regarded by the Dodds as a product of the negative consequences wrought by the Great War and the loss of Empire on certain dominant ideas of manliness. The attempt to re-gender the nation also had an important geographical element in that the vision of heroic masculinity perpetrated by the documentary was to be found in images of non-southern peripheral regions such as Yorkshire, Teeside or the North Sea. This scenario clearly contrasts with some of the dominant constructions of Scotland discussed in the earlier chapters of this book with regard to conceptions of fantasy and desire that can be coded both metropolitan and feminine. It may also suggest a reason why those critics who have championed the documentary, such as Grierson, Wilson and Hardy, have tended to be dismissive of the romantic and fantasy images of Scotland perpetrated by the 'story film'.

Significant Developments in the Documentary Form

The techniques of documentary production were affected by the coming of sound, although the impact was not as great as on the fiction film where the desire for synchronised dialogue more or less rendered montage techniques redundant. In the case of documentary, images continued to be shot silently with a soundtrack created separately, allowing the various elements, including images, wildtrack ambient sounds, voice-over narration and music, to continue to be conceived in terms of montage. One of the most successful documentaries to use sound/image montage creatively was *Night Mail*. Like *Drifters* this is a much-discussed production, particularly with reference to the use of W.H. Auden's poetic narration, the lines composed to work in rhythmic conjunction with the images of the locomotive hurtling through the night, and Benjamin Britten's music. But *Night Mail* is also particularly relevant to considerations of the positioning of Scotland within the construction of a unified British national culture. Alastair Michie, for example, regards the central trope of the railway journey from South to North, England to Scotland, as appropriate to the national unification project of both the documentary movement and also British cinema in general – invoking similar journeys (albeit with different dramatic purposes) depicted in feature films like *The Thirty-Nine Steps* and *I Know Where I'm Going*.[11]

Harry Watt, the major creative force behind *Night Mail*, was responsible for another landmark film in the documentary canon with a Scottish connection. A celebration of the Post Office's ship-to-shore radio service, *North Sea* is based on a real event drawn from the records of the Post Office and shipping companies, depicting the plight of an Aberdeen trawler crew who become caught up in a fierce storm. It featured non-professional actors cast from the labour exchange in Aberdeen and was shot on location in Aberdeen and at sea with some studio interiors filmed at Blackheath in London. Unlike most of the documentary movement's output, *North Sea* was widely distributed in Britain and was popular with audiences, Rachael Low noting that the film 'delighted and impressed documentarists as well as the public, the critics and the trade'.[12] *North Sea* has also been regarded by some commentators as marking a turning point in the development of the documentary towards more story-based productions utilising a naturalistic approach to dramatic narrative and continuity editing rather than the poetic montage techniques advocated by Grierson.

This notion of a split in the movement initiated by the emergence of the story documentary has been challenged by Brian Winston who suggests that dramatisation was always an essential element of the Griersonian documentary, arguing that 'the *Night Mail* sequences, whether shot in studio or in Crewe, were every bit as much a drama documentary as ... *North Sea*'.[13] And it is significant that Grierson also actively steered some film-makers towards story documentary, including Jenny Gilbertson whose film *The Rugged Island – A Shetland Lyric* (1934) successfully integrates a narrative featuring the relationship a young couple with a depiction of the harsh life of the islanders. The narrative relies on the conventions of conflict – Andrew and Enga's quarrel over the promise of a new life in Australia – and its resolution (Andrew is freed from his responsibilities to look after his parents). There is even a suitably dramatic climax featuring the rescue of a lamb before Andrew and Enga are reunited. *The Rugged Island*'s formal construction may be rather crude, relying heavily on voice-over for narrative information and coherence, but as an early example of the use of story form, and as a poetic representation of the landscape and people of Shetland in its own right, Gilbertson's contribution to the history of Scottish documentary is an important and significant one.

Winston also draws attention to the profound influence of Robert Flaherty on the British documentary tradition, an influence played down by Grierson and subsequent commentators. Yet Flaherty's romantic conception of 'man against nature', epitomised by films like *Nanook of the North*, *Moana* and *Man of Aran* (the latter made for the GPO Film Unit) is clearly evident in many Scottish documentary subjects from *Drifters* to *The Rugged Island* to *North Sea*. The fascination with the struggle for existence, whether given a traditional or modern context, in wild, remote and inhospitable environments is particularly resonant in representations of Scotland as one of the last great wildernesses in western Europe. Consequently, life on the Caledonian peripheries had interested many film-makers, both Scots and non-Scots, resulting in a tradition that includes several films about the remote island of St Kilda[14] – such as Oliver Pike's 1908 production, *St. Kilda, its People and Birds*, and *St. Kilda, Britain's Loneliest Isle* (1923) made by the Glasgow-based Paul Robello – and the 1935 documentary *Eriskay – a Poem of Remote Lives*, made by the German anthropological photographer Werner Kissling, a figure very much in the Flaherty mould of film-maker as explorer.

Another illuminating element of Winston's sustained critique of the Griersonian documentary is his assessment of the profound influence of sponsorship. Despite claims to political radicalism by the movement, the governments involved in the documentary enterprise were, with the one exception of the Labour administration between 1929 and 1931, Conservative.[15] The Tories had not only been quick off the mark in appreciating the political potential of film-making, their willingness to sponsor the documentary movement during the 1930s was an indication that the promotion of a reformist social democratic state was clearly in line with their own political thinking. It is certainly impossible to conceive of the official documentary movement producing such a radical statement as *Hell Unlimited* (1936), Norman McLaren and Helen Biggar's anti-war film made under the auspices of the Glasgow School of Art. This powerful combination of images of death, destruction, disease and poverty, drawing upon exciting footage, actors, animation and diagrams, presents a forceful plea against rearmament and the power of the arms manufacturers. It also remains one of the most important Scottish contributions to oppositional political film-making in the 1930s of the kind that could only be made beyond the constraints of state-supported film production.[16]

The First Films of Scotland Committee, 1938

Whatever the importance of films like *Drifters*, *Night Mail* and *North Sea* to any consideration of the representation of Scotland in the documentary film, these remain isolated moments within a broader production programme, resolutely British in orientation and constrained by the interests of the paymasters in Whitehall. As even Grierson was forced to admit, such films ultimately 'suited the London purpose (and) ... have been at best indirect in their service to Scottish expression'.[17] But an important new initiative emerged in the late 1930s with the formation of a committee to commission a programme of films on contemporary Scottish life for the 1938 Glasgow Empire Exhibition. Set up by the Scottish Development Council and chaired by Sir Gilbert Archer, the first Films of Scotland Committee was made up of an impressive array of individuals with an interest in Scottish cultural life including Grierson, Norman Wilson, Charles Oakley, novelist Neil Gunn and playwright O.H. Mavor (James Bridie). Alexander B. King, the leading Scottish independent distributor, was also made a member of the committee to ensure that the resulting films would have some access to distribution. To help finance the production programme, £5,000 was provided by the Glasgow industrialist Sir John McTaggart.

Grierson's role in the initiative was crucial in facilitating the production of seven films through Film Centre, the London-based consultancy he had recently set up to mediate between sponsors and film-makers. Paul Swan notes that the programme of films was not only intended as a celebration of contemporary Scotland, but also as an advertisement for Scottish social and economic reconstruction that would be screened not only in Glasgow and the rest of the UK but also abroad. This initiative constituted 'the only occasion when complete responsibility for the national screen projection of an entire country was to be delegated to the documentary movement'.[18] Such sentiments echo Grierson's own judgement:

> Founded in a deliberate attempt to use the film for national purposes, the Films of Scotland Committee was, for Britain, unique. Nowhere as in Scotland was there a public body using the cinema to maintain the national will and benefit the national economy. After twelve years spent in preaching and teaching the power of the cinema to national authorities, I found it very satisfactory that my own country should set this example.[19]

Despite the unionist hegemony that dictated political life during the 1930s, this was also a moment of crisis in Scottish national identity. The demise of British colonial power, the traumatic experience of the World War I and the effects of the depression combined to threaten the stability of the unionist bond. The call for Home Rule had been forcefully articulated by radicals in both liberal and labour parties before the war, and the subsequent demise of the liberals and the greater national orientation of labour led to the creation of the National Party of Scotland in 1928 (which subsequently became the Scottish National Party six years later). But as Richard J. Finlay notes, the rise in nationalist sentiment during the 1930s was exacerbated by anxieties on the part of traditional unionist supporters in industry and commerce that their control of Scotland's economic destiny was slipping away.[20] The depression had hit Scotland particularly hard and the over-reliance on heavy industry was hampering any major recovery. New industries were not coming north, unemployment remained higher than the national average and living conditions in the overcrowded cities were a cause for concern. The notion that Scotland was getting a raw deal from Westminster was exacerbated by concern over levels of public spending and the amount of time dedicated by parliament to Scottish affairs.

One major response to this growing dissatisfaction was administrative devolution, signified by the Scottish Office moving to Edinburgh in 1932. New agencies such as the Scottish Development Council and the Scottish Economic Committee were also created to promote industrial diversification and new employment opportunities, and one of the direct outcomes of this programme was the 1938 Empire exhibition, described by Finlay as 'an effort to combine the memories of better times with an attempt at economic regeneration'.[21] The figure responsible for launching this initiative was the Scottish Secretary of State, Walter Elliot. Although a unionist, Elliot had consistently identified himself with Scottish affairs, even in his previous post as Minister for Agriculture, and thus embraced a recognition that the reconstruction of Scotland's economy required nothing less than massive state intervention. Christopher Harvie suggests that 'Elliot was conscious of the need to legitimate the Unionists as a party of moderate, statist reform, one that could both incorporate the liberal tradition and attract the working class.'[22] Such views had much in common with those of Elliot's close friend and associate John Grierson.

The Films of Scotland programme consisted of four major documentaries, *The Face of Scotland*, *Wealth of a Nation*, *They Made the Land* and *The Children's Story*, celebrating respectively the Scottish character and people, Scottish industry old and new, the development of agriculture, and the history and achievements of Scottish education. These were supplemented by three shorter instructional films: *Sea Food*, *Sport in Scotland* and *Scotland for Fitness*. The following year, the Committee funded *Dundee*, a depiction of one of Scotland's major industrial centres, directed by Donald Alexander. The programme was seen by twelve million people during the six months it was screened in Glasgow. But a controversy arose when the British Council excluded the films from the British programme for the 1939 New York World Fair on the grounds that they failed to conform to the stereotypical idea of 'Bonnie Scotland' to complement the image of an England represented by the Trooping of the Colour, the Crown Jewels and Buckingham Palace. Yet the vision projected by the programme is hardy a radical one. Made very much within the dominant modes of the Griersonian documentary, the films all rely on an authoritative male voice to supply narrative coherence to the images. They emphasise the positive processes of development and modernisation while avoiding any reference to the economic and social problems affecting contemporary Scotland that had prompted action by the national government in the first place. As Ian Aitken suggests, this clearly illustrates the constraints imposed by state sponsorship:

> although the films made for the Films of Scotland committee were concerned with important social problems, they were obliged to present a generally optimistic account of the steps being undertaken to resolve those problems. The overall tone of the films is not one of uncritical enquiry but of an

optimistic exposition of faith in the ability of the nation to surmount its problems.[23]

Taking a cue from the romantic tradition of Flaherty, the films also tend to convey a sense of development and change as a 'natural' and even inevitable phenomenon, rather than the consequence of complex social, economic and political struggle. Neil Blain notes that *The Face of Scotland*, directed by Basil Wright, embodies a problematic conception of Scottish history in its attempt to assert certain continuities between a mythical past and the realities of the present, positing the image of a timeless desolate rural Scotland waiting to be discovered beneath the surface of modern industrial society.[24] Beginning with the imaginary reminiscence of a Roman soldier posted at Hadrian's wall, *The Face of Scotland*'s whistle-stop tour through history touches on such defining issues as Calvinism, egalitarian education, the role of Scottish inventors in the modernisation process and the Scottish sacrifice in the Great War. Scotland's future is circumscribed by typically naturalistic allusion to 'the character of her people' over images of an all-male football crowd, before the film ends on a final shot of Edinburgh castle, an enduring symbol of national identity.

They Made the Land, directed by Mary Field, fashions a similar narrative in relation to the development of modern agriculture in Scotland, the problems of cultivating a wild inhospitable landscape gradually solved by innovations such as draining, planting new trees, and new techniques in animal husbandry, ploughing and cultivation. The positive role of science in agricultural development is also stressed to underline the modern dimension of farming. Again this is posited as a romantic struggle of man against nature, with no references to the kind of economic, political or social upheavals that transformed the Highland landscape in the aftermath of the 1745 Jacobite rebellion and resulted in the large-scale clearance of the land for sheep farming and the rearing of deer for hunting purposes. Donald Alexander's film *Wealth of a Nation*, applies the same thesis to industry, charting the (inevitable) decline of the old traditional industries such as fishing, shipbuilding, coal, iron and steel before examining initiatives to modernise Scottish industry: new trades, the building of new roads, railways, airports and hydro-electric power stations in the Highlands. The social ramifications of these developments are also noted with new houses and leisure initiatives solving the squalor and health problems associated with overcrowding and slum living. But despite acknowledging the existence of such major social problems, once again there is no attempt to analyse their origins. *The Children's Story*, directed by Alexander Shaw, functions as a companion piece to *Wealth of a Nation*, stressing the central importance of education to the production of a modern Scotland.

The first Films of Scotland Committee made a minor but significant impact on indigenous film production in Scotland. While five of the eight films were made by London-based film units such as Realist Films (*The Face of Scotland*), Strand Films (*The Children's Story*) and by newsreel companies like Gaumont British Instructional (*They Made the Land, Scotland for Fitness*) and Pathé (*Sea Food*), the remaining three commissions were given to a Scottish company.[25] *Wealth of a Nation, Dundee* and *Sport in Scotland* were all made by the Glasgow-based Scottish Film Productions which had been set up in 1928. The company's output also included *The River Clyde* (Stanley L. Russell, 1938), a survey of the industry and activities of the Clyde Trust written by the novelist George Blake, and several productions sponsored by the Ministry of Information during the Second World War. Another Scottish production unit extremely active during the 1930s was the team of John C. Elder and J. Blake Dalrymple who made a series of teaching films, primarily on industrial and agricultural subjects, for Gaumont British Instructional.

The Scottish Documentary during the 1940s

During World War II, documentaries made in Scotland or featuring Scottish subjects continued to be funded by the government, primarily through the Ministry of Information and the Scottish Office. Some of the MOI films addressed issues related directly to the Scottish experience of the war such as *Scotland Speaks* (Jack Ellitt, 1941) produced by Strand, *Land Girl* (1941) directed by Donald Alexander for Paul Rotha Productions and *Freedom of Aberfeldy* (Alan Harper, 1943), a film depicting the hospitality enjoyed by Commonwealth troops stationed in Scotland, made by the Edinburgh unit Campbell-Harper Films. Other films were concerned with various social and infrastructural issues, three of the most important being made by Paul Rotha Productions: *Highland Doctor* (Kay Mander, 1943), *Power for the Highlands* (Jack Chambers, 1943) and *Children of the City* (Budge Cooper, 1944). The latter film, shot principally in Dundee, deals with the problem of juvenile delinquency. While it suffers from the by now familiar paternalistic and condescending mode of address in its depiction of the fate of three boys convicted of robbery, *Children of the City* nevertheless features some powerful images of dark oppressive tenements enclosing an urban environment marked by substandard living conditions and stark poverty.

Writing in 1945, Norman Wilson described the wartime MOI/Scottish Office films as 'the authentic voice of Scotland discussing its problems', favourably contrasting these with a series of documentaries sponsored by the British Council 'content to portray the surface pattern of contemporary life and to record in an attractive light the achievements of British industry and science'.[26] Despite Wilson's antipathy, some of the British Council productions are interesting, particularly in their use of Technicolor and the story form. *Western Isles*

(Terence Bishop, 1941), featuring some fine cinematography by Jack Cardiff, combines a dramatic narrative with a descriptive account of island life in the tradition of *The Rugged Island*. In this case, the focus is on the production of Harris tweed, depicting the various stages in the process from the shearing of the island sheep and the washing of the wool to the waulking and spinning. Colour is used to create a powerful visual link between environment and product, the greens and browns of the landscape recurring as the predominant colours of Harris tweed – adding a new dimension to the dominant natural conception of industrial processes in documentary. This is itself interwoven with a story based on an actual sinking of a British ship, the *Atlantic Queen*, by a German U-boat – a scenario anticipating the first British feature-length documentary to be made in colour, *Western Approaches* (Pat Jackson, 1944). Dispensing with voice-over, *Western Isles* constructs its narrative primarily through image and editing, the mobile camera seeking out the action rather than relying on the usual combination of image and voice-over to create meaning. There is also some effective parallel editing between the rituals of life and work on the island and the dramatic plight of the sailors on the high seas.

But the aesthetic tradition epitomised by *The Face of Scotland*, *Wealth of a Nation* and *They Made the Land* continued to resonate during the 1940s. It is central to the construction of *The Crofters* (Ralph Keene, 1944) and *North East Corner* (John Eldridge, 1946), both made by the London-based Green Park company for the MOI. *The Crofters* examines life in the remote community of Achriesgill in Sutherland, the tight-knit and hardy community eking a living from sheep farming, livestock rearing and some fishing against a magnificent backdrop of rugged hills and moorland. This time the typically patrician narrator is juxtaposed with voices of the community, providing a more empathetic account of the inhabitants of Achriesgill and their way of life. Largely an account of a former Aberdeenshire fisherman, *North East Corner* explores developments in the fishing industry and agriculture but once again largely with a discourse of modernisation and progress. The final part of the film turns the attention towards Aberdeen, a bustling city built from the local granite and site of various thriving industries and educational institutions. During this section the old fisherman's voice-over gives way to a range of strong regional voices, but unfortunately the dislocation between voice and image tends to work against any attempt to create a sense of real people telling their own stories.

But there is also a hint of a more poetic, imagistic approach in the urban sequences of *North East Corner*, an impulse to be more forcefully articulated in Eldridge's major contribution to documentary, *Waverley Steps* (1947). In its depiction of life of the Scottish capital over a weekend, the film owes a great deal to Arne Sucksdorff's *Rhythm of a City* on Stockholm which Forsyth Hardy had screened for Eldridge and his colleagues.[27] The narrative structure of *Waverley Steps* is constructed through a series of interwoven incidents featuring a range of recurring characters, including a young railway fireman who spends the weekend with his wife, a Danish sailor on shore leave, a coalman who wins money on the dogs and subsequently celebrates in a local pub, a budding romance between two medical students who attend a university dance, a clerkess in the Royal Bank of Scotland who has a disagreement with her crusty old boss, and a bigamist who is tried and found guilty in the city courts. The action begins early in the morning with the arrival of the train and ends at night with a series of departures: the sailor boarding his ship, the train pulling out of the station, the couple kissing goodnight. This time there is no voice-over and while there is some (post-synchronised) dialogue, this tends to add detail rather than provide vital information.

The narrative is primarily driven by the fluid array of images shot by Eldridge and his cameraman Martin Curtis. The interaction between characters and environment evokes the poetic naturalism of the Italian neo-realist films of the same period and the later British 'Free Cinema' documentaries (with the odd jarring moment such as the unlikely drunken piper busking outside the pub). The urban environment plays a major role in the drama, the streets, buildings and bridges conveying a vibrant sense of place and an arena in which the various strata of society work and play. The broad social mix of Edinburgh's population is also conveyed, from the coal merchant placing his bet to the banker in his gentleman's club. While this representation is generally unpatronising and non-judgemental, Eldridge cannot resist taking a gentle swipe at the pompous banker, cutting from a shot of him sipping tea (having just complained about his female colleague), to the merchant's horse drinking from a trough. As a poetic depiction of a modern city, *Waverley Steps* remains one of the most accomplished examples of the Scottish documentary. Its impressionistic aesthetic and rejection of the more didactic techniques of the Griersonians affords the spectator space to interpret the images and draw a variety of meanings and inferences from them, bringing the city to life in the progress.[28]

The Second Films of Scotland Committee, 1954–82

The Scottish documentary was dealt a major blow when the Scottish Office decided to discontinue any direct financial support for film-making after *Waverley Steps*. The situation was exacerbated by the subsequent closure of the Crown Film Unit by a new Conservative administration elected in 1951, effectively signalling an end to the movement established in 1929. Documentary film-making continued but the major work was now carried out by units directly supported by industry such as British Transport Films[29] and the National Coal Board Film Unit. But a major new initiative was to come in the resurrection of Films of Scotland in 1954 with a remit 'to promote, stimulate and encourage the production of Scottish films of national interest'.[30] Under chairman Sir Alexander B. King and director Forsyth Hardy, the new committee included several other familiar faces from Scottish film culture such as John Grierson, Norman Wilson and Charles Oakley. Established with a donation of £10,000 from the businessman Hugh Fraser, the new Films of Scotland Committee was charged with persuading industry and other national organisations to sponsor individual documentary film projects with the Committee's own running costs covered by commissions charged to the sponsors. Films of Scotland also retained rights in the productions, guaranteeing that any box-office profit would also be ploughed back into the administration. But the sponsor exercised a great deal of influence on the creative process, including agreement over all stages of the scripting, the choice of film-makers, editing, voice-over commentary and choice of narrator. The completed films were showcased every year at the Edinburgh Film Festival and the Royal Festival Hall in London, effectively presenting, as Jo Sherrington puts it, an annual report of the organisation's activities.[31]

The initial batch of commissions give some sense of the kind of priorities that were established with regard to suitable subjects. They included *Festival in Edinburgh* (1955), *Enchanted Isles* (1957), depicting Bonnie Prince Charlie's route through the Hebrides, *A Land Lived In* (1957), a film on National Trust properties, *Life in the Orkneys* (1957) and *Scotland Dances* (1957). The subsequent Films of Scotland output can be roughly categorised in three broad areas: the projection of Scotland as a physical environment or tourist destination, the promotion of Scottish culture, and the celebration of Scottish industry. These emphases are reflected in the profile of the major sponsors including local authorities (city corporations, town and county councils), government agencies concerned with economic development (Scottish Development Department, Highlands and Islands Development Board) and culture (the Scottish Arts Council), and various private and public companies (including nationalised utilities like NSHEB and SSEB).[32] The collective output also served to consolidate and extend the repertoire of familiar images of landscape and cityscape, culture and industry already discussed in earlier chapters of this book.

The important contribution made by representation to the promotion of Scotland as a tourist destination had been demonstrated in the early nineteenth century with the dramatic impact of the publication of Scott's poem 'Lady of the Lake' on the number of visitors to Loch Katrine and the Trossachs. But a concerted institutional effort to establish tourism as a major industry did not begin until 1969 when the Scottish Tourist Board was founded. David McCrone *et al.* suggest that heritage has had a particular resonance in the Scottish context: 'There is no shortage of myth-making icons with which to imagine

Scotland. The importance of tourism, and around it, the heritage industry, gives commercial expression to national identity.'[33]

The Films of Scotland documentaries concerned primarily with Scotland as a physical place are split between those projecting the familiar rural vision of a picturesque land of Highlands and islands, and those concentrating on urban spaces. Around thirty films were made on rural themes, including *Busman's Holiday* (1959), *Perthshire Panorama* (1959), *A Song for Prince Charlie* (1959), *Holiday Scotland* (1966), *Loch Lomond* (1967), *Islands of the West* (1972), *A Pride of Islands* (1973), *Travelpass* (1973) and *Clydescope* (1974). Many of these take the form of the travelogue, with visitors moving through magnificent natural landscapes dominated by mountains, lochs and rugged seashores. The vision of Scotland presented has a direct continuity with the kinds of images explored in the first part of this book, images that are still central to the marketing strategies of the Scottish Tourist Board.[34]

But the representation of Scotland as physical environment by Films of Scotland goes beyond the image of the picturesque wilderness. There are almost as many films on major cities and towns like Edinburgh, Glasgow, Aberdeen, Inverness, Stirling, Perth, Ayr, Paisley, Kirkcaldy and Dunfermline, in addition to a number promotional documentaries for the five Scottish new towns. The representation of Edinburgh and Glasgow is particularly interesting in terms of the very different kind of emphasis placed on the two cities (that in some ways echo the dominant images perpetrated in feature films). Documentaries on Edinburgh, such as *George IV's Edinburgh* (1960), *Prospect for a City* (1967), *Walkabout Edinburgh* (1970) and *Castle and Capital* (1979), tend to focus on the history, architecture and culture of Scotland's capital, including several that concentrate specifically on the annual arts festival: *Festival in Edinburgh* (1955), *The Edinburgh Tattoo* (1959), *The Edinburgh Festival* (1965) and *Edinburgh on Parade* (1970). In contrast, Glasgow is presented as a modern industrial city embracing process of social and physical change in films like *Health of a City* (1965), on the work of the city Medical Officer, *If Only We had the Space* (1974), dealing with home improvement in the tenements, *Glasgow 1980* (1971) and *Places ... or People* (1975), both exploring the physical processes of urban redevelopment. The city also features in several of the industrial films made by Films of Scotland, reinforcing the intimate connection between Glasgow, industrial activity and working-class life already forged by fictions like *The Shipbuilders* and *Floodtide*.

The representation of Scottish culture in the Films of Scotland output has many continuities with the depiction of the environment, epitomised by a number of documentaries concentrating on either traditional cultural activities such as Highland dancing, music and sporting activities and events, or on Scotland's contribution to the arts. The former group can be seen as an exten-

sion of the kind of discourse perpetrated by the travelogues in their representation of cultural activities closely associated with the Highland environment,
while the latter group owe much to the form of the Arts Documentary pioneered by the BBC programme *Monitor* in the late 1950s and early 1960s.
Adopting a similar biographical approach, Films of Scotland produced numerous works on major Scottish artists in collaboration with the Scottish Arts
Council. This output includes films on writers: *Practical Romantic, Sir Walter
Scott* (1969), *Hugh MacDiarmid: No Fellow Travellers* (1972), *Neil Gunn – Light
in the North* (1972), *Sorley Maclean's Island* (1972) and *Norman MacCaig: A
Man in My Position* (1977); on architects, most notably Murray Grigor's *Mack-
intosh* (1968) and *Hand of Adam* (1975); and on painters: *Three Scottish Painters*
(1963) featuring John Maxwell, Joan Eardley and Robin Philipson, and *Still Life
With Honesty* (1970), Bill Forsyth's film on the work of Sir William Gillies.
There were even documentaries on the photographic arts, *The Sun Pictures*
(1965) celebrating the pioneering photographers David Octavius Hill and
Robert Adamson, and *I Remember, I Remember* (1968), an autobiographical
film by John Grierson made in association with Scottish Television.

A particularly high-profile area for Films of Scotland was the subject of
industrial activity, with more than fifty documentaries produced on traditional
and heavy industries such as distilling, fishing, textiles, steel, coal, shipbuilding
and transport, and more modern activities like hydro-electric power and North
Sea oil. Some of the most high-profile and critically successful productions
made by Films of Scotland come into this category, including the Oscar-winning *Seawards the Great Ships* (1960), on the Clydeside shipbuilding industry,
and *The Heart of Scotland* (1961), a film dealing with the history and industrial
development of Stirlingshire, both initiated by John Grierson. The international success of *Seawards*, directed by the American Hilary Harris, has also
meant that this production has received considerable critical scrutiny. As many
of the travelogues can be related to an earlier cinematic tradition, so this film
can be placed firmly in the context of features dealing with shipbuilding, projecting the familiar discourse of national unity through the stress on the
importance of shipping to Britain as opposed to Scotland. The influence of Grierson, who wrote the initial treatment, is also discernible in the approach to the
subject-matter: the industrial process from drawing office to launch is conveyed
in heroic, masculine, lyrical terms, dominated by the spectacle of sheer scale
conveyed by the monster ships under construction and the awesome power of
the finished vessel being launched. This aestheticism, described by Neil Blain as
'a concern with "shape" and "beauty" ',[35] is fetishised at the expense of any
acknowledgement or engagement with economic or political issues relevant to
the shipbuilding, and there is no indication of the conflicts and insecurities rife
in an industry that had long passed its heyday.[36] As Blain puts it: 'An absorption

with the shapes of materials, components and part-completed vessels, a general intention to eulogise and mysticise, and a script disposed to personification and hyperbole combine to emphasise tradition, timelessness and destiny over the specificities of work, history and class structure.[37]

A rather different set of functions are performed by *The Heart of Scotland*, a documentary that appears to be a hybrid of two very different kinds of film. The opening sequences, with their evocation of history and agricultural progress, through images of Stirling Castle, the Wallace Monument and the surrounding agricultural landscape, appear to rerun parts of *The Face of Scotland* and *They Made the Land*. But this romantic vision of progress gives way to an engagement with the oil refinery at Grangemouth, and while there are clearly similarities with the aesthetic approach of *Seawards*, this time the representation of industry as spectacle is rather more interesting. This may be partly due to the fact that in the early 1960s petro-chemicals signify future possibility rather than past glory. But, at the same time, the direction by Laurence Henson and photography by Eddie McConnell, utilising a range of extreme angles, whip pans and editing, serves to formalise the architecture of the refinery in an almost abstract manner. This not only conveys a modernist celebration of industrial beauty and awe, as *Seawards* does, it also creates an other-worldly strangeness that is faintly unsettling and would seem to belong to the realms of science fiction rather than informative documentary.

The Emergence of an Independent Production Sector

By the early 1980s, the production of documentary films primarily for theatrical distribution was becoming impossible to sustain, forcing Films of Scotland to cease trading in 1982. As Forsyth Hardy recalls:

> The Committee was faced with an increasingly difficult situation: a decline in
> the revenue from the distribution of short films, the resistance of audiences
> and cinema managements to any film with a promotional purpose, the
> eagerness of the Scottish film companies to make films, including full-length
> fiction films, independently and the fact that television had materially altered
> the opportunities for film production and exposure.[38]

Over a period of twenty-seven years, the second Films of Scotland Committee had been involved in the production of some 160 films. This in turn had a major impact on the stimulation of an indigenous independent film production sector in Scotland, nurturing and sustaining a number of companies specialising in instructional and industrial film-making, including two who were to play a major role in the development of independent production in Scotland from the 1950s onwards. Templar Films had been set up in Glasgow in 1949 to make films for local authorities and industry and between 1959 and 1971 the company produced sixteen documentaries for Films of Scotland, including such high-profile productions as *Seawards the Great Ships, The Heart of Scotland, The Big Mill* (1963), *Weave Me a Rainbow* (1962) and *Three Scottish Painters*. Meanwhile, three of the first five films commissioned by Films of Scotland, *A Land Lived In, Life in the Orkneys* and *Scotland Dances,* had been made by the Edinburgh-based Campbell-Harper films, founded in the 1930s by Alan Harper. Campbell-Harper were subsequently able to take advantage of the demand for government-sponsored films during the war and subsequently became a major player from the 1950s onwards, making some twenty-two films for Films of Scotland between 1957 and 1972, including *Construction of the Forth Bridge* (1965), *The Sun Pictures, Holiday Scotland* and a number of films about Edinburgh.

Both companies also provided an important training ground for new talent, with several individuals subsequently going on to form their own production units. Among the most important graduates of Templar films were the team of Laurence Henson and Eddie McConnell, who made *The Heart of Scotland* and *The Big Mill* for the company. Henson had been John Grierson's assistant on the STV series *This Wonderful World,* leaving with his mentor's encouragement in 1961 to direct *The Heart of Scotland,* with McConnell, a Glasgow School of Art graduate, as his cameraman. Having established a reputation for striking image-making, the two subsequently formed their own company, International Film Associates (Scotland) Ltd, the name taken from John Grierson's own North American registered company. IFA proved to be an extremely active unit, securing twenty-nine commissions for Films of Scotland over a twenty-year period, in addition to numerous projects for British Transport Films, the Children's Film Foundation and television companies. Templar, and in turn IFA, provided a training ground for a host of other Glasgow based film-makers including Bill Forsyth, Charles Gormley, Oscar Marzaroli, Michael Coulter and Gordon Coull. This activity consequently spawned more independent companies such as Ogam Films, who made a number of films directed by Marzaroli, including *Glasgow 1980* and *A Pride of Islands* and Forsyth's *Still Life With Honesty,* and Tree Films, formed by Forsyth and Charles Gormley, which produced films like *Islands of the West, If Only We had the Space* (1974), *Keep Your Eye on Paisley* (1975) and *Places ... or People* (1975).

Campbell-Harper provided a similarly fertile environment for emerging Edinburgh talent. Cameraman Mark Littlewood photographed several documentaries for the company in the late 1960s before joining forces with Mike Alexander, another Campbell-Harper employee, Murray Grigor and Patrick Higson, in the short-lived Martvr Films. Littlewood and Alexander subsequently formed Pelicula which soon became a major force, producing eleven films for

Films of Scotland in a decade including *Iona – Dove Across the Water* (1982), one of the last productions made by the committee. A former editor at the BBC and an energetic and innovative director of the Edinburgh Film Festival between 1967 and 1973, Murray Grigor also quickly established himself as a major film-maker, his debut being the celebrated documentary *McIntosh*, made under the auspices of IFA (Scotland). This film afforded Grigor the opportunity to work with a number of other ambitious film-makers like McConnell, Marzaroli and Forsyth. With his wife Barbara, Grigor subsequently formed his own company, Viz, based in Inverkeithing in Fife, and set about making several innovative films such as *Clydescope* and *Hand of Adam*. Like Pelicula, Viz continued to be a major force after the demise of Films of Scotland, the Grigors' interest in Scottish culture and in the arts guiding the direction of their work which included a number of biographical films on various iconoclastic characters from Billy Connolly to Eduardo Paolozzi to George Wyllie. Another significant east coast film-making partnership that emerged in the 1960s was Edinburgh Film Productions, founded by Robin and Trish Crichton. In 1969 the Crichtons opened a small studio facility at Nine Mile Burn near Penicuik from which they produced a number of films for Films of Scotland and other clients.

The Lure of Fiction

Writing in 1960, John Grierson made clear his view that an indigenous Scottish film industry was impossible, citing among other factors a lack of native film-making talent: 'I can't see what there is, both distinguished enough to be national and powerful enough to make its mark internationally, which has not already been decently accommodated by the more dashing entrepreneurs you find in an international metropolis like London.'[39] Yet many of the key people involved in this new independent production sector stimulated by Films of Scotland harboured ambitions to move beyond the constraints of the documentary. The first opportunities in this direction materialised in the late 1960s in the guise of the Children's Film Foundation. The CFF had been set up in 1951 'to ensure a supply of good quality, moral (but not moralising) films for young people'.[40] As David Bruce notes, the director of the Foundation in the 1960s was Dundonian Henry Geddes who, concerned that the CFF's films tended to be biased towards the south of England, began to explore the possibility of commissioning a Scottish company. This resulted in Laurence Henson and Eddie McConnell making their first dramatic subject in 1967, *Flash the Sheepdog*, a tale of a young London boy who comes to stay on a farm in the Borders. This was quickly followed by *The Big Catch* (1968), featuring the adventures of a group of boys in Ullapool during a slack period in the local fishing industry. The boys 'borrow' an idle fishing boat to rescue another boy who has gone off to capture one of the wild ponies on the Summer Isles and on the

The first steps beyond the documentary. *Flash the Sheepdog*, a production by Laurence
Henson and Eddie McConnell for the Children's Film Foundation

way back they also locate a large shoal of fish, a discovery that saves them from
the wrath of the adults. In 1972 Henson and McConnell made a third CFF film,
Mauro the Gypsy, about a gypsy boy who saves a young girl from drowning, set
this time on the east coast in Angus. Four years later Mike Alexander and Mark
Littlewood also received a commission from the Foundation for *Nosey Dobson*,
the story of a boy on the Isle of Arran who foils a robbery.

While this activity can be seen as representing a modest cinematic break-
through for Scottish film-makers, the work produced was subject to certain
fundamental constraints. At around one hour in duration, the CFF productions
all fall short of the full-length feature. Subject-matter and aesthetic modes were
also largely prescriptive, relying heavily on the familiar devices of resourceful
children and picturesque rural locations. Charlie Gormley, who co-wrote *The
Big Catch* with Henson, recalls both the generic limitations imposed but also
the magical lure of the opportunity to make 'real cinema':

> the Children's Film Foundation offered a crack at minutely budgeted 35mm
> 'theatrical production. The kind they showed at the Saturday morning matinees.
> But before you got near those ABC Minors and the Rank equivalent, you had to
> undertake a post-graduate course in the Henry Geddes school of film-making

which ignored how visually sophisticated the young audience had become, and insisted you opened every sequence with a wide shot so the kids would know for sure where they were. But it was 'pictures' and we littered the Scottish landscape with young Londoners holidaying with uncles and aunts in the Highlands, learning to guddle salmon and befriend sheepdogs before the coastguard and the police and the fire brigade rushed in for the grand slam ending.[41]

While Mike Alexander notes:

> there were certain things you couldn't say and couldn't do, and you had a producer appointed by the CFF to look over your shoulder. I was keen to work again with Charles Rees, who came up to Scotland and stayed in my house while he was editing it. But in the end the film was finished off in London without Charles. I was pleased with the final results but this was my first dose of reality as a film-maker. … I also became aware of the problem of not planning big set pieces properly, where you have 50 or 60 extras in a scene. So it was a pretty harsh learning experience at times.[42]

Alexander had already made a number of short dramas prior to *Nosey Dobson*, including *The Bodyguard* (1969) and *The Family* (1970), both commissioned by Bruce Beresford, head of production at the British Film Institute. In 1966 the BFI had assumed responsibility for the Experimental Film Fund set up in 1952 by producer Michael Balcon to nurture new film-making talent via the financing of short films, an initiative that had helped to kick-start the careers of film-makers like Lindsay Anderson, Tony Richardson, Ken Russell, Tony Scott and Stephen Frears. Alexander's third film for the BFI, *Home and Away*, is a sensitive semi-autobiographical account of the experiences of a lonely young boy at boarding school. The rather austere aesthetic employed in the film was partly inspired by Alexander's fondness for the work of Ingmar Bergman. But the resulting stillness and minimalism also bears the mark of fellow Scottish film-maker Bill Douglas, who collaborated on the writing of *Home and Away* at the behest of new BFI production chief Mamoun Hassan. Douglas had already made *My Childhood*, the first part of his celebrated autobiographical trilogy for the BFI, and was editing the second part, *My Ain Folk*, when he was brought on to the project. But his input was extremely important, as Alexander recalls:

> I went to London for two or three weeks to work on the script. I met Bill every morning to discuss how the film might be and what interested him about it. He cut things out and did what he always did with his own films, accepting that reality could be pretty boring and what you needed was to bring in other

things to convey how you felt. So we ended up with a framework which, apart from the fact that the boy goes to Rothsay to school, didn't bear much relationship to what actually happened to me. He also taught me a lot about dialogue, particularly how to make it work with hardly any.[43]

In addition to his BFI films, Alexander made a number of other short productions in the 1970s, including *The Poet* (1970), *The Gardener* (1972), *The All Rounder* (1974), *The Tent* (1978) and *The Adman* (1979), some of which were made with the help of the BBC. After leaving Campbell-Harper, Alexander had joined the corporation as an assistant cameraman and was able to get support for his own productions in the form of crews and editing facilities. This allowed him to build up a body of work outside the confines of the documentary. It also made him an inspiration for other ambitious Scottish film-makers like Bill Forsyth: 'We really admired someone like Mike Alexander, for instance, who pursued a very steady course. He made narrative films with his own resources. … You could see him steadily moving in one direction.'[44]

Films of Scotland also contributed directly to the development of indigenous Scottish drama production in their own small way. Recognising the constraints imposed by sponsorship, the committee had responded by making it possible for the occasional film to be made without sponsorship. Initial examples included two experimental films by Eddie McConnell – *A Kind of Seeing* (1967), inspired by the colours and shapes of the Scottish landscape, and *Amazing Moments of the Great Traction Engines* (1969), a fantasy about a small boy who inherits a steam road roller – and *Sisyphus* (1971), the first Films of Scotland cartoon film, based on the Greek legend.[45] The committee also commissioned three longer dramas, beginning with *The Duna Bull*, made appropriately by the by now relatively experienced Henson–McConnell team in 1972. This tentative step towards fiction was an inevitable development from the 'experimental' works noted above and reflected the kind of growing ambition within a Scottish film-making community increasing restricted by the parameters of the sponsored documentary.

Scripted by Clifford Hanley from an original idea by Forsyth Hardy, *The Duna Bull* is set on a fictional remote Hebridean island. Dependent on the annual export of livestock for survival, the island faces disaster after the sudden death of the local bull. On the mainland, a new specimen is selected and is to be sent under the charge of Charlie Johnson (Richard Harbord), a reluctant Englishman employed by the Scottish Office. When the delivery of the bull is delayed, the media take an active interest in the story, leading to a direct intervention by the Secretary of State. Meanwhile, Johnson's initial antipathy towards Duna and its inhabitants is gradually overcome by the amorous attentions of Helen (Juliet Cadzow), the island schoolteacher. In addition to brief appearances by veteran Scottish actors like Alex McCrindle and Jean Taylor-Smith, *The Duna Bull* also draws heavily on familiar narrative ingredients – a rural community facing disaster, plucky islanders, an antagonistic Englishman who falls for local lass, top-level government intervention – that relate it closely to the tradition of whimsical comedy epitomised by features like *Laxdale Hall* and *Rockets Galore*.

The second Films of Scotland drama was directed by Robin Crichton also from a Clifford Hanley script. A pastiche of the famous Hollywood comedy *The Great Race* (Blake Edwards, 1965), *The Great Mill Race* features a competition between various textile mills to produce and deliver a suit to Galashiels in the quickest time. The competitors include the devious Gordon Blackadder, head of the major manufacturer Scotia Rampant who steals the idea for the event from Thistle Mills, a small family firm. Unsurprisingly, after various thrills, spills and mishaps, Thistle pip their larger rivals at the post. *The Great Mill Race* contains footage of the industrial process that would not be out of place in a sponsored documentary, recognised by the assistance given to the production by the National Association of Scottish Woollen manufacturers and the Scottish Woollen Trade Employers Association. The third and final dramatic subject was to be made under the auspices of Films of Scotland, *The Boat* (Laurence Henson, 1975), another comedy featuring Chic Murray. It is perhaps significant that all three 'story films' made by Films of Scotland were comedies, a particularly appropriate genre for such low-budget production.

These tentative experiments in moving beyond the confines of the documentary by Scottish film-makers were augmented in a characteristically idiosyncratic and innovative way by Murray Grigor. Rather than seeking commissions for the CFF, Grigor decided that an alternative strategy was to subvert the system of documentary production from within. Consequently his films *Travelpass* (1973) and *Clydescope* (1974) parody the conventions of the Films of Scotland travelogue – epitomised by productions like *Holiday Scotland*. *Travelpass*, a film made to celebrate the Highland Board's 'Rover' ticket is an exercise in extreme kitsch, while *Clydescope* is an innovative pot-pourri of archive footage, animation sequences by John Byrne, music by Ron Geesin, a wonderfully arch voice-over by Michael MacLiammuir, and the central comic persona of Billy Connolly travelling the great river from source to mouth. Grigor's eclectic and irreverent approach won many admirers, including Colin McArthur who praises the radical deconstruction of the dominant regressive representational conventions of Scotland:

> *Clydescope's coup de grâce* to the discourse of Tartanry is to take on and defeat Loch Lomond. This shrine of Tartanry (and Kailyard) represented on scores of unspeakable postcards, shortbread tins and table mats, and celebrated in

popular song and in the Ur-Tartan documentary, is represented in *Clydescope* by a bear-garden on its shore while, on the soundtrack, the song 'Loch Lomond' is sonorously played on what sounds like a ship's foghorn as *The Maid of the Loch* cruises in frame.[46]

The production's sponsor was the Clyde Tourist Association and it is a mark of Grigor's skills as film-maker that he produced a film that simultaneously met the promotional requirements of its sponsor while sending up the conventions of the genre.[47]

The legacy of the Scottish documentary tradition and Films of Scotland in particular is consequently a mixed one. Very few films were produced that can be held up as classics, the majority being either extended advertisements or instructional films for various industries, corporations and institutions. More-over the kind of images created of contemporary Scotland demonstrate a heavy reliance on pre-existing and often stereotypical representations and associ-ations with little or no attempt to either challenge convention or explore alternatives. Yet at the same time the documentary provided a crucial continu-ity of indigenous film-making, facilitating a small but sustainable production sector to emerge in Scotland. Despite the creative limitations sponsored film-making entailed, ambitious film-makers now had an opportunity to learn and practise their craft in Scotland. This in turn provided the impetus for ambition to be nurtured, leading some to move beyond the confines of documentary towards the world of fiction and the possibility of a new Scottish cinema.

Notes

1   Forsyth Hardy, *Scotland in Film* (Edinburgh: Edinburgh University Press, 1990), p. 33.

2   *Cinema Quarterly* was also the second major serious film periodical to be published in English after *Close Up*, which ran from 1927–33. *Cinema Quarterly* adopted a similar ideological stance to *Close Up*, anti-Hollywood, pro-European cinema. But as Forsyth Hardy, who was the reviews editor for the magazine, argues, *Cinema Quarterly* also represented a reaction to the limitations of *Close Up* which he regarded as 'a comic publication … an avant garde thing that had no real relationship to the total development of movies.' Interview with Forsyth hardy, in Colin McArthur (ed.), *Scotch Reels: Scotland in Cinema and Television* (London: BFI, 1982), p. 76.

3   Including such ground-breaking features as *Paisà* (Roberto Rossellini, 1946), *Farrebique* (George Roquier, 1947), *Louisiana Story* (Robert Flaherty, 1948) and *La terra trema* (Luchino Visconti, 1948).

4   John Grierson, 'Edinburgh and the Documentary Idea', from Forsyth Hardy (ed.), *Grierson on Documentary*, 2nd edn (London: Faber & Faber, 1966),

pp. 346–7. Initially published in *Documentary Newsletter*, August 1948. For a detailed discussion of the history of the EIFF, see Colin McArthur, 'The Rises and Falls of the Edinburgh International Film Festival' in Eddie Dick (ed.), *From Limelight to Satellite: A Scottish Film Book* (London: BFI/SFC, 1990).

5   Lewis Grassic Gibbon, 'A Novelist Looks at the Cinema', *Cinema Quarterly*, vol. 3, no. 2, Winter 1935.

6   Hugh MacDiarmid, 'Poetry and Film', *Cinema Quarterly*, vol. 2, no. 3, Spring 1934.

7   Roderick Watson, *The Literature of Scotland* (Basingstoke: Macmillan, 1984), p. 326.

8   Ian Aitken (ed.), *The Documentary Film Movement: An Anthology* (Edinburgh: Edinburgh University Press, 1998), pp. 12–15.

9   John Grierson, '*Drifters*' (1929) in Aitken (ed.) *The Documentary Film Movement*, p. 79.

10 Kathryn Dodd and Philip Dodd, 'Engendering the Nation' in Andrew Higson (ed.), *Dissolving Views: Key Writings on British Cinema* (London: Cassell, 1996), p. 50.

11 Alastair Michie, 'Scotland: Strategies of Centralisation' in Charles Barr (ed.), *All Our Yesterdays: 90 Years of British Cinema* (London: BFI, 1986). Ian Aitken takes a rather different view, arguing that while 'the narrative architecture of *Night Mail* is concerned with issues of national communication and distribution, its thematic centre is linked to representations of regional accents, forms of behaviour, place names and environments'. 'Introduction' in Aitken (ed.), *The Documentary Film Movement*, p. 19. Grierson himself recalls that what he wanted was the production of 'a film dedicated poetically to the crossing of the Scottish border', a symbolic act suggesting a sense of national difference rather than continuity. John Grierson, 'I Remember, I Remember' (1970) in Aitken (ed.), *The Documentary Film Movement*, p. 150.

12 Rachel Low, *Documentary and Experimental Films of the 1930s* (London: Allen & Unwin, 1975), pp. 144–5.

13 Brian Winston, *Claiming the Real: The Documentary Film Revisited* (London: BFI, 1995), p. 54.

14 The evacuation of the island was also the inspiration for Michael Powell's feature *Edge of the World* and Bill Bryden's *Ill Fares the Land*, discussed in Chapters Two and Six respectively.

15 Brian Winston, *Claiming the Real*, p. 36.

16 For a detailed consideration of oppositional film-making in Britain during the 1930s, see Don MacPherson (ed.), *Traditions of Independence* (London: BFI, 1930).

17 John Grierson, 'A Scottish Experiment' in Forsyth Hardy (ed.), *Grierson on Documentary*, 1st edn, (Glasgow: Collins, 1946), p. 146. Originally published in the *Spectator*, 6 May 1938.

18 Paul Swan, *The British Documentary Film Movement 1926–1946* (Cambridge: CUP, 1989), p. 135.

19 John Grierson, 'A Scottish Experiment' in Forsyth Hardy (ed.), *Grierson on Documentary*, p. 147.

20 Richard J. Finlay, 'National Identity in Crisis: Politicians, Intellectuals and the "End of Scotland"', *History*, vol. 79, no. 256, June 1994.

21 Ibid., p. 259.

22 Christopher Harvie, *No Gods and Precious Few Heroes* (London: Edward Arnold, 1981), p. 100. Elsewhere Harvie describes Elliot as a 'White Marxist', Elliot's own term for 'someone who understood Marx and argued against him on his own terms', 'Walter Elliot – the White Marxist' in *Travelling Scot* (Glendaruel: Argyll Publishing, 1999), p. 127.

23 Ian Aitken, 'Introduction' in Aitken (ed.), *The Documentary Film Movement*, p. 23.

24 Neil Blain, 'A Scotland as Good as any Other? Documentary Film 1937–82' in Eddie Dick (ed.), *From Limelight to Satellite*, p. 60.

25 Beyond the centrality of government sponsored film-making, the documentary movement had also successfully attracted sponsorship from major industries such as the Gas Council, oil companies and various transport companies operating shipping, airline and rail services. This led to the establishment of independent units such as Strand Films, Realist Films and Paul Rotha Films, all of which made films in Scotland. In addition to their contributions to the Films of Scotland Committee programme, Strand were responsible for *The Key to Scotland*, Marion Grierson's homage to Edinburgh in 1935, while Realist Films subsequently made *Paraffin Young* (Ralph Bond, 1938) and *Cargo for Ardrossan* (1939), directed by Grierson's other sister Ruby.

26 Norman Wilson, *Representing Scotland* (Edinburgh: Edinburgh University Press, 1945), p. 15. The British Council films dealing specifically with Scotland included *Land of Invention* (Andrew Buchanan, 1940), *Border Weave* (John Lewis Curthoys, 1941), *Western Isles* (Terence Bishop, 1941), *Steel Goes to Sea* (John E. Lewis, 1941), *Song of the Clyde* (Jimmy Rogers, 1941), *Royal Mile, Edinburgh* (Terence Bishop, 1943) and *The New Mine* (Donald Carter, 1944).

27 Forsyth Hardy, *Scotland in Film*, p. 57.

28 Following the critical success of *Waverley Steps*, John Eldridge subsequently graduated to feature-film production via the Group 3 initiative, directing *Brandy for the Parson* (1951), *Laxdale Hall* (1952) and *Conflict of Wings* (1954).

29 British Transport Films made several films about Scotland from the 1950s to the 1980s, including *The Heart is Highland* (1952), *The Land of Robert Burns* (1956), *Scotland for Sport* (1958), *Coasts of Clyde* (1959), *Wild Highlands* (1961) and *Glasgow Belongs to Me* (1966), *Next Stop Scotland* (1968), *Golfers in a Scottish Landscape* (1971) and *A Line for All Seasons* (1981).

30 Quoted by Forsyth Hardy, *Scotland in Film*, p. 104.

31 Jo Sherrington, *'To Speak Its Pride': The Work of the Films of Scotland Committee* (Glasgow: SFC, 1996), p. 14.

32 The single largest sponsors include the Scottish Arts Council which supported thirteen Films of Scotland documentaries during the period, and the Highland and Islands Development Board which sponsored eight films. Forsyth Hardy recalls that the HIDB were 'one of the most understanding of the government financial bodies served by Films of Scotland', *Scotland in Film*, p. 122.

33 David McCrone, Angela Morris and Richard Kiely, *Scotland the Brand: The Making of Scottish Heritage* (Edinburgh: Edinburgh University Press, 1995), p. 197.

34 Ibid. See Chapter 4.

35 Neil Blain, 'A Scotland as Good as Any Other?' in Dick (ed.), *From Limelight to Satellite*, p. 59.

36 Christopher Harvie notes that between 1954 and 1968 Scotland's share of world shipbuilding fell from 12 per cent to a mere 1.3 per cent. *Scotland and Nationalism* (London: Allen & Unwin, 1977), p. 174.

37 Neil Blain, 'A Scotland as Good as Any Other?' in Dick (ed.), *From Limelight to Satellite*, p. 65.

38 Forsyth Hardy, *Scotland in Film*, p. 130.

39 John Grierson, in Forsyth Hardy (ed.), *John Grierson's Scotland* (Edinburgh: Ramsay Head Press, 1979), pp. 171–2.

40 David Bruce, *Scotland the Movie* (Edinburgh: Polygon, 1996), p. 216.

41 Charlie Gormley, 'The Impact of Channel 4', in Eddie Dick (ed.), *From Limelight to Satellite*, p. 186.

42 Interview with Mike Alexander, Glasgow, 21 January 2000.

43 Ibid.

44 Bill Forsyth, quoted by Allan Hunter, 'Bill Forsyth: The Imperfect Anarchist' in Eddie Dick (ed.), *From Limelight to Satellite*, p. 155.

45 In 1974 the Scottish Film Production Trust was established to finance films independently of sponsorship restrictions. This initiative resulted in three productions, *Castle and Capital* (1980), on Edinburgh, *The Grand Match* (1981), on curling, and *Iona – Dove Across the Water* (1982).

46 Colin McArthur, 'Scotland and Cinema: The Iniquity of the Fathers' in McArthur (ed.), *Scotch Reels*, p. 65.

47 Although Grigor did run into trouble with his next project, a tourist film on the north-west of Scotland in Spring. *Assynt*, featuring Bill Paterson as the Victorian eccentric Sir Charles St John travelling round the Highlands in an amphibious craft was, according to Grigor, a film with no discernible purpose. Consequently it was never shown. Interview with Murray Grigor, Inverkeithing, 22 January 2000.

Chapter Six
The Role of Television

The First Steps Towards a New Scottish Cinema

Inspired by the first tentative steps beyond documentary, the second half of the 1970s witnessed a concerted attempt to intensify this momentum towards the production of indigenous feature films in Scotland. As Robin Macpherson notes:

> By 1976 there was a clear sense of ambition tempered by frustration amongst the 'second generation' of Scottish film-makers, people like Douglas Eadie, Charlie Gormley and Bill Forsyth. A series of key developments suggest that this was a critical moment in the formation of a 'project' to establish what, if not a separate Scottish film industry, may be termed a Scottish film 'sector'.[1]

The developments Macpherson alludes to here include 'Film Bang', a initiative in 1976 that brought together the film-making community to debate the problem of funding and create a sense of identity within the sector that had previously been lacking. 'Film Bang' also resulted in the publication of what amounted to a manifesto for a Scottish film-culture,[2] and instigated the annual publication of a directory of Scottish film personnel, facilities and production companies. The following year saw 'Cinema and the Small Country', a conference focused on the attempt to find solutions to the problems hindering the creation of a film industry in Scotland, in particular the identification of new sources of finance. This initiative occurred at a politically opportune moment marked by growing support for a devolved Scottish parliament,[3] and, as Macpherson argues, it was effectively the midwife of the newly created Scottish Association of Independent Producers. Along with the main film industry union, the ACTT, the SAIP helped considerably to consolidate the collective voice of the Scottish film community and, crucially, facilitate the forging of connections with key industry players in London.

This new sense of purpose also resulted in the making of the first truly indigenous Scottish feature film since the 1920s. Written and directed by Bill Forsyth and produced on a minuscule budget with the collaboration of members of the Scottish Youth Theatre, *That Sinking Feeling* generated enormous excitement when it was premièred at the 1979 Edinburgh Film Festival. Paddy Higson, the production manager on the film who would subsequently become a major Scottish producer in her own right, recalls the haphazard manner in which *That Sinking Feeling* was realised:

> Bill had somehow or other raised £2,000. We all had cars. I think the camera came from Ogam. Alex Mackenzie and Alisdair Campbell provided the lights. Louise Coulter's dad had a grocery business and provided the food. Eddie Burt was able to provide a van. So it was scraped together, no-one was paid anything. We did it over three weeks and a number of weekends. John Gow cut it and the lab bills were paid by Bill and Charlie [Gormley] on the back of Tree films. But later it was sold to Goldwyn.[4]

Described by Forsyth as 'a fairy tale for the workless',[5] *That Sinking Feeling* tells the unlikely story of a gang of unemployed Glasgow teenagers who relieve the boredom of their existence by planning and a carrying out a robbery of ninety-three stainless steel sinks from a factory. Despite obviously limited production values, the film is driven along by Forsyth's keen observation, wit and charm, and by the sheer exuberance of the inexperienced cast. But whatever its symbolic value, *That Sinking Feeling* did not provide a viable model for a putative Scottish film industry. This required regular and reliable sources of finance that would allow production companies to survive and develop their potential beyond the previous limitations imposed by Films of Scotland. A solution to this impasse was just around the corner, however, in the form of the new fourth terrestrial television channel, a broadcaster that was to pioneer a new relationship between cinema and television in Britain.

The Channel Four Effect

The advent of Channel Four, which began broadcasting on 2 November 1982, was to usher in the first major wave of Scottish feature-film production. The company had been established with a remit to cater to tastes and interests largely ignored or neglected by the existing broadcasters and to encourage innovation and experiment in the form and content of programmes. It was also to operate as a publisher rather than a producer, commissioning all its product from independent producers and the existing ITV companies. This clearly presented a major new opportunity for the Scottish independent sector to secure commissions across a wide range of programme genres. The fact that the first chief executive of Channel Four, Jeremy Isaacs, was also a Scotsman intensified the optimism, as Mike Alexander suggests:

> I think he made a big difference. For a start he came from outside the London village mentality and was aware of the developments that had been happening outside London. If there was any potential film community it was in Scotland, and I think Jeremy recognised that. He persuaded us there should not be a Scottish quota,[6] that we should be good enough to do it on merit. Isaacs gave us a real sense of something to aim for.[7]

This view is echoed by Paddy Higson:

> When Channel Four was set up Jeremy very consciously brought all the commissioning editors up to Scotland. And I think that was the first time that anyone had taken the trouble to say that there might actually be people up here who can do things. It helped film culture in Scotland and allowed people to make relationships with various commissioning editors.[8]

Isaacs had also signalled that his priority for drama would be to commission feature-length works originated on film, the implication being that these would have the opportunity of some theatrical exposure before being broadcast. And with £6 million to invest in up to twenty new films in the first year of operations, Channel Four immediately positioned themselves as a vital new source of finance for established film-makers and newcomers alike. Isaacs appointed David Rose, formerly head of the BBC regional drama unit at Pebble Mill in Birmingham, as his commissioning editor for drama.[9] The establishment of Pebble Mill in 1971 had marked the first major devolution of BBC drama production to the regions, a process subsequently extended with the setting up of national drama centres in Glasgow and Cardiff in 1976 and 1979 respectively. Rose's background in regional production was to have a major impact on the kind of work subsequently commissioned by the Channel.

Channel Four appeared to bode well for the cultivation of Scottish film-making with four of the first twenty-eight films commissioned by David Rose for 'Film on Four' being Scottish projects.[10] But, interestingly, only one of these was a contemporary urban subject despite Rose's expressed interest in this area.[11] Set in a world of bars and night clubs, *Living Apart Together* (Charles Gormley, 1983) is a musical drama featuring B.A. Robertson as a Scottish rock singer returning home to Glasgow in the hope of patching up a failed relationship with his wife (Barbara Kellerman), the casting of Robertson following the now familiar strategy of utilising stars from other spheres of entertainment. In stark contrast, Barney Platts Mills's *Hero* (1982), based on J.F. Campbell's *Tales of the*

Western Highlands, a collection of Arthurian-like myths and legends collected in the 1860s, grew out of a community project, Platts Mills casting a group of young amateurs from the deprived Drumchapel neighbourhood in Glasgow. It was also the first feature to be made in Gaelic, but as the already inexperienced cast did not understand the language this strategy served only to draw attention to the amateur basis of the production. Consequently *Hero* failed to win admirers either in the Gaidhealtachd or with Channel Four viewers, recording by far the lowest audience figures for the first season of 'Film on Four'.[12]

The other two productions are both melancholic and poetic narratives of the rural Scottish experience set in the recent past. *Ill Fares the Land* (1983), the first feature written and directed by celebrated playwright Bill Bryden, is a sombre dramatisation of the events leading up to the evacuation of the last thirty-six inhabitants of St Kilda in 1930 which had also inspired Michael Powell's feature *Edge of the World*. It is effectively constructed as a drama-documentary, opening with a series of aerial images of the isolated rocky outcrop of St Kilda accompanied by an informative voice-over explaining the circumstances of the evacuation. (Despite this transparent appeal to truth, the production was actually filmed on the mainland peninsula of Applecross in Wester Ross.) Aided by a fine ensemble cast including Fulton Mackay and David Hayman and experienced cinematographer John Coquillon, Bryden

Looking back on the last of St Kilda: Bill Bryden's *Ill Fares the Land*

A taste of freedom: Phyllis Logan in Michael Radford's Film on Four, *Another Time, Another Place*

concentrates on the human drama in which the islanders struggle to keep their way of life alive before finally succumbing to inevitability. The fourth Scottish 'Film on Four', *Another Time, Another Place* (1983), is another cinematic debut, this time by writer/director Michael Radford. A delicate and moving portrait of the wartime experiences of a frustrated young farmer's wife on the Black Isle who has an illicit love affair with an Italian prisoner of war, the film is one of the most accomplished of the early Channel Four productions and will be examined in detail in the next chapter.

Another important Scottish production made for Channel Four was Murray Grigor's *Scotch Myths*.[13] Recalling the formal experimentation and carnivalesque absurdity of Grigor's earlier documentary *Clydescope*, *Scotch Myths* is a tongue-in-cheek deconstruction of the dominant discourses governing the historical representation of Scotland from Macpherson's *Ossian*, Robert Burns, Walter Scott and Harry Lauder to whisky and the Loch Ness Monster. The various comic set-pieces are constructed in a way that recalls the anarchic energy and intertextuality of the music hall, with Grigor utilising his small group of actors, including John Bett, Bill Paterson, Juliet Cadzow and Alex Norton, in a variety of roles. Femi Folorunso points out that until the 1940s not only was the music hall 'the most important and richest form of entertainment in Scotland: it is also important to note that it has declined more slowly in Scotland than anywhere else in the United Kingdom.'[14] Another important element of

Grigor's Rabelaisian brew is the absurd appearance of cigar-chewing Hollywood director Samuel Fuller (one of several neglected 'auteurs' celebrated at
the Edinburgh Film Festival during Grigor's period as director) wandering
around the Highlands in search of his own 'Brigadoon'. *Scotch Myths* was broadcast appropriately on Hogmanay in 1982 as a welcome and ironic antidote to
the traditional 'tartan and bagpipes' variety shows welcoming the New Year.[15]

While this first batch of features appeared to herald a new dawn of opportunity for Scottish film-makers, not everything was totally rosy in the garden,
however. In the early days of Channel Four, David Rose found himself desperately short of product and consequently several films had to be screened almost
immediately, wrecking any possibility of even a limited run in cinemas. This is
precisely what happened to *Living Apart Together,* which Gormley had shot on
Super-16 expecting a theatrical release. This disappointment did help his position however when he went back to Channel Four with his project *Heavenly
Pursuits*. Gormley had learned to think bigger from his experiences with *Living
Apart Together*, and this time the package contained two *bona fide* 'stars' in Tom
Conti and Helen Mirren, an experienced producer in veteran Michael Relph
and a budget which at £1,150,000 was more than double that the previous film.
Heavenly Pursuits was consequently released theatrically in 1987 and broadcast
the following year. The only other Scottish 'Film on Four' production commissioned in the 1980s was *Conquest of the South Pole* (1990), Gillies
Mackinnon's innovative and resourceful adaptation of Manfred Karge's stage
play filmed in the port of Leith. Made on a minuscule budget of £300,000, the
film demonstrates the assuredness of a neophyte director who would become
one of the most productive British film-makers of the 1990s, particularly in the
on-screen choreography of the ensemble cast and the inspired use of the
locations. The docks, warehouses, stockyards and coldstores are transformed
into an imaginary landscape within which the protagonists re-enact Amund-
sen's polar expedition as a temporary distraction from the hopelessness and
misery of their lives on the dole.

Beyond the 'Film on Four' slot the Channel also commissioned a number of
significant Scottish films. These include *Every Picture Tells a Story* (1984), James
Scott's lyrical biopic about the life and work of his father, the painter Willie
Scott. After an auspicious period working in theatre, the radical film-maker
John McGrath returned to the screen with *Blood Red Roses* (1986), the story of
a Clydeside female political activist played by Elizabeth MacLennan, which was
given a limited theatrical release in Scotland and then broadcast in three one-
hour parts. While *Tickets for the Zoo* (1991), a didactic television film
dramatising the desperate plight of young homeless people in Edinburgh written by Christine Winford and directed by Brian Crumlish, was an interesting
attempt to inform the audience about how easily vulnerable members of society

can fall into destitution. In doing so it recalled the interventionist impulse of Ken Loach's celebrated 1996 TV play *Cathy Come Home*. Channel Four also contributed indirectly to another flourish in Scottish production activity via their annual subvention to the British Film Institute Production Board initiated in 1986. Over a short period, the BFI commissioned four Scottish projects: *Play Me Something* (Timothy Neat, 1989), *Silent Scream* (David Hayman, 1990), *Venus Peter* (Ian Sellar, 1990) and *Blue Black Permanent* (Margaret Tait, 1993), all debut features for the film-makers concerned. Neat and Tait were both established documentarists in their own right; the former's films *Hallaig* (1984) and *Tree of Liberty* (1987) had already been screened by Channel Four, while the latter had made her reputation with a series of poetic films in the 1950s and 1960s before embarking on her first feature production at the age of 73.

Channel Four made a further significant intervention in its support for a number of franchised independent film and video workshops, enshrined in the 'Workshop Declaration' of 1984. The first Scottish workshop to be founded was the Edinburgh Film Workshop Trust in 1977 and within six years it had begun producing broadcast work, establishing a relationship with Channel Four's Independent Film and Video Department. EFWT was followed in 1981 by the community-oriented Video in Pilton, also in Edinburgh, and in 1983 by the Glasgow Film and Video Workshop. There have also been two less well developed initiatives in the form of the Stirling-based Alva Films and the Gaelic workshop Fradharc Ur on the Isle of Lewis. As Robin Macpherson notes, the workshop sector in Scotland tended to concentrate on offering a range of production, training, facilities and support covering basic introductory experience right up to broadcast documentary production.[16] The workshops consequently had a limited impact on the kind of developments examined in this chapter, a consequence of the meagre level of resourcing available. This was exacerbated when Channel Four decided to abandon revenue funding for the workshops in 1991 in favour of one-off commissions. As John Caughie puts it, this decision was clearly informed by 'an increasingly entrepreneurial logic as Channel Four moved towards autonomy in the market and faced the prospect of a reliance on its own ability to sell advertising' and making the Workshops 'a charitable anachronism in a market economy'.[17] The Scottish workshops, particularly the EFWT and GFVW, have nevertheless continued to provide crucial entry-level opportunities for film-makers.

This shift in emphasis also had implications for the Channel's involvement in more mainstream film production, particularly considering that fact that despite a generally favourable critical response, very few Channel Four-backed films had actually made any money. This prompted certain policy changes by a new chief executive, Michael Grade, and a new drama head, David Aukin, including, as John Hill notes, a reduction in equity investments in productions, with a correspondingly greater emphasis on buying television rights.[18] During Aukin's tenure, Channel Four scored a number of commercial and critical successes, including two high-profile Scottish projects, *Shallow Grave* (1995) and *Trainspotting* (1996), made by the team of director Danny Boyle, producer Andrew MacDonald and writer John Hodge. The kind of film-making represented in particular by *Trainspotting* marks a shift towards a more market-driven imperative, in this case trading on both the underground notoriety of Irvine Welsh's original novel and a soundtrack featuring many of the top stars of Britpop and contemporary dance music. In this way, the commissioning focus had subtly shifted from the creative expression or innovation of the film-maker to the potential marketability and audience appeal of the finished product.[19] Aukin articulated his own (characteristically upbeat) assessment of the situation in the following way:

> We can now make films for ourselves … occasionally these films will travel … we need no longer feel overwhelmingly dependent on overseas markets to finance our films … we can remain true to our stories, to our casting and to our way of making films. The proviso is that films must be made for a price that can be recouped from our own audiences.[20]

This new economic realism would be consolidated with the creation in 1999 of a separate company, Film Four, headed by Paul Webster, with a brief to produce a slate of productions that will be able to survive in the market place.

Scotland and the Television Play

Channel Four's conception of film had been influenced as much by a well-established tradition of single dramas made for television as any preceding cinematic heritage. The idea of serious television drama in Britain is often synonymous with the long-running BBC strands 'The Wednesday Play' and 'Play for Today' which ran from the early 1960s to around the time Channel Four began broadcasting. The individual most closely associated with the cultivation of the single play in Britain is Sydney Newman, the Canadian producer who ran 'Armchair Theatre' for the ITV company ABC from 1958 before becoming head of drama at the BBC in 1963. At the Canadian Broadcasting Corporation Newman had acquired a reputation for commissioning original contemporary drama written for television, rather than relying on the adaptation of pre-existing theatrical works, a policy he was to continue after taking over 'Armchair Theatre.' However, Newman's interest in socially progressive television, engaging with contemporary British social life and problems lives was to find its fullest expression at the BBC.[21] Such a project recalls the mildly progressive and socially inclusive rhetoric of the documentary movement, and can be related, however tangentially, to the important influence exerted over the young New-man at the National Film Board of Canada in the 1940s by John Grierson, who had been instrumental in persuading the Canadian government to establishing the NFB in 1939.[22] While finding Grierson a rather domineering boss, Newman nevertheless appreciated his ability to nurture new talent, recalling an 'incredible faculty of bringing out in us deep wells of understanding and responsibility'.[23] The two men consequently developed an enduring friendship that lasted until Grierson's death in 1972.[24]

It would be misleading to suggest that Newman was single-handedly responsible for revolutionising British television drama. Like his mentor, he relied heavily on the contribution of others to extend, refine and bring to life his general ideas. One of the most important figures in this respect was the Glaswegian James MacTaggart, who became one of the first two producers of the 'Wednesday Play' along with Peter Luke. The two had very different inclinations and this is reflected in the kind of plays they commissioned, MacTaggart's tastes being much more towards original work addressing controversial issues like race, homosexuality, capital punishment and abortion.[25] Despite returning to direction after only two seasons as a producer, MacTaggart's legacy was to live on particularly in the work of Tony Garnett, story editor on many of his productions, who would help to pioneer the development of drama productions shot entirely on film, as opposed to being recorded on video in the studio.

The development of broadcasting in Britain had been governed from the start by a strongly metropolitan impulse. Like his fellow Scot Grierson, John Reith's project as the first director-general of the BBC was governed by a strong belief in centralisation and the nation. As Kevin Robbins and James Cornford note:

> His greatest achievement was to create a system that was in all respects 'British': a nationalised industry, functioning as a national public sphere and articulating a popular conception of national culture and identity. That this came to appear for so long, and not just in Britain, the natural form and existence for broadcasting is testimony to what was accomplished.[26]

This assumption of national unity, presided over by a centralised bureaucracy, for a long time militated against any significant development of regionalism within the BBC, let alone the various national configurations within the United Kingdom. The introduction of commercial television in 1955, as a network of geographically specific franchises, did involve an explicit conception of regionalism, however, resulting in, among other things, the establishment of the independent Scottish broadcasters, Scottish Television (STV) and Grampian

Television. But, as Jean Seaton argues, during the formative years of independent television companies were expensive to run and consequently the smaller franchises, with their limited audiences, attracted little commercial interest.[27] This allowed Roy Thompson to acquire the franchise for STV at a very low price, giving rise to his notorious statement that the operation amounted to 'a licence to print money'.[28] Seaton concludes that while the creation of ITV entailed an explicit commitment to regional commercial broadcasting, this emerged and developed in a form essentially governed by economic rather than cultural considerations.

All of this has had serious implications for the development of indigenous television drama in Scotland, the most expensive and prestigious genre in television production. Some period drama was produced at the BBC's studio in Glasgow in the 1960s, including series such as *Madame Bovary*, *Scarlet and Black*, *For Whom the Bell Tolls* and *Witch Wood*, but these were effectively London projects using the new 625-line facility adopted by BBC2 when it began transmission in 1964. The actual representation of Scotland in television drama during the period was restricted to popular series like *Para Handy* and *Dr Finlay's Casebook*, produced by the BBC and STV respectively, which unsurprisingly relied heavily on familiar but increasingly tired iconography and aesthetic conventions synonymous with various films of the 1950s. While certain Scottish writers such as Eddie Boyd and Alan Sharp began to establish themselves as TV dramatists in the 1960s,[29] it was during the following decade that a more serious dramatic engagement with Scotland began to emerge that served to extend the existing repertoire of images and representations created by the cinema.[30]

This more distinctively Scottish voice inevitably entailed a number of high-profile adaptations, including several elegiac works rooted in the rural experience. Adapted by John McGrath and directed by James MacTaggart, *Orkney* (1971) comprises a trilogy of George Mackay Brown stories reflecting Orcadian life during the nineteenth century, between the wars, and the present day. In the same year the BBC also produced a serialised adaptation of Lewis Grassic Gibbon's classic novel *Sunset Song*, starring Andrew Keir and Vivien Heilbron. (The other parts of his *Scots Quair* trilogy, *Cloud Howe* and *Grey Granite* were subsequently serialised in 1982 and 1983 respectively.) Other island-located dramas produced during the period include the STV adaptations of Lavina Derwent's *Sula* (1975) and *Return to Sula* (1978), and *Andrina* (1981) Bill Forsyth's BBC adaptation of a short story by George Mackay Brown. Scottish television drama also benefited greatly in the 1970s from recent developments in the theatre, most notably a number of works concerned with the kind of social engagement pioneered by the Glasgow Unity theatre group in the 1940s.[31] A number of successful stage plays in this tradition were quickly adapted for the small screen by their original authors, including two productions by Bill Bryden: *Willie Rough* (1976) inspired by the experiences of the playwright's grandfather as a riveter and radical shop steward, during the First World War, and *Benny Lynch* (1976), based on the life of the Scottish world fly-weight boxing champion and produced by Granada. Another significant contribution in this context is *The Bevellers* (1974), Roddy McMillan's depiction of the harsh experience of a young man's first day in the bevelling shop of a Glasgow glass factory. While a similar workplace scenario is presented in John Byrne's play, *The Slab Boys* (1979), set in a Paisley carpet factory in the late 1950s, although this time there is a greater emphasis on the energising and potentially liberating force of working-class humour, artistic expression and new forms of youth culture like rock 'n' roll. [32]

Whatever the novelty value of these images of working-class Scottish masculinity, the resulting television plays tended to be rather orthodox in construction. A much more radical approach to form was adopted by writer John McGrath and director John Mackenzie in *The Cheviot, the Stag and the Black Black Oil* (1974), a 'Play For Today' adaptation of the acclaimed stage production by McGrath's socialist theatre company 7:84 Scotland. [33] Praised by Colin McArthur as 'the most interesting attempt thus far to unite television and radical historiography in a dramatic mode which promotes both pleasure and analysis', [34] *The Cheviot* critically examines the history of economic exploitation of the Highlands – from the mass clearing of the land for the rearing of sheep and subsequently the breeding of deer for hunting to the North Sea oil exploration of the early 1970s. McGrath's innovation in the original play was his appropriation of the traditional ceilidh form (bearing many similarities to music hall), an eclectic and frequently comic combination of song, dance and storytelling utilising a small group of actors in a variety of roles, to address this history of exploitation. [35] The television adaptation of *The Cheviot* not only retained the virtues of the original by way of footage of a performance of the play in front of a Highland audience in Dornie, it also added new elements to the mix, including filmed reconstruction of dramatised episodes from the history of the clearances and documentary scenes examining working conditions in the North Sea oil industry. The final combination serves to produce a particular effect as John Caughie observes:

> The elements are not integrated to confirm and support each other, but are clearly separated out and allowed to play against each other. The risk which the theatrical production always ran of being overwhelmed by the exuberance of its own performance is tempered by the possibility which the separation of discourses allows of continually unsettling the spectator's position. The documentary on the present oil industry produces a contemporaneity of history which both undercuts the romanticism of a 'Celtic twilight', and offers

a way of seeing this struggle in terms of other struggles. It is the possibility of this collision, of the refusal of integration, which makes the documentary drama a potentially interesting political form.[36]

Despite this formal radicalism, *The Cheviot, the Stag and the Black Black Oil* remained something of an isolated experiment in television drama, although similar techniques of ironic distancing and bricolage can also be discerned in Murray Grigor's *Clydescope,* made around the same time, and his own subsequent radical exercise in playful cultural commentary, *Scotch Myths.*

Tales of the West: the Work of Peter McDougall

But as we have seen, the single play also created an opportunity for original drama conceived and written for the small screen and one of the most significant Scottish contributions to this tradition remains the hard-edged work of Peter McDougall. Like Sharp and Bryden before him, McDougall was strongly influenced by his formative experiences in Greenock where he had worked in the shipyards before moving to London to become a painter and decorator. This led to a chance encounter with the actor and writer Colin Welland who encouraged McDougall to realise his own creative ambitions, initiated by *Just Your Luck* (1972), a raw work focusing on Scottish proletarian life blighted by restricted opportunity, drink and despair. The play centres around the plight of Alison Hawkins (Lesley Mackie), a 17-year-old who has become pregnant to Alec Johnson (David Hayman), a young sailor she has only just met having split from her previous boyfriend. To make matters worse, Alison is Protestant and Alec is Catholic and much of the play is concerned with how the problem of religious division are negotiated by the respective families. But while the acknowledgement of the deep-rooted sectarianism in Scotland is a welcome change after an almost universal evasion of the issue in the cinema, it is ultimately secondary to McDougall's focus on Alison's entrapment within the expectations of her role as a working-class wife and mother.

The portrayal of the Scottish working class in *Just Your Luck* not only avoids sentimentality, it verges at times on contempt: both families wallowing in a state of domestic squalor and mutual antagonism with weak drunken fathers constantly berated by their sly, sharp-tongued wives while dirty children cry and run amok in the background. But whatever the novelty of unadulterated west coast Scottish accents discussing the relative virtues and vices of Protestants and Catholics in a television drama, the form of *Just Your Luck* is solidly traditional. Directed by Mike Newell, the play is shot largely on multi-camera video with the bulk of the action confined to the studio sets of the Hawkins and Johnson families. There are a small number of filmed exteriors, but these serve only to link the major scenes and to provide the merest hint of the existence of an environment of squalid grey council tenements and shipyard cranes in the background. Consequently, *Just Your Luck* remains very much in the theatrical tradition, physically restricted and heavily reliant on dialogue.

From the mid-1960s onwards, the use of 16mm film had gradually transformed television drama, a process pioneered by landmark productions such as *Up the Junction* (1965) and *Cathy Come Home* (1966), both directed by Ken Loach and the latter produced by Tony Garnett. Their innovation was to bring drama production much closer to the techniques of the cinema, including single-camera shooting and film editing replacing multi-camera set-ups and vision mixing. This in turn created a very different kind of drama, oriented much more towards the aesthetics of cinema than the stage. The use of film also brought television into a very different relationship with the real world. Whether concerned with contemporary social issues or not, all studio-bound drama was heavily dependent on dialogue. Film on the other hand allowed visual action and location to play a more significant role in the drama, facilitating a greater exploration of the relationship between characters and their environment. It has been suggested that this represented a break-away from a prevailing naturalist tradition towards a greater realism, M.K. MacMurragh-Kavanagh arguing that Garnett's particular commitment to film was an aspect of his interest in portraying 'real life as it is lived':

> He realised that dealing with the issues of abortion or homelessness in the necessarily alienated environment of the studio looked and, more importantly, *felt* entirely different to dealing with them in the streets where these issues were daily concerns. When placed in the 'real world', and filmed in a way to emphasise this reality, these daily concerns were transferred into urgent problems requiring immediate attention.[37]

While the single play continued to be regarded as primarily a writer's medium, this shift towards a more cinematic mode of production also indicated the increasingly significant creative contribution of those responsible, particularly the director, cameraman and editor.

McDougall's second television play for the BBC, *Just Another Saturday*, benefited greatly from precisely this kind of formal construction. The director John Mackenzie had also been a production assistant to Loach and Garnett before making his own directorial debut in 1967 with *The Voices in the Park*, a 'Wednesday Play' written by Leon Griffiths.[38] *Just Another Saturday* (1975) centres around John (Jon Morrison) a young stick thrower in a Glasgow Protestant flute band taking part in his first city-wide Orange parade. Over the course of twenty-four hours his sectarian fanaticism is brought into question as he begins to perceive the unsavoury underside of militant Protestantism. On the way back

Urban tribalism: Jon Morrison leads the Protestant flute band in Peter McDougall's 'Play For Today', *Just Another Saturday*

from Glasgow Green the band passes through 'Fenian Alley', a neighbourhood populated by Catholics, and during the subsequent battle John witnesses the various acts of unnecessary brutality. Violence also erupts later when he his accosted by an angry Catholic who pulls a knife on him outside the pub where he has been drinking with three workmates, led by big Paddy (an early role for Scottish comedian Billy Connolly), who also happen to be Catholics. Another key concern in the work is John's relationship with his father Dan (Bill Henderson), who cautions his son about the dangers of religious fanaticism and the ways in which sectarianism serves only to split the working class, preventing them from uniting against the 'real' enemy. But despite his political radicalism, Dan is portrayed as a useless drunk, considerably weakening his authority and credibility in the eyes of John.

The cinematic sensibility of Mackenzie is evident throughout *Just Another Saturday*, the opening montage of Protestant iconography – Rangers scarves, a picture of William of Orange, the flute band regalia, John's tattoos – quickly and powerfully establishing a certain set of dramatic and thematic expectations. But the most potent images are of John during the parade, ecstatically leading the band with his frenzied stick throwing. The physicality of Jon Morrison's performance combines with the dynamic direction, the fluid camerawork (a combination of hand-held shots in the thick of the action and a variety of camera angles including some very effective overhead shots) and the fragmented editing to convey the visceral excitement of the parade. The Glasgow locations are equally central, framing the action and alluding to the complex geographical and social meanings attached to the parade. The urban streets serve to normalise the action, but also to point up the territorial contestation at the heart of sectarianism. Skilful use is also made of a real Orange parade, into which the drama is insinuated by way of *cinéma vérité* techniques. The use of film also allows a greater sense of realism in the interiors which are largely restricted to John's home and the pub. The pub environment in particular is as emblematic as the streets, a homosocial domain synonymous with a complex mixture of communality, humour, sentimentality and aggression defining a particular vision of working-class Scottish masculinity.

After *The Elephant's Graveyard* (1976), a more gentle and reflective drama featuring Jon Morrison and Billy Connolly as a couple of men bunking off work who run into each other in the woods outside Greenock, McDougall and Mackenzie turned their attention towards the mythical figure of the urban Scottish 'hard man', an element of the discourse of 'Clydesidism' noted in Chapter Four. *Just A Boy's Game* (1979) features rock singer Frankie Miller as Jake McQuillan, a shipyard worker with a reputation for violence. Despite having 'gone straight', Jake remains a target for local lads desperate to establish their own credentials. Once again McDougall returns to his obsession with familial relations and the continuity of fate across the generations. Jake retains a great deal of admiration for his ailing grandfather (Hector Nicol), a brute of a man who in his youth also had a reputation as a street fighter and who, it transpires, has served time for murdering Jake's father, something that does nothing to tarnish Jake's feelings towards the old man. Glimpsed briefly in *The Elephant's Graveyard*, the shipyards of Greenock dominate the environment of *Just a Boy's Game* with the massive cranes visible through almost every window. Yet all the characters, particularly Jake and his friends Dancer (Ken Hutchison) and Tanza (Gregor Fisher), display a profound ambivalence towards the world of work. Jake's shift as a crane operator is interrupted by Dancer who turns up with alcohol and the assertion that 'Friday has been declared a holiday', and the two go off to the squalid flat of Bella (Jan Wilson), the local prostitute, to get drunk. Labour in this context is regarded as tedious and repetitive, and there is no hint of the kind of sentimentality towards the yards as a source of masculine pride and meaning that would arise in a context of soaring unemployment during the 1980s.

Much of the action in *Just a Boy's Game* takes place at night with Mackenzie making a virtue of this in creating an atmosphere of uncertainty and danger. This is particularly effective in the use of the environs of the dark shipyards during the denouement of the drama when Jake, Dancer and Tanza are attacked by members of the 'young team' gang, led by McCafferty (Billy Greenlees), an ambitious thug who covets Jake's crown. Chased by two of the gang, Dancer runs into a mooring cable and falls to his death into the dry dock. Had this been an industrial accident the setting would have taken on a particular political meaning, but as it stands the location and circumstances of Dancer's demise can be read as a direct consequence of his own failure as a husband, father and responsible employee. In this way, he represents an echo of John's father Dan in *Just Another Saturday* as yet another casualty of working-class Scottish masculinity.

McDougall and Mackenzie relied even more heavily on a cinematic model for their next collaboration. Adapted from the autobiography of reformed Glasgow gangster Jimmy Boyle, *A Sense of Freedom* is a feature-length production commissioned by STV. The first fragmented and elliptical part of the film depicts a series of events in Boyle's violent career as a gangster on the streets of Glasgow: loan sharking, terrorising 'clients', the savage skirmishes with rival gangs and the inevitable run-ins with the law. The city in which this activity takes place is a dark and grubby place governed by violence and fear, the intimate hand-held camera technique used effectively to render both the chaos and cold brutality of the violence. After being convicted for murder, Boyle receives a life sentence and the focus shifts to his subsequent experiences in prison. A reluctant and troublesome captive, he is repeatedly beaten and brutalised by the wardens and locked up in solitary confinement. His resistance involves 'dirty' protests and repeated escape attempts, met by more and more severe punishment, including one incident when both his arms are broken. Finally, after a riot in which a prison officer loses an eye, the authorities decide to adopt a different approach, transferring Boyle to the new 'Special Unit' at Barlinnie prison, an experiment geared towards the rehabilitation of prisoners through creative stimulation. The film ends with a freeze frame of an incredulous Boyle opening his parcel of belongings with a knife freely given to him by a warden, accompanied by the information that the unit was where he would write the autobiography on which the film was based.[39]

Mackenzie and his cameraman, Chris Menges, one of the most adept exponents of *vérité* cinematography in Britain,[40] adopt a much more claustrophobic style in the prison sequences. The camera is persistently placed uncomfortably close to its subject, unflinchingly recording the process of pain and gradual dehumanisation. But the revelation of the work is the powerful central performance of David Hayman in his first major film production after a decade on stage. In the opening sequences, his persona is firmly locked behind a hard shell, but this gives way to a palpable sense of a physical body and a spirit being gradually worn down by the years of beatings and abuse. Hayman conveys an intense vulnerability in the process, eliciting sympathy for someone we have seen is capable of the most horrendous acts. In one poignant sequence, he comes close to cracking, pacing frantically up and down in his tiny cell with an insane grin on his face, the unsettling strains of Frankie Miller's acoustic guitar pounding away on the soundtrack. While in another he lies helpless, his arms broken, calling out for his mother. But perhaps the most enduring image of all is of a defiant Boyle, covered in his own excrement, taunting the guards, a blistering evocation in human degradation initiated on the mean streets of Glasgow and consolidated within the prison system.

While *A Sense of Freedom* marked the final collaboration between McDougall and Mackenzie,[41] the former was to remain a potent force within Scottish television, writing a further three major works for the BBC. *Shoot for the Sun* (1987) is a bleak portrayal of the hard-drugs scene in Edinburgh featuring Jimmy Nail and Brian Cox as a couple of ex-cons who become involved as dealers. The film was directed by Ian Knox who was also responsible for *Down Where the Buffalo Go* (1988), a drama marking McDougall's return to the struggle of ordinary people in Greenock, this time set against the backdrop of the closure of the shipyards and the presence of the American nuclear submarine base in the nearby Holy Loch. The production was given added distinction by way of the casting of Harvey Keitel as a US serviceman whose marriage to a local woman has broken down. Unfortunately, the rather sentimental lament for the destruction of an industry and with it a traditional way of life sits uncomfortably with McDougall's previous contemplation of employment in *The Elephant's Graveyard* and *Just a Boy's Game*. McDougall's last work to date, *Down Among the Big Boys* (1993), a black comedy about a successful Glasgow criminal, Jo Jo Donnelly, whose daughter is about to marry the rising star of the local CID signals a change in direction. As directed by Charlie Gormley, this is much lighter piece, foregrounding the black humour and absurdity which had always been present in McDougall's work, the Glasgow milieu this time reflecting the materialism of Billy Connolly's upwardly mobile gangster, enjoying the spoils of a successful career.

The raw visual power and energy of McDougall's work, *Just a Boy's Game* and *A Sense of Freedom* in particular, served to consolidate a very different set of mythical representations of Scotland. Eschewing the romantic fantasies of the cinema, McDougall and Mackenzie create an alternative dark, urban world blighted by poverty, machismo and violence. But, despite the use of a naturalistic aesthetic, this vision is no more real than *Brigadoon*. Neither is it political in the manner of John McGrath; no coherent analysis of the social forces that have created men like Jake McQuillan and Jimmy Boyle is offered. Rather, their plight is rendered in mythic terms, enshrining the image of the working-class hard man as a contemporary 'Wild West hero' or 'gangster'. Ian Spring notes the

transparent motivation of the Western in *Just a Boy's Game*, with Jake McQuillan cast as the gunfighter who has 'hung up his guns'.[42] While *A Sense of Freedom*
– despite points of connection with a British tradition epitomised by films like
Get Carter (Mike Hodges, 1971), *Villain* (Michael Tuchner, 1971) and Mackenzie's own *The Long Good Friday* (1981) – evokes the powerful influence of
numerous Hollywood prison dramas and the violent urban thrillers of Martin
Scorsese.

The Changing Face of Scottish Television Drama

The film policies initiated by Channel Four encouraged other television
companies to become more directly involved in feature production in the
1980s, but in most cases this proved to be a brief flirtation.[43] The BBC proved
to be initially more reluctant to move in this direction, but the appointment of
producer Mark Shivas to the drama department in 1988 initiated a change in
direction. Under Shivas, the single drama tradition associated with 'Play For
Today' was recast in the 'Film on Four' mould, the BBC even adopting a similar branding with the slots 'Screen One' and 'Screen Two'. It is worth noting,
however, that only a small proportion of productions made it into the cinema,
one of the obstacles being the persistence of different union regulations governing production at the BBC for cinema and television. But the situation began
to improve as those involved became more confident and comfortable with the
process, leading to a string of theatrical releases including *The Snapper* (Stephen
Frears, 1993), *Priest* (Antonia Bird, 1995), *Land and Freedom* (Ken Loach, 1995)
and *Jude* (Michael Winterbottom, 1996). Shivas also collaborated with the BBC
Scotland Drama department's first venture into feature-film production with
Gillies Mackinnon's *Small Faces* (1996), initiating what was to prove a limited
but very significant involvement in the development of a Scottish film industry
in the latter half of the 1990s.

During the 1980s the drama department at BBC Scotland began to assert
itself more vigorously under the leadership of Bill Bryden who was appointed
head of drama in 1984. Whereas his predecessors Pharic McLaren and Roderick Graham had tended to produce material initiated and controlled by the
drama department in London, Bryden began to mount a serious challenge to
this highly centralised state of affairs. David Hayman notes that Bryden brought
a creative energy to the BBC drama department ('he kept calling it a studio'),[44]
while Mike Alexander recalls: 'What Bill was brilliant at was going down to
London and getting the money. He took people under his wing like Peter
McDougall and William McIlvanney. I don't know how many new people got
in but he certainly created a substantial body of work when he was there. And
of course he loved writers, television drama for him was writer driven.'[45]

In addition to Peter McDougall's last three major works, Bryden also commissioned *Dreaming* (1990), an anti-Thatcherite musical/fantasy written by acclaimed novelist McIlvanney and directed by Alexander. Featuring newcomer Ewan Bremner as Sammy Nelson, an unemployed teenage fantasist in the mould of 'Billy Liar', this innovative production boasted the participation of Billy Connolly and Scottish rock band Deacon Blue (brought to life by Sammy's vivid imagination) and incorporates a number of exuberant fantasy sequences including parodies of Busby Berkeley musicals, silent slapstick comedy and the 1970s TV series *Kung Fu*. Bryden's contract with the BBC also enabled him to write and produce one of his own works every year and, while he rarely exercised this option, this led to the production of *The Holy City* (1986), a controversial modern reworking of the Passion, featuring David Hayman as a Christ figure who appears in Glasgow. This is used to convey a contemporary political message combining elements of socialism and nationalism in both lamenting the destruction of the Glasgow shipyards by Thatcherite economics (in a similar vein to *Down Where the Buffalo Go*), and drawing parallels between the oppressive English establishment and the Roman occupation of the Holy Land.

But perhaps the most interesting new talent to be nurtured during Bryden's tenure at the BBC was the writer David Kane. After establishing himself in theatre, Kane's first television drama, *Shadow on the Earth* (1988), is a homage to numerous sci-fi paranoia movies set in a small village during the 1950s. It tells the story of a young boy who becomes convinced that the strange pale-skinned man who observes the skies through a telescope is an alien. Kane followed up with *Dream Baby* (1989), a contemporary comedy set in Edinburgh in which a young girl, Annie (Jenny McCrindle), contrives to trick the two men in her life that she is pregnant. Her plan is to use the money she collects from them to escape from the grim realities of a life on the dole and travel the world with her friend Sheena (Mandy Matthews). After writing a couple of mini-series, *Jute City* (1991) and *Finney* (1994), Kane directed his own script of *Ruffian Hearts*, one of three contemporary dramas dealing with the complexities of romantic attachment made by the BBC in 1995 under the label 'Love Bites'. The success of this black comedy lies in Kane's finely observed writing and his skilful handling of an ensemble cast including Peter Mullan, Ewan Bremner, Jenny McCrindle, Vicki Masson, Maureen Beattie, Clive Russell, Gary Lewis and Bronagh Gallagher among others. The style and tone of *Ruffian Hearts* also anticipated Kane's first cinema film, *This Year's Love*, released in 1999.

The 1980s and 1990s also witnessed important developments within the realm of series and serials. By far the most successful long-running Scottish series is the police drama *Taggart*, created in 1983 by Glenn Chandler. The three-episode pilot, *Killer*, introduced the granite-faced, lugubrious and cynical figure of Jim Taggart, a Glasgow detective dedicated to the job played by former boxer Mark McManus. Ian Spring regards Chandler's creation as influenced by the character of Jack Laidlaw from William McIlvanney's novels, *Laidlaw* (1977) and *The Papers of Tony Veitch* (1984).[46] *Taggart's* popularity led to the production of a number of ninety-minute feature-length specials, beginning with *Cold Blood* in 1987. The series even survived McManus's death in 1994, continuing with Taggart's former sidekick Mike Jardine and his assistant Jackie Reid as the new leading characters. In addition to its sheer popularity, *Taggart* also helped to establish a new image of Glasgow as a vibrant, heterogeneous modern city, a space defined as much by culture as heavy industry, populated by different ethnic as well as socio-economic groups.[47]

Music was central to the other major contribution to network drama by BBC Scotland in the 1980s: the celebrated *Tutti Frutti*, John Byrne's wry drama about the reformation and come-back tour of a 1960s Scottish rock 'n' roll band. Once again Bill Bryden was central to the project, devising the basic idea for a series which, as Hugh Herbert notes, would 'answer a felt need to inject a new, strong, popular Scottish/regional presence into BBC network drama'.[48] With the backing of BBC1 controller Michael Grade, Bryden approached Byrne, a former colleague from STV in the 1960s. The resulting six-part series, starring Robbie Coltrane, Emma Thompson, Maurice Roëves and Richard Wilson, returned to the theme of the influence of American popular culture on working-class Scotland which Byrne had previously explored in his *Slab Boys* trilogy. *Tutti Frutti* also managed to present a broad view of contemporary Scotland, from the cosmopolitan environment of Glasgow to the grim reality of frontier towns like Methil and Buckie, two of the venues for the Majestics tour. In common with many of the Scottish dramas already discussed in this chapter, *Tutti Frutti* explores questions of culture, place, belonging and identity. But Byrne's examination of flawed masculinity is a long way from Peter McDougall in its deconstruction of the myth of the hard man (represented in *Tutti Frutti* by the character of Vincent Diver, played by Roeves) and attendant affirmation of both a different kind of masculinity offered by 'new boy' Danny McGlone (Coltrane) and what Adrienne Scullion refers to as 'the structural role of woman in the translation and the deconstruction of the signs of (traditional) masculinity'.[49] In critical terms *Tutti Frutti*, was a major success, winning numerous plaudits including a number of BAFTA awards.[50]

In both *Tutti Frutti* and his subsequent series *Your Cheatin' Heart* (1990), Byrne provided an alternative version of working-class urban Scottish culture perpetrated not only in the dramas of Peter McDougall and Bill Bryden, but also in the novels of Alan Sharp, William McIlvanney and James Kelman and the paintings of Peter Howson and Ken Currie. Despite the undoubted importance of such a direct engagement with the struggle, frustration and pain of

individuals and communities at the sharp end of economic and social instabil-
ities wrought by advanced capitalism, this tradition inevitably ends up
wallowing in pessimistic self-defeat. Roderick Watson describes the heroes of
McIlvanney's and Kelman's fiction as 'lonely men essentially sealed off (even
from their lovers) given to physical action, but held rigid by the male ethos and
a sense of socio-political futility in an existential realm of pain and courage,
and masochistic or homo-erotic martyrdom,'[51] contrasting this with the image
of feminine creativity and engagement with the land in Grassic Gibbon's *Sunset Song*. In a similar way, the work of Byrne and arguably David Kane has
initiated a less overtly masculinist direction in television drama. A major institutional development in this respect was the appointment in 1993 of Andrea
Calderwood as the new head of drama at the BBC to replace Bill Bryden, a move
greeted with incredulity in certain quarters. Nevertheless, this signalled the
dawning of yet another new chapter in Scottish film production, one in which
women were to assume an increasingly high profile.[52]

Notes

1   Robin Macpherson, 'Independent film and television in Scotland: a case of
    independent cultural reproduction?' Unpublished M.Litt dissertation,
    University of Stirling, 1991, p. 172.
2   See *Film Bang* (Glasgow: Film Bang, 1976). This was followed by a special
    edition of *New Edinburgh Review* entitled 'Scottish Cinema?', vol. 34, no. 2,
    1976.
3   In the second general election of 1974 the SNP won eleven seats, capturing
    30.4 per cent of the Scottish vote. This enabled the party to exert pressure on
    the Labour government to take their demands for devolution seriously,
    culminating in the 1979 referendum.
4   Interview with Paddy Higson, Glasgow, 19 January 2000. The sale to Goldwyn
    not only gave *That Sinking Feeling* exposure, it also provided some
    retrospective payment to some of the major participants in the production.
5   Quoted by Allan Hunter, 'Bill Forsyth: The Imperfect Anarchist' in Eddie
    Dick (ed.), *From Limelight to Satellite: A Scottish Film Book* (London:BFI/SFC,
    1990), p. 154.
6   The debate over a Scottish quota was based on the operation of the Goshen
    quotient, a formula whereby 11 to 12 per cent of the public funding for the
    arts in Britain is apportioned to Scotland. As Robin Macpherson notes, the
    SAP had estimated that applying this to Channel Four commissioning would
    generate sixty-five hours and a £2 million increase in Scottish film and
    television production. Robin Macpherson, *Independent Film and Television in
    Scotland*, p. 210.
7   Interview with Mike Alexander, Glasgow, 21 January 2000.

8   Interview with Paddy Higson, Glasgow, 19 January 2000.

9   At Pebble Mill Rose, had been responsible for such major single dramas as *Pentad's Fen* (1974), *Black Christmas* (1977) and *Licking Hitler* (1978) and series like *Gangsters* (1976, 1978) and *Empire Road* (1978).

10 See John Pym, *Film on Four: A Survey 1982/1991* (London: BFI, 1992), pp. 28–9.

11 See Jeremy Issacs, 'Film on Four' in *Storm Over 4: A Personal Account* (Weidenfeld & Nicolson, 1989).

12 *Hero* was watched by 382,000 viewers when it was broadcast on 29 December 1982, compared to the next lowest audience of 1,386,000 for *Bad Hats*. The highest viewing figures during the first year of Film on Four was generated by *The Country Girls* at 4,230,000. All figures in John Pym, *Film on Four*, p. 29.

13 *Scotch Myths* was an arts commission by David Scott and was made under a union agreement covering documentary production. Interview with Murray Grigor, Inverkeithing, 22 January 2000.

14 Femi Folorunso, 'Scottish Drama and the Popular Tradition' in Randall Stevenson and Gavin Wallace (eds), *Scottish Theatre Since the Seventies* (Edinburgh: Edinburgh University Press, 1996), p. 177.

15 During his formative years at the BBC, Grigor worked on *The White Heather Club*, the epitome of Scottish variety kitsch. Interview with Murray Grigor.

16 Macpherson's account of the Scottish workshop sector is the most extensive available on the subject, see *Independent Film and Television in Scotland* pp. 327–30. Margaret Dickinson draws upon this material in her book *Rogue Reels: Oppositional Film in Britain, 1945–90* (London: BFI, 1999).

17 John Caughie, *Television Drama: Realism, Modernism and British Culture* (Oxford: Oxford University Press, 2000), p. 200.

18 These television rights were bought for a figure of around £500,000. John Hill, 'British Television and Film: The Making of a Relationship' in John Hill and Martin McLoone (eds), *Big Picture, Small Screen: The Relations Between Film and Television* (Luton: University of Luton Press, 1996), p. 169.

19 For a detailed discussion of this issue and its implications for television, see John Caughie, 'Television and the Art Film: The Logic of Convergence' in Caughie, *Television Drama: Realism, Modernism and British Culture*.

20 David Aukin, in Duncan Petrie (ed.), *Inside Stories: Diaries of British Film-Makers at Work* (London: BFI, 1996), p. 3.

21 Among the many writers who were commissioned during the 1960s were Dennis Potter, John Hopkins, David Mercer, Troy Kennedy Martin, John Mortimer, Simon Gray, Jeremy Sandford, Nell Dunn, Fay Weldon, David Rudkin, Alan Plater, Jim Allen and John Osborne, practically a role call of all the brightest talents in Britain at the time, many with a particular engagement with contemporary social experience.

22 In an attempt to recreate the kind of stimulating and creative environment he

had formed at the EMB and GPO film units, Grierson brought in a number of established international figures such as Stuart Legg, Norman McLaren, Joris Ivens and Boris Kaufman. Such luminaries provided inspiration and guidance to the many newcomers, such as Newman, attracted by the possibilities the NFB seemed to offer.

23 Sydney Newman, in James Beveridge (ed.), *John Grierson: Film Master* (New York: Macmillan, 1978), p. 157.

24 After spending twelve extremely productive years in British television, Newman returned to Canada as Commissioner of the National Film Board, the post held by Grierson when Newman had first joined the NCB.

25 These themes are explored in plays like *Fable* and *Horror of Darkness*, both written by John Hopkins, James O'Connor's *Three Clear Sundays* and Nell Dunn's *Up the Junction*, all of which were broadcast in 1965. The important influence of the producer in the Wednesday Play is discussed by Irene Shubick in her memoir *Play for Today: The Evolution of Television Drama* (London: Davis-Poynter, 1975), esp. pp. 75–6.

26 Kevin Robbins and James Cornford, 'Not the London Broadcasting Corporation? The BBC and the New Regionalism' in Sylvia Harvey and Kevin Robbins (eds), *The Regions, the Nations and the BBC: The BBC Charter Review Series, Volume 3* (London: BFI, 1993), p. 9.

27 James Curran and Jean Seaton, *Power Without Responsibility: The Press and Broadcasting in Britain*, 3rd edn (London: Routledge, 1988).

28 Quoted by Seaton, ibid., p. 196

29 Alan Sharp had established himself in the 1960s, both as a novelist with *A Green Tree in Gedde* (1965) and *The Wind Shifts* (1967) and a playwright with *A Knight in Tarnished Armour* (1965) and *The Long Distance Piano Player* (1970), for the 'Wednesday Play' and 'Play for Today' slots respectively, before moving to Hollywood. While Eddie Boyd had started writing radio plays before moving to television with 'Wednesday Play' commissions like *A Black Candle for Mrs Gogarty* (1967) and *The Lower Largo Sequence* (1968) and series made in Glasgow such as *The View from Daniel Pike* (1971–73) and *Badger by Owl Light* (1981).

30 Ironically, this is a period regarded by some commentators as a period of decline in the single play due to a combination of economic and cultural factors that favoured the historical series over the contemporary single drama. See for example Carl Gardner and John Wyver, 'The Single Play: From Reithian Reverence to Cost-Accounting and Censorship', *Screen*, vol. 24, nos. 4–5, 1983, p. 118.

31 For an analysis of this theatrical tradition from the 1940s to the 1990s, see Randall Stevenson, 'In the Jungle of the Cities' in Stevenson and Gavin Wallace (eds), *Scottish Theatre Since the Seventies*.

32 First performed on stage in 1978, *The Slab Boys* inaugurated a trilogy of plays by Byrne including *Cuttin' a Rug* (1979) and *Still Life* (1982).

33 Linda Mackenney notes that the company, formed in 1973, took their name from a statistic published in the *Economist* claiming that in Britain 7 per cent of the population owned 84 per cent of the wealth. A sister company, 7:84 England, had been established by McGrath two years earlier. Linda Mackenney, 'The People's Story: 7:84 Scotland' in Randall Stevenson and Gavin Wallace (eds), *Scottish Theatre Since the Seventies*.

34 Colin McArthur, *Television and History*, BFI Television Monograph No 8 (London: BFI, 1980), p. 51.

35 McGrath discusses this in an interview with Olga Taxidou, 'From Cheviots to Silver Darlings' in Randall Stevenson and Gavin Wallace (eds), *Scottish Theatre Since the Seventies*, pp. 152–3.

36 John Caughie, 'Progressive Television and Documentary Drama' in Tony Bennett *et al.* (eds), *Popular Television and Film* (Oxford: Oxford University Press/BFI, 1981), p. 349.

37 M.K. MacMurragh-Kavanagh, ' "Drama" into "News": Strategies of Intervention in "The Wednesday Play" ', *Screen*, vol. 38, no. 3, Autumn 1997, p. 249.

38 Mackenzie was also one of a number of talented television directors including Ken Loach, John Boorman, Kevin Billington and Jack Gold who were afforded the opportunity to move into feature production in the late 1960s. But the British cinema was just about to enter a major period of crisis, and Mackenzie returned to television after directing just two features, *One Brief Summer* (1969) and *Unman, Wittering and Zigo* (1971).

39 When first screened in 1981, *A Sense of Freedom* was followed by a televised debate on Boyle and the Special Unit at Barlinnie. Boyle was subsequently released on parole in 1983 after sixteen years' incarceration.

40 Initially a documentary cameraman, Menges had established his reputation with a number of dramas, for both cinema and television, directed by Ken Loach and Stephen Frears.

41 After *A Sense of Freedom*, Mackenzie became increasingly involved in feature production. He returned to Scottish television drama in 1998 with the four-part series *Looking After Jo Jo*, a bleak portrait of an Edinburgh family's involvement in the hard-drugs scene of the early 1980s written by Frank Deasy and starring Robert Carlyle.

42 Ian Spring, *Phantom Village: The Myth of the New Glasgow* (Edinburgh: Polygon, 1990), pp. 76–8.

43 In the Scottish context, STV's involvement in Bill Forsyth's *Gregory's Girl* (1981) preceded the Channel. The company also invested in *Ill Fares the Land* (Bill Bryden, 1983), *Comfort and Joy* (Bill Forsyth, 1984) and *The Big Man* (David Leland, 1990).

44 Interview with David Hayman, Glasgow, 24 January 2000.

45 Interview with Mike Alexander.

46 Ian Spring, *Phantom Village: The Myth of the New Glasgow*, p. 80.

47 In recent years, the crime theme has inspired a number of other serials, many of which draw heavily on the ambience and stylish aesthetics of *film noir* including Frederick Lindsay's political thriller *Brond* (1987), produced by Channel Four, David Kane's *Jute City* (1991), a conspiracy tale involving the Masonic order set in Dundee, and the more recent adaptation of Iain Banks's popular thriller *The Crow Road* (1996).

48 Hugh Herbert, 'Tutti Frutti' in George W. Brandt (ed.), *British Television Drama in the 1980s* (Cambridge: Cambridge University Press, 1993), p. 178.

49 Adrienne Scullion, 'Feminine Pleasures and Masculine Indignities: Gender and Community in Scottish Drama' in Christopher Whyte (ed.), *Gendering the Nation: Studies in Modern Scottish Literature* (Edinburgh: Edinburgh University Press, 1995), p. 197.

50 This paved the way for both Byrne's follow-up series *Your Cheatin' Heart*, another six-part, musical-based drama which this time took the Glaswegian penchant for country and western as its central theme, and a subsequent move into directing, first his 1993 BBC production *Boswell and Johnson's Tour of the Isles* followed by a cinema version of *The Slab Boys* (1997).

51 Roderick Watson, 'Maps of Desire: Scottish Literature in the Twentieth Century' in T.M. Devine and R.J. Finlay (eds), *Scotland in the 20th Century* (Edinburgh: Edinburgh University Press, 1996), p. 302.

52 For example, Peter McDougall's reported response was his disbelief that Bill Bryden's job had been given to a 'wee lassie'.

Chapter Seven
A Scottish Art Cinema

... there have been very few national cinemas. In my opinion there is no Swedish cinema but there are Swedish movie-makers – some very good ones such as Stiller and Bergman. There have been only a handful of cinemas: Italian, German, American and Russian. This is because when countries were inventing and using motion pictures, they needed an image of themselves. (Jean-Luc Godard, in conversation with Colin MacCabe, National Film Theatre, London, 7 June 1991)[1]

A British Art Cinema?

Despite the production of a significant number of Scottish features in the 1980s, many funded by Channel Four, Godard's characteristically provocative remarks offer a useful caution to any claim that this somehow constituted the emergence of a new national cinema in Scotland. Indeed, the application of the concept of national cinema has been far from straightforward in the broader context of British cinema, as film historians like Andrew Higson and John Hill have demonstrated.[2] For Higson, one of the key markers of a national cinema is the idea of product differentiation, mobilised by the British cinema as a strategy in its historical struggle to compete with Hollywood, which he explores by way of a number of examples of popular cinema from the 1920s to the 1940s. Product differentiation has continued to be a relevant concept for British cinema in more recent times, but with a new emphasis on the integration of traditions of television drama and post-war European art cinema. Such a construction not only applies to the general direction of the British cinema as a whole, it also suggests a useful way of approaching developments in Scottish film-making.

Some commentators have suggested that the reinvigoration and rebranding of British cinema in the 1980s has served to consolidate the idea of a distinctive British art cinema. John Hill for example argues that the advent of 'Film on Four' served to integrate the stylistic concerns of the European art film with the preoccupations of, what Christopher Williams has identified as, a tradition of 'social art cinema' in Britain. Characterised by 'an almost frenzied curiosity about social life and its systems, differences and observances'[3] this tradition is associated with the documentary movement, Michael Balcon's stewardship of Ealing Studios and the international films produced by David Puttnam in the 1980s. Hill notes:

> It is undoubtedly the case that this process gathered momentum in the 1980s and was given a particular impetus by Channel Four as a result of its joint commitment to the support of a 'national cinema' (which would win prestige internationally by circulating as 'art') and to the fulfilment of a public service remit (which favoured a degree of engagement by cinema with matters of contemporary social concern).[4]

The concept of art cinema tends to be linked to particular aesthetic and industrial developments in Europe during the post-war period and is generally deployed to signify an alternative to the Hollywood classical narrative film. David Bordwell describes art cinema as 'a distinct film practice, possessing a definite historical existence, a set of formal conventions, and implicit viewing procedures.'[5] The label 'art' serving to differentiate European production by recourse to a notion of cultural value or seriousness regarded as absent from populist American entertainment. But art cinema can also be defined as a particular kind of commodity subject to certain structures and institutional practices. As Steve Neale observes:

> Art cinema ... in its cultural and aesthetic aspirations, relies upon an appeal to the 'universal' values of culture and art. And this is very much reflected in the existence of international film festivals where international distribution is sought for these films, and where their status as 'Art' is confirmed and re-stated through the existence of prizes and awards, themselves neatly balancing the criteria of artistic merit and commercial potential.[6]

Despite the existence of particular kinds of market relations, art cinema is usually produced with an appeal to a cultural rather than a commercial imperative. Consequently, many of the major achievements of the post-war European art cinema have been predicated on systems of state subsidy and other forms of support for film-making. In the 1970s, in Britain the only institutional space within which innovative film practice could be supported was the British Film Institute's production board, which took its first tentative steps towards the production of feature films in the early 1970s under Mamoun Hassan. Among the films supported by the BFI during this period were the first two parts of Bill

Douglas's acclaimed autobiographical trilogy *My Childhood* (1972) and *My Ain Folk* (1973), *Pressure* (Horace Ove, 1974), *Winstanley* (Kevin Brownlow and Andrew Mollo, 1975), *A Private Enterprise* (Peter Smith, 1975) and *Requiem for a Village* (David Gladwell, 1975). Collectively, this body of work signalled a new vitality in cinema aesthetics and storytelling from Brownlow and Mollo's examination of the seventeenth-century 'digger' riots, to Ove and Smith's engagement with the respective experiences of the Afro-Caribbean and Asian communities in Britain, to the intensely contemplative aesthetic of Douglas that also signalled new possibilities for an alternative cinematic construction of Scotland.

Hassan left the BFI in 1974 to become head of the publicly funded National Film Finance Corporation, established in 1949 as a kind of film bank for British producers, where he continued to promote a particular kind of socially engaged and formally innovative British cinema. Hassan was also an important figure in the development of Scottish film-making through his enthusiastic support of both Bill Douglas and Bill Forsyth, in addition to being Douglas's staunchest supporter at the BFI, he ensured that the third part of the trilogy, *My Way Home,* would be made after his departure from the Institute. Before the NFFC was wound up in 1985 Hassan was also able to commit £2 million to Douglas's only other major film, *Comrades,* a project finally released in 1987 which had taken a painful eight years to realise. Prior to this, Hassan had also backed the then relatively unknown Forsyth, the NFFC providing half of the £200,000 budget for *Gregory's Girl* (1981), the film that was to firmly establish the Scottish film-maker as a major new talent.

After a period of intense internal debate over policy in the late 1970s, the BFI intensified its support for feature projects. Chris Petit's *Radio-On* (1979), an existential road movie inspired by the work of German auteur Wim Wenders, is often cited as the break-through production, suggesting, as Steve Neale puts it, the possibility of 'penetrating a sector of the commercial industry at the level of exhibition and, perhaps, of opening a space within that sector for the development of a kind of British art cinema'.[7] This ambition was subsequently realised by a number of high-profile BFI productions including *The Draughtsman's Contract* (Peter Greenaway, 1982), *Caravaggio* (Derek Jarman, 1986) and *Distant Voices, Still Lives* (Terence Davies, 1988), all of which were also produced with the financial participation of Channel Four who had agreed to provide an annual subvention for BFI production in the mid-1980s. For John Hill, this achievement served to elevate the art film tradition to a position of pre-eminence in British cinema.[8] The circulation and consumption of British films also entailed a heightened critical emphasis on individual film-makers:

> as British cinema has increasingly occupied the terrain of art cinema at the
> level of production and distribution, so it has become more common for

British cinema to be characterised, and promoted, in terms of personal approaches and styles. As a result, it is not just the overtly 'authored' films of directors like Derek Jarman and Peter Greenaway that have circulated internationally as 'art' films but also the less artistically self conscious work of Stephen Frears, Mike Leigh, Ken Loach, and, even, James Ivory.[9]

It is within this institutional context that the applicability and relevance of the idea of art cinema to the emerging indigenous Scottish feature film can be contemplated.

The Scottish Dimension

The Scottish contribution to British cinema in the 1980s is clearly subject to the same broad pattern of determinations but it is possible to identify certain tendencies that suggest a particular relation to the European art film tradition. While the relatively small number of films makes any kind of generalisation problematic, there does appear to be a particular interest in cinema as personal expression, marked by certain recurring themes such as the alienated or isolated subject, the significance of the environment in relation to subjectivity and a preoccupation with biographical and autobiographical modes of narrative. The distinctive qualities of art cinema can be further illustrated by way of a comparison between two roughly contemporaneous features, *The Big Man* (David Leland, 1990) and *Silent Scream* (David Hayman, 1990). Both films have a basic superficial similarity in their focus on a problematic working-class Scottish male who becomes embroiled in criminal activity, but the subsequent elaboration of both narrative and theme provides a striking contrast.

Adapted from the novel by William McIlvanney, *The Big Man* tells the fictional story of an unemployed miner who becomes inadvertently caught up in a web of crime, corruption and manipulation. *Silent Scream*, in contrast, is based on the memoirs of convicted murderer Larry Winters, an inmate of the Barlinnie special unit who died of a drug overdose in 1977. *The Big Man* is constructed around a classical linear narrative charting the fluctuating fortunes of Danny Scoular, a flawed but fundamentally honourable hero lured by a ruthless gangster into an illegal and violent world of bare-knuckle boxing. Recognising the depths to which he has sunk, Danny endeavours to rebuild his self-esteem and by the end of the film is rewarded by way of a reconciliation with the wife and community he had let down, providing the kind of satisfying resolution associated with mainstream commercial cinema. *Silent Scream* on the other hand signals an affinity with the conventions of art cinema through its utilisation of a fractured and fragmented narrative structure motivated by a preoccupation with the acute psychological turmoil of Larry Winters, a man suffering from a severe psychic disorder. This is powerfully conveyed by the

The anguish of incarceration:
Iain Glen as convicted
murderer Larry Winters in
The Silent Scream

rejection of temporal or causal linearity in favour of almost arbitrary cutting between significant moments in his life and the surreal hallucinatory visions of his tortured psyche, serving to blur the distinctions between objective and subjective worlds, reality and fantasy. The temporal ordering of events compress past and present, the 'real' time of the film corresponding with Winters' last night on earth broken up by a myriad of flashbacks depicting a parole visit home, an interview with a prison psychiatrist, episodes in a troubled childhood, and his experiences in the Parachute Regiment that led to the slaying of a London barman. Such a construction also prevents any easy audience identification or empathy with Winters who remains something of an enigma throughout. While the visual stylisation, including distorted and surreal sets, animation and extreme lighting and compositional devices, serves to further undermine the stability of the subjective world represented.

These fundamental aesthetic differences can be related to the different economic and institutional context of each production. *The Big Man* is an overtly commercial project financed by Palace Productions, the short-lived British Satellite Broadcasting company, Scottish Television Enterprises and the American independent studio Miramax. In addition to a reliance on narrative strategies rooted in familiarity and reassurance, the film features several estab-lished or up-and-coming stars including Liam Neeson, Joanne Whalley, Ian Bannen and Billy Connolly. The pressure on *The Big Man* to appeal to an inter-national audience – manifest in the casting, the melodramatic motivation of the narrative and the representation of the working-class community – under-mines its ability to engage with the specificities of the subject-matter and to speak to and for a particular kind of social experience. In comparison, *Silent Scream* was produced in line with a cultural rather than a commercial imper-ative, financed by the BFI, Channel Four and the Scottish Film Production Fund, and consequently engages directly with the subjective 'reality' of Larry Winters's life. The screenplay by Bill Beech draws on both his personal acquain-tance with the subject and Winters's own writings, including the prose poem which gives the film its title. It also captures a sense of the emotional and material hardships and the tight familial bonds characterising working-class Scottish society. As such, *Silent Scream* is much more rooted in a particular cul-tural milieu, yet at the same time its construction profoundly relates it to broader aesthetic traditions informed by particular aspects of art cinema.

The Strange Case of Bill Forsyth

The writer-director Bill Forsyth offers an interesting if rather perplexing case study in terms of the discussion of the emergence of a new Scottish art cinema in the early 1980s. During this period, Forsyth not only established himself as the pre-eminent Scottish film-maker of his generation, he was also for some critics the most important figure in the short-lived revival in British cinema. Nick Roddick for example argues that Forsyth's films 'provided many of the brightest moments of the renaissance … they have shown the development of a film-maker of unique talent, able to observe the behaviour of real people, then turn that behaviour into the heightened reality of a dramatic story'.[10] After his initial foray into feature film-making with the DIY production of *That Sinking Feeling* (1979), Forsyth enjoyed a period of unbridled productivity resulting in three further cinema films, *Gregory's Girl* (1981), *Local Hero* (1983) and *Com-fort and Joy* (1984), and one television play, *Andrina* (1981). The surprise commercial success of *Gregory's Girl* also made Forsyth bankable in the eyes of investors and consequently both *Local Hero* and *Comfort and Joy* were funded as commercial propositions by Goldcrest and Thorn-EMI respectively.

The critical construction of Bill Forsyth as a mainstream film-maker is informed by an association with a particular brand of popular warm-hearted comedy. Forsyth Hardy's identification of 'a quirky sense of humour, a prefer-ence for amiable eccentricity, a reluctance to identify anything remotely evil in his characters and situations'[11] being a typical assessment. But such a benign reading of the comedic mode serves to obscure or misrecognise the more serious elements lurking just below the surface of Forsyth's world, a depth that certain perceptive commentators had begun to recognise early on. In 1983, John Brown was already suggesting that the films had been largely misread, critics missing the 'cool and detached style with which Forsyth presents his characters' obsessiveness, [and]... the ironic bitterness which surfaces discomfortingly from time to time'.[12] While Allan Hunter, a consistent champion of Forsyth's work over the years, makes a similar argument: 'viewers latch on to certain elements and assume that they have unlocked the door to his entire psyche never looking beyond the qualities of charm and humour to examine the recurring themes of loss, loneliness and isolation.'[13]

It is certainly the case that this 'darker persona' is less evident in Forsyth's first two features. *That Sinking Feeling* may gesture towards the despair of the young unemployed, but any serious contemplation is undercut by humour of a farcical rather than an ironic nature, the scene when one character attempts suicide by drowning himself in a bowl of cornflakes being a typical example. *Gregory's Girl* also relies heavily on a surface wit and charm, although this time with a greater underlying complexity and intelligence. The tale of a gawky 16-year-old schoolboy (John Gordon Sinclair) infatuated with a girl who is also the newest member of the football team, is a perceptive study of adolescent male obsession. While Gregory dreams wistfully of Dorothy (Dee Hepburn), his friends Andy and Charlie attempt a series of woefully pathetic chat-up lines in their desperation to make some kind of connection with the female of the species. There are several other exquisite character studies in adolescent sublimation, the channelling of libidinal energy into various infatuation with photography, numbers or, in the case of the wonderfully ambiguous Steve (Billy Greenlees), cookery. While the boys are at the mercy of their hormones, the girls are portrayed as infinitely more socially competent and self-aware, although just as interested in sex. Gregory is ultimately manipulated by a formidable female conspiracy as he is subtly but firmly guided away from the disappointment of being stood up by Dorothy, to a joyful date and potentially serious relationship with Susan (Clare Grogan). The naïve energies of *Gregory's Girl* recall certain strains in continental film-making, including Ermanno Olmi's 1961 film *Il Posto*, which features a similar scenario and emotional tone, and the zest and playful absurdity of the early French *nouvelle vague* and the Czech 'new wave'.[14]

The BBC production of *Andrina*, Forsyth's adaptation of short story by George Mackay Brown, begins to suggest a rather different emotional emphasis, however. It tells the story of an old Orcadian sailor Bill Tarvald (Cyril Cusack) who one night meets a mysterious young woman (Wendy Morgan) while staggering home drunk from the pub. Over the following winter months, Andrina becomes a regular evening visitor to Bill's isolated cottage, cooking, cleaning and coaxing stories from him. She is interested in a particular story and eventu-

Teenage obsession: Dee Hepburn and John Gordon Sinclair in Bill Forsyth's *Gregory's Girl*

ally Bill discloses the long repressed memory of an idyllic summer romance with a girl called Sigrid that culminated in the girl becoming pregnant and his running away to sea. This painful disclosure causes Bill to take to bed with a bad cold and Andrina's visits cease. On recovering, he attempts to find out what has happened to his mysterious guest, only to discover that no one else on the island has heard of her. An answer is provided however in the form of a letter from Sigrid, now living in Australia, informing Bill that the child he rejected had her own daughter who was determined to visit her Scottish grandfather. Tragically, the girl had recently died and would be unable to realise her ambition. Her name was Andrina and the letter contains a photograph that Bill immediately recognises as his recent guest, a supernatural visitation come to force the old man to confront his own ghosts. Not only did *Andrina* signal a new departure for Forsyth in terms of being an adaptation rather than an original screenplay, but the concern with quiet melancholy and loss initiated a theme that would resonate in most of his subsequent films.

Admittedly, such a dour sensibility was not an obvious aspect of Forsyth's next major venture, *Local Hero*. At £2.5 million, more than ten times the cost of *Gregory's Girl*, this was his most commercial and expensive production to date. The basic plot concerning the plans of an American oil company to establish a giant refinery on the site of the West Highland village of Furness, recalled a number of Scottish films including *I Know Where I'm Going*, *The Maggie*, *Laxdale Hall* and *Rockets Galore* in its familiar scenario of the confrontation between a remote Scottish community and the forces of modernity. Rather than resisting the outsiders, however, the avaricious natives of *Local Hero* collaborate enthusiastically in their own 'exploitation'. But despite this twist, ultimately the film conforms to the established tradition in terms of a reliance on the romantic and elemental appeal of the beauty and remoteness of the landscape.

This exoticisation extends to the inhabitants of Furness who appear to exist largely outside the stresses and complications of modern life, while the main female characters – Marina and Stella – are directly associated with the beguiling elemental forces of the stars and the sea. Such a resurrection of the externally constructed romantic vision of Scotland explored in Chapter Two serves to overpower the additional theme of existential loneliness and isolation associated with the character of MacIntyre (Peter Reigert), the young American who unlike his predecessors in the genre fails to cement his relationship to the magical environment by winning the girl, a theme crystallised in the relatively downbeat and somewhat unresolved ending with Mac back home in Texas pondering the superficiality of his materialistic existence. Yet even this coda assumes the form of sentimental longing, stimulated by a romantic encounter with an idealised vision of Scotland.

The theme of loneliness is more effectively elaborated in *Comfort and Joy*, the story of a Glasgow radio DJ who becomes involved in a violent dispute between two rival ice cream vendors. The predicament of the central character, Dickie Bird (Bill Paterson), is a more substantial study in contemporary alienation, beginning with the departure of his kleptomaniac girlfriend, along with almost the entire contents of their shared flat, just before Christmas. This misfortune is compounded by Bird's increasing dissatisfaction with the banality of his professional life, consisting mainly of inane banter and the recording of embarrassing commercial jingles. He regains some sense of meaning, however, via the territorial dispute between the rival Italian families, becoming involved when he distractedly follows a beautiful woman (Clare Grogan) in an ice cream van. In brokering a reconciliation, Bird comes to terms with his existential crisis and the film ends with him back at work on Christmas Day. Yet nothing materially has changed in his life, the bittersweet conclusion being that survival depends on an acceptance of circumstances that human beings can do very little to alter. Unfortunately, these virtues are partly undermined by the rather whimsical representation of the conflict between Mr Bunny and Mr McCool, solved by a collaborative venture making ice cream fritters. This is far removed from the brutality and murder that marked the real ice cream war in Glasgow that came to light around the same time as the film was released.

After *Comfort and Joy* Forsyth broadened his film-making horizons beyond Scotland with *Housekeeping*, an adaptation of a novel by Marilynn Robinson set in a remote community in the American North West in the 1950s. Although financed by Columbia Pictures, the film is much closer in theme and style to independent American cinema than Hollywood convention. It is also more successful in conveying a weightier, serious side to Forsyth and the focus on female characters marked a welcome departure from the preoccupation with self-absorbed males.[15] This was followed by two further American-backed films:

Breaking In (1989), from a John Sayles script concerning the relationship between two unlikely burglars played by Burt Reynolds and Casey Siesmazko, and *Being Human* (1994), an irredeemably flawed $30 million production that almost ended Forsyth's career. *Being Human* charts the predicament of a character who appears in five different incarnations at various points in history. The film begins in prehistoric Scotland where a cave-dweller called Hector loses his wife and children to a group of strangers who arrive one day in their ships. The subsequent episodes, set in ancient Rome, medieval France, a prospective African colony during the age of exploration, and contemporary New York/New Jersey, depict different versions of Hector (all played by Robin Williams) desperately attempting to be reunited with his lost family. After protracted re-editing and the addition of an explanatory voice-over, *Being Human* was finally distributed theatrically in America where it grossed a mere $1.5 million. In Britain it suffered a worse fate, being released only on video. The failure of the film serves to underline the contradictions of the expectations of Warner Bros. and the sensibility of the film-maker, the fundamental opposition between Hollywood convention and European art cinema played out in the mangled body of the film.[16]

The initial success of Bill Forsyth in the early 1980s had an almost immediate effect on Scottish film-making, marked by the appearance of a number of light comedies clearly attempting to replicate the same kind of wry humour. The perceived popular appeal of 'Forsythian comedy', is signified by the fact that the first examples, *Restless Natives* (Michael Hoffman, 1985) and *The Girl in the Picture* (Cary Parker, 1985), were backed by mainstream commercial producers Thorn-EMI and Rank respectively. The connections with Forsyth are immediately obvious in both films. The plot of *Restless Natives*, scripted by the fifteen-year-old Ninian Dunnet and charting the escapades of two unemployed Edinburgh teenagers (Vincent Friel and Joe Mullaney) who become unlikely latter-day highwaymen by using a moped to prey on coach parties of tourists visiting the Scottish Highlands, bears some striking similarities with the absurd heist in *That Sinking Feeling*. While *The Girl in the Picture* functions as a distant sequel to *Gregory's Girl*, with John Gordon Sinclair's photographer reprising many of the mannerisms of his previous character in a tale of romantic misunderstanding set in the bourgeois West End of Glasgow. But while aspiring to the gentle, the quirky and the mildly absurd, these productions conspicuously lack the underlying ambiguity that gives substance and depth to Forsyth's work.

Heavenly Pursuits (1986), written and directed by Forsyth's former documentary partner Charlie Gormley, can be viewed in a similar context. But while still firmly in the charming romantic comedy mode, the film is more original in its conception and substantial in terms of its cinematic realisation than either *Restless Natives* or *The Girl in the Picture*. Gormley's narrative centres on the apparent working of miracles in a Glasgow secondary school by remedial teacher Vic Matthews (Tom Conti). Vic's essential rationality distances him from attempts by the local Catholic priest to use the miraculous progress of one of his pupils as evidence of divine intervention by 'the blessed Edith Semple', the girl after whom the school has been named. But having establishing this potentially controversial theme, *Heavenly Pursuits* ultimately colludes in the existence of the supernatural when Vic's undisclosed terminal brain tumour miraculously vanishes. The narrative is also sweetened by the developing relationship between Vic and a fellow teacher, Ruth Chancellor (Helen Mirren), and Gormley's depiction of Glasgow as a bright and ultimately optimistic environment presents an interesting contrast with the darker representation of the city by Forsyth in *Comfort and Joy*.[17] The Forsythian legacy is also discernible in the 1992 road movie *Soft Top, Hard Shoulder*, directed by Stefan Schwartz and written by Peter Capaldi who also plays the leading role. Capaldi had appeared in *Local Hero* as the gauche Danny Olsen and, as Philip Kemp notes, *Soft Top, Hard Shoulder* shares Forsyth's characteristically 'dry, slightly pixilated Scots humour and ... edgy attitude to sexual politics'.[18] The film even directly quotes both *Local Hero* (a rabbit on a deserted Scottish road and an isolated red phone box) and *Comfort and Joy* (the Italian/Glaswegian ice cream family). But ultimately Schwartz and Capaldi struggle and fail to overcome the basic obstacle facing any attempt at a British road movie: how to spin out a relatively short and unexciting journey – in this case the 400 miles from London to Glasgow – into a credible and engaging feature film.

Biography, Memory and Cultural Expression

If Forsyth's own ambivalent relationship to the categories and concerns of the art film spawned a sub-genre of mainstream light comedy, an alternative tradition emerged in Scottish film-making constituting a much more substantial engagement with some of the central tenants of European art cinema. The founding moment here is Bill Douglas's iconoclastic autobiographical trilogy, *My Childhood* (1972), *My Ain Folk* (1973) and *My Way Home* (1978). Produced under the auspices of the BFI production board, these films recount the harrowing experiences of Jamie, a child growing up in the Scottish mining village of Newcraighall in the 1940s and early 1950s. *My Childhood* depicts Jamie's life with his cousin Tommy and their maternal grandmother towards the end of the war, the harsh material and emotional impoverishment being alleviated only by his friendship with a German prisoner of war. After the grandmother's death, Tommy is sent away to a children's home and Jamie is taken in by his father's family. The harrowing privations endured by him at the hands of his cold and vindictive paternal grandmother becomes the primary focus of *My Ain Folk*, ending with Jamie following his cousin by being carted off to a children's home. *My Way Home* moves the story on a few years with Jamie about to leave the

The poetry of suffering: Stephen Archibald as Jamie in Bill Douglas's *My Childhood*

home. After an ill-fated attempt to live first with his father and then with a foster mother, Jamie spends a period in a hostel before being called up for national service. It is during his posting in Egypt that Jamie finds redemption through his friendship with Robert, a young middle-class Englishman who introduces him to books and the possibility of a more optimistic and fulfilling future.

What is immediately striking about Douglas's *Trilogy* is its aesthetic distance from the kind of cinema produced in the 1970s. The austere black and white images embody a stillness and intensity recalling the world of silent cinema and reinvesting in the medium what Andrew Noble describes as 'that pristine capacity to see the objects of the world as if for the first time'.[19] This intensely contemplative aesthetic shows a striking affinity with the great French critic André Bazin's identification of a tradition of silent cinema characterised by film-makers such as Flaherty, Dreyer, Murnau and Stroheim who essentially put their faith in the power of the image to reveal reality.[20] Bazin contrasted this progressive tendency with those approaches that alluded to an event rather than showing it, exemplified by the exponents of montage cinema such as Eisenstein and Pudovkin. But Douglas dissolves this essential opposition by drawing equally on the potential of montage to complement and extend the visceral power of his images. John Caughie explores the construction of the *Trilogy* as a work:

> built in blocks which exist in dialectical rather than causal relationship with one another … a montage of scenes and frames, read backwards and forwards in relation to each other, rather than a linear narrative leading to a resolution and

closure ... At the level of the scene, each block has its own shape, held
characteristically in the film in a static camera or a still composition, a still life.[21]

This close attention to both image and editing permits the audience to
observe the objective fact of Jamie's impoverished existence while simultaneously gaining access to his subjective sense of confusion and powerlessness.
The unblinking gaze of Douglas's camera reflects the surface of the world, while
his use of contrapuntal imagery, narrative ellipses and symbolism combine to
prise open the interior realm of retarded emotion and understanding, creating
an effect described by Caughie in terms of a dialectical tension between 'aesthetic distance and intense intimacy'.[22] The use of non-professional actors in
several key roles serves to enhance this, the pain palpably etched on the face of
young Stephen Archibald as Jamie conveying infinitely more about the human
condition than the most skilful 'acting' could ever hope to. A further distin-
guishing characteristic of Douglas's innovative approach to film-making is his
use of sound. There is no extra-diegetic music in the *Trilogy* and the spare dialogue conveys very little narrative information. But just as the stillness of the
image forces the audience to look, so the relative silence encourages greater
attention to those sounds which are in evidence – boots scraping on asphalt,
the chirping of birds, the rumble of vehicles, the timbre of voices – granting
them much more emotional significance as a result.

Despite a wealth of critical plaudits and numerous international awards, the
cumulative effect of Douglas's idiosyncratic approach to film-making has
served to isolate his achievement. Such was the struggle to raise finance for subsequent projects that he was able to make only one further feature film before
his untimely death in 1991. *Comrades* (1987) recounts the story of the Tolpud-
dle martyrs, a group of Dorset farm labourers who were arrested, tried and
transported to Australia for forming a trade union. The film continued Douglas's interest in the perseverance of the human spirit in the face of material
adversity and his attachment to intense contemplation and the construction of
elliptical narrative. *Comrades* also alludes to his fascination with the world of
optics and image making, conveyed by way of a number of references to various forms of pre-cinematic optical toys and media such as the magic lantern,
the zoetrope, the peep show and the camera obscura. The story itself is ostensibly mediated by the character of an itinerant magic lanternist played by
Scottish actor Alex Norton, who appears in a number of roles throughout the
film connected to the various allusions to particular optical devices or effects.[23]

Despite his undoubted achievements, Douglas's relationship to other film-
makers has appeared somewhat muted beyond perhaps an apparent influence
on Terence Davies's own autobiographical trilogy, *Children* (1976), *Madonna
and Child* (1980) and *Death and Transfiguration* (1983), produced by the BFI.

More recently, the spirit of Douglas has been enthusiastically invoked in the critical response to Lynne Ramsay's debut feature *Ratcatcher*, which will be discussed in the last chapter of this book. But there are a number of other Scottish films which can be productively examined as part of a tradition of deeply personal autobiographical cinema exemplified by the Douglas trilogy, a legacy that also points much more resolutely towards the 'sustained, hard-edged and diverse *European* tradition of art cinema'.[24] It is this European dimension that serves to tentatively distinguish the following strand of Scottish art cinema from the broader definitions of art employed by John Hill and Christopher Williams in relation to the British cinema of the 1980s.

One of the most accomplished of the early 'Film on Four' commissions noted in the previous chapter is Michael Radford's *Another Time, Another Place* (1983). Like Bill Douglas before him, Radford was drawn to the poetic possibilities offered by personal reminiscence, in this case the memoirs of septuagenarian Scottish writer Jessie Kesson that provided the material for his first two dramatic films.[25] *The White Bird Passes* (1980), a television production made by BBC Scotland, recounts the grim childhood of 9-year-old Janie (Vicki Masson), the daughter of an Elgin prostitute between the wars. Forced to live in a single room with a mother (Isobel Black) who is regularly visited by clients, young Janie seeks escape in books and adventures with her friend Gertie with whom she regularly plays truant from school. This behaviour alerts the attention of the authorities who send Janie to a residential school in the country where she will remain for the next seven years. *The White Bird Passes* is structured as a series of impressionistic recollections by the 16-year-old Janie looking back to her formative experiences in the dark streets of Elgin, conveyed throughout by Radford with economy and sensitivity. The carefree nature of childhood is evoked by an image of the two little girls proudly marching through a field carrying giant hogweeds like grand parasols; while the melancholic weight of Janie's situation is reflected in her weary and resigned expression as she stares out of the window of the train that is taking her away from her mother and into institutional care, her misery recalling the earlier image of old Annie Frick peering out at the world, the weight of a life of drudgery palpably etched on her face.

The larger canvas of *Another Time, Another Place* provided Radford with the opportunity to develop as a film-maker and this time both characterisation and relationships are more carefully and subtly drawn. The film is effectively a sequel to *The White Bird Passes* with the adult Janie (played by Phyllis Logan who had appeared as the 16-year-old Janie in the previous film) now married to a dour and unresponsive farmer, Dougal (Paul Young). It is wartime and three Italian POWs have been billeted on the farm to help in the fields. From the moment they arrive, Janie is fascinated by the exotic foreigners. Initially attracted to the tall, dark and handsome Paulo, it is the passionate Neapolitan Luigi who breaks down her inhibitions, providing the physical and emotional fulfilment her husband is apparently incapable of. Their brief affair inevitably ends in tragedy when Luigi is mistakenly arrested for the rape of a farm servant, an incident taking place when he was making love to Janie on the hillside. She decides to confess to the authorities to save him, but it transpires that he is still guilty of the crime of 'fraternising with a civilian female'. The film ends with an emotionally devastated Janie seeking comfort from Jess the neighbour who had refused to work with the Italians after her husband had been killed at Monte Casino.

Another Time, Another Place conveys a kind of poetic realism closer to continental cinema with Radford's aesthetic influenced in particular by the Italian director Ermanno Olmi's *The Tree of Wooden Clogs* (1978), a film about the rural peasantry in nineteenth-century Lombardy. The rural landscape of the Black Isle plays a central role in *Another Time, Another Place*, although rather than providing a picturesque backdrop, the low grey skies, endless winter rain, and ploughed fields convey a sense of claustrophobia circumscribing the lives of those living under it. There are some documentary-inspired touches, such as the intimate fly-on-the-wall camerawork during the ceilidh, but the overall style is much more contemplative, concerned to penetrate and convey the psychological and emotional states of the characters. The acute attention to detail at times recalls the intensity of Bill Douglas, but Radford is ultimately less austere, deploying both colour and music to enhance his depiction of both emotional and physical landscapes. The Scottish dimension is also more thoroughly interrogated in *Another Time, Another Place*. While the German in *My Childhood* provided Jamie with much-needed human contact, the Italian POWs serve to exacerbate the cultural difference between northern and southern Europe, the contrast between the ceilidh and the Italians' Christmas celebrations instructive in this respect. The former delineates the social structure of the rural Scottish community: the men and women immediately split up on entering the hall. Janie's enthusiasm for dancing sets her apart from the other women but she must wait to be asked to dance by a man, her youthful exuberance linking her with the children who share her curiosity with the foreigners in their midst. The Italian celebration is marked by the men playing and singing, Luigi's soulful song a contrast to the sweet but rather frigid rendition of 'Rowan Tree' by Meg at the ceilidh,[26] while Janie's dance with him is more overtly wild and passionate than the carefully choreographed Scottish jigs and reels.

One writer-director with a more direct connection to the legacy of Bill Douglas is Ian Sellar, having worked on both *My Childhood* and *My Ain Folk*[27] before enrolling at the National Film and Television School. He took a year out to make his debut film, *Over Germany*, for the German broadcaster ZDF, and since graduating has written and directed two major features, *Venus Peter* (1989) and

Prague (1992). Like Douglas's *Trilogy* and Radford's *The White Bird Passes*, *Venus Peter* centres around the experiences of a child. Based on Christopher Rush's biographical novel, *A Twelvemonth and a Day*, it recounts the experiences of a young boy growing up in a rural fishing community in Orkney in the late 1940s.[28] From the moment Peter (played by 9-year-old Gordon R. Strachan) is baptised with salt water, his world is dominated by the sea – a close identification with boats almost resulting in tragedy when he attempts to hold his breath indefinitely under water. But Peter also displays profound wisdom in his observation that 'the sea is everything', preserving a sense of hope in the face of the collapse of the local fishing industry. Once again the child's life is marked by the absence of a father, but unlike Douglas's Jamie and Radford/Kesson's Janie, Peter at least has the benefit of a loving and supportive family network facilitating greater opportunity for him to indulge his powers of imagination. He is aided and abetted by his grandfather (Ray McAnally), a fisherman who spins poetic yarns about the sea and gives the boy a telescope through which he observes both the world about him and imaginary glimpses of his returning father, a handsome captain of a boat decked out in brightly coloured sails. Peter's love of poetry is fuelled by the venerable old landlady, Epp, who gives him a poetry book just before she dies, and subsequently by his teacher, Miss Balsilbie (Sinead Cusack), an irrepressible romantic with whom he becomes infatuated. Peter also identifies with the ethereal Princess Paloma (Juliet Cadzow), the most exotic member of the gallery of local eccentrics, a mad woman rumoured to be the offspring of Thai

Orcadian elegy: *Venus Peter*

royalty who lives alone in a big house and who is cared for by the local minister, the kindly Reverend Kinnear (David Hayman).

Like Douglas and Radford before him, Sellar achieves a similar sense of the
interconnections between objective and subjective dimensions in *Venus Peter*,
although this time Peter's immersion in the world of his imagination sets him
apart from the emotional and economic realities of a community confronting
the imminent demise of its main industry. Christopher Rush notes that the
process of adaptation from novel to film enhanced the objective elements of his
original story:

> Where *Venus Peter* perhaps succeeds more emphatically than *Twelvemonth* is
> in its presentation of two distinct levels of experience: the realistic and the
> poetic. I believe that *Twelvemonth* is wholly submerged in its own poetry.
> *Venus Peter*, on the other hand, shows a boy of heightened sensibilities
> experiencing poetic fantasies, while all around him is a world of hard
> economic fact, a world falling apart financially.[29]

Venus Peter's affinity with Bill Douglas can be discerned in the observed
moments and gestures: Epp smashing a boiled sweet with a poker to make it
easier for Peter to eat, Peter carelessly breaking the eggs wrapped in the pages
of a poetry book. Sellar makes a similar use of narrative echoes and repetitive
imagery, most strikingly in the connection between the dying beached whale
(an almost mythical figure symbolising the power and the bounty of the sea)
and grandfather's boat, the *Venus*, also destined to end its life on dry land. But
the major difference between *Venus Peter* and Douglas's *Trilogy* lies in the
experiences of childhood and the meanings associated with the past. While
Peter's innocence and fantasy insulate him against the harsher aspects of a
changing world (and, as Roderick Watson has indicated, Rush's original novel
constitutes 'a sustained elegy to childhood and a lost past'),[30] Jamie's unremit-
ting suffering can only be alleviated by leaving his childhood, his community
and indeed Scotland behind him.

A more ambivalent contemplation of the profound influence of environment,
in this case the sea, on successive generations is the central premise of Margaret
Tait's *Blue Black Permanent*. The film explores a daughter's struggle to come to
terms with the haunting legacy of a mother who died by drowning. In a series
of flashbacks it is revealed that Barbara's (Celia Imrie) grandmother was also
claimed by the sea, the effects of this prior tragedy ultimately leading to her own
mother's death. What is unclear is whether Greta (Gerda Stevenson) deliberately
committed suicide or accidentally wandered into the sea while sleepwalking,
making her daughter's anguish all the more difficult to cope with. Unfortunately,
despite the fascinating premise, Tait is clearly out of her depth working within

the conventions of the feature film, the actors appearing extremely uncomfortable in the leaden dialogue scenes, which do little more than provide narrative information. Ironically Tait's poetic short films made in Orkney and Edinburgh in the 1950s and 1960s earned her a deserved reputation as poet with an acute eye for the details of the world, yet robbed of the intimacy of narrow gauge filmmaking in *Blue Black Permanent* she fails almost totally to capture or convey the elemental and ominous power of the sea. There is a more characteristic and effective accumulation of images in the charged closing montage, but otherwise the vital Orcadian environment is rendered as rather flat and lifeless.

But whatever their particular merits or demerits, films like *Blue Black Permanent*, *Venus Peter* and *Another Time, Another Place* marked a new phase in the representation of peripheral and rural Scottish experience, founded on indigenous internal cultural expressions rather than externally imposed metropolitan fantasies. Another important contribution in this context is Mike Alexander's Gaelic-language film *As An Eilean/From the Island* (1993), the first and to date only feature funded by the Comataidh Telebhisein Gaidhlig (CTG), the Gaelic Television Committee.[31] With Douglas Eadie's script derived from two short stories by Iain Crichton Smith, *The Last Summer* and *The Heart*, *As An Eilean* reflects the bilingual realities of the contemporary Gaelic experience, and is therefore a very different proposition to *Hero*, Barney Platts Mills's 1982 Gaelic evocation of Celtic myth. Crichton Smith's upbringing on the island of Lewis is central to his poetic vision of island life and Mike Alexander's sensitive direction is clearly influenced by his own formative years on Arran. Consequently, *As An Eilean* projects a deep sense of the complexities of the remote community's relationship to the mainland, exploring the specific intensities and problems from an insider point of view – including issues of loneliness, repressed desire, the absence of significant others and a fear of the unknown. At the centre of the narrative are two characters linked together through their shared introspection and creative aspiration. Callum (Iain F. Macleod), a brooding teenager soon to leave the island for university in Aberdeen, is encouraged in his love of poetry by his teacher MacAlasdair (Ken Hutcheson), a lonely widower whose interaction with the island takes place largely through his camera lens. But unlike the external romantic view of peripheral life, *As An Eilean* also manages to convey the community's direct connection with the modern world, particularly through the teenage brothers Callum and Colin, with their interest in rock music, football and cinema.

A Search for Identity: Scotland and Europe

The opposition of core and periphery structuring the island–mainland relationship is also relevant in locating Scotland in relation to Europe. Scotland's historical affinities with the continent are frequently contrasted with

English isolationism, running from the 'auld alliance' with Catholic France, through the various mercantile links with Calvinist Holland, Germany and the Baltic states, to the more recent espousal of a 'Scotland in Europe' policy by the Scottish National Party.[32] The European dimension of contemporary Scottish identity is forcefully articulated in some recent Scottish films. Ian Sellar's 1983 film *Over Germany* is an autobiographical account of a young Scottish boy, the son of a bomber pilot and a Jewish refugee, who visits his German grandmother for the first time. In Hamburg, a city his father bombed, the boy is confronted with the limitations of his comic-book preconceptions of Germany and crucially of his own relationship to her history. Sellar subsequently returned to the thorny question of cultural identity with his second feature film *Prague* (1992) which is similarly concerned with a young Scotsman attempting to connect with continental roots. Alexander Novak (Alan Cumming) travels to the Czech capital in search of a fragment of old newsreel from 1941 apparently showing members of his family attempting to evade arrest and transportation to the Nazi death camps shortly before they disappeared. Alexander's progress is hampered by the Byzantine procedures of the national film archive. When he does eventually find the film it is destroyed in a freak accident before he can view it. On the point of returning to Scotland, Alexander is informed by Elena (Sandrine Bonnaire) the enigmatic archivist with whom he has a brief relationship, that the film depicted a little girl floating away in the river. That little girl was Alexander's mother and the fragment of film tangible proof of her escape and his connection to the past.

The formal construction, mode of address and thematic preoccupations of *Prague* are once again clearly those of art cinema. Alexander is a complex and allusive central character, his encounters with others continually hampered by an inability to communicate successfully. In addition to the obvious problems of language, much of the dialogue in the film is oblique and evasive, adding to the general sense of confusion which surrounds Alexander as he tries to negotiate this foreign city and culture to which he claims a bond. As his quest becomes increasingly frustrated, so Sellar subtly switches focus towards a consideration of the way Alexander uses the past to evade confronting his feelings for Elena, who has announced that she is pregnant with his child, and embracing his opportunity to be a father. His emotional neediness is exacerbated by his inability to deal with Elena's closeness to Josef (Bruno Ganz), her superior at the film archive. But it is ultimately the fear of giving himself and taking responsibility for the future, rather than being fixated in that past, that constitutes the dilemma he is finally forced to confront.

A genuine European co-production, *Prague* was developed by the Scottish Film Production Fund and £2 million budget came from a combination of the British Screen, BBC Films, the SFPF and the French broadcaster Canal+. The production team included Scots, Czechs, a French camera team headed by the distinguished cinematographer Darius Khondji and a cosmopolitan cast including three leading roles played by a Scot, a German and a French actress. But inevitably this eclecticism drew criticisms with the film being described in some quarters as a 'Euro-pudding' with only a tenuous connection with Scotland.[33] While there may be some justification in questioning the decision of the SFPF to invest £130,000 of Scottish public money in a project to be made entirely in another country, *Prague's* preoccupations provide a welcome and timely alternative to the conception of Scottish identity within rather limited cultural and geographical boundaries. As Trevor Johnston perceptively remarks: 'At a moment when the concept of an independent Scotland in Europe has become part of the currency of political debate, *Prague's* narrative presents a young Scot, tangibly linked to the European experience of the Holocaust and the legacy of Communism, rethinking his own identity.'[34]

Scotland's relationship to Europe is also central to Timothy Neat's *Play Me Something* (1989), produced by the BFI. Co-written by the novelist and art critic John Berger and adapted from *Once in Europa*, his collection of stories about European peasant life, *Play Me Something* is a fascinating meditation on cultural transmission and the art of story-telling. A group of travellers are stranded at the airport on the Hebridean island of Barra, the plane from Glasgow having been delayed by fog. Into their midst walks a strange man (played by Berger) who sits down and begins to recount a story, a simple tale about the encounter between Bruno, an Italian peasant from a mountain village, and Marietta, a shop worker from Mestre, on a visit to the city of Venice. Despite their differences, the two spend the day and night together, chatting and drinking in a café, dancing at a Communist festival on the island of Guidecca, making love in an abandoned boat. Berger's spoken narrative is illustrated by a combination of 16mm colour 'documentary' footage of Venice, black and white images of a rural mountain village, and a series of still photographs by Jean Mohr featuring the two main protagonists. The 'story' of *Play Me Something* is consequently woven out of these disparate elements, with the audience providing the necessary coherence, returning at various points to the waiting room on Barra where the various occupants have become immersed in the tale, offering the occasional comment or contribution.

As Philip Schlesinger observes, *Play Me Something* explicitly constructs itself as a European text invoking a particular relationship between Scotland and other peripheral cultures in Europe:

> [The film] is evolved from a quintessentially Scottish island scene, where self conscious use is made of the traditions of Celtic story-telling. The marginal rural settings of Italy and Scotland are brought into a common frame, a

'European' one, as are Venice's tidal city and Barra's tidal airport. At one level we are being informed that the power of a tale well told can compare, contrast and also transcend cultures, to produce transformative effects on those who attend in the right way.[35]

The sophistication of this dialogue is echoed in the framing story in other ways. The character of the storyteller is dressed in a dark suit and hat, the festive garb of an Italian peasant. But he is summoned into existence by the eccentric TV repairman whose arrival and departure by horse and cart opens and closes the film; the casting here is significant in that the repairman is played by Hamish Henderson, a well-known specialist in Scottish folk culture. As a self-conscious attempt to locate Scotland within a contemporary European framework in a way that expresses the value of the local and the particular at the same time as demonstrating the virtues of cross-cultural communication, *Play Me Something* represents a major achievement. Constituted very much as experimental art cinema, Neat and Berger's film is also a testament to the ongoing importance of cinemas that address national specificity in an expressly outward-looking manner.

As an essentially self-reflexivity piece of work, *Play Me Something* invokes another key impulse of the art cinema tradition. In drawing attention to the nature of its own construction, the film also challenges the seamless invisibility perpetrated by the classical narrative film, offering a simultaneous commentary and analysis on the very story it is telling. Consequently, it can be related to other examples of self-reflexive film-making such as *The Cheviot, the Stag and the Black Black Oil* and *Scotch Myths* discussed elsewhere in this book. But the most tangible link between Scotland and the traditions of art cinema is provided by the small but significant range of films reflecting a powerful and poetic sense of personal experience and biographical narrative. While a filmmaker like Bill Forsyth has existed on the margins of mainstream and art house cinema, a dualism that has possibly been more of a hindrance than a virtue, a number of others like Bill Douglas and Ian Sellar have operated resolutely with a European art cinema tradition. The personal vision informing their work, and that of Mike Alexander, Mike Radford, Timothy Neat, Margaret Tait and David Hayman, also discussed above, constitutes the first major attempt to construct a cinematic alternative to the decades of external representations of Scotland. In projecting a different engagement with questions of identity, culture, history and landscape these film-makers began collectively to reconfigure the relationship between the metropolitan core and Celtic periphery, opening up the possibility of a distinctive Scottish 'voice' comparable to a range of other forms of contemporary creative expression from the novel to the theatre.

Notes

1   Jean Luc-Godard in conversation with Colin MacCabe in Duncan Petrie
    (ed.), *Screening Europe: Image and Identity in Contemporary European Cinema*
    (London: BFI, 1992), p. 98.

2   See in particular Andrew Higson, *Waving the Flag: Constructing a National Cinema
    in Britain* (Oxford: Clarendon Press, 1995) and John Hill, 'The Issue of National
    Cinema and British Film Production' in Duncan Petrie (ed.), *New Questions of
    British Cinema* (London: BFI, 1992). Hill returns to the question in his later book,
    British Cinema in the 1980s (Oxford: Oxford University Press, 1999).

3   Christopher Williams, 'The Social Art Cinema: A Moment in the History of
    British Film and Television Culture' in Williams (ed.), *Cinema: The Beginnings
    and the Future* (London: University of Westminster Press, 1996), p. 191.

4   John Hill, *British Cinema in the 1980s*, p. 67.

5   David Bordwell, 'The Art Cinema as a Mode of Practice', *Film Criticism*, vol.
    4, no. 1, Autumn 1979, p. 56.

6   Steve Neale, 'Art Cinema as Institution', *Screen*, vol. 22, no. 1, 1981, p. 35.

8   John Hill, *British Cinema in the 1980s*, pp. 64–5.

9   Ibid., p. 66.

10 Nick Roddick, 'The British Revival' in Fenella Greenfield (ed.), *A Night at the
    Pictures: Ten Decades of British Film* (Bromley: Columbus Books/British Film
    Year, 1995), p. 110.

11 Forsyth Hardy, *Scotland in Film* (Edinburgh: Edinburgh University Press,
    1990), p. 177.

12 John Brown, 'A Suitable Job for a Scot', *Sight and Sound*, Summer 1983, p. 158.

13 Allan Hunter, 'Bill Forsyth: The Imperfect Anarchist' in Eddie Dick (ed.), *From
    Limelight to Satellite: A Scottish Film Book: (London: BFI/SFC, 1990)*, p. 156.

14 Forsyth himself was greatly inspired by Malle and Godard in the 1960s. As he
    put it in 1981: 'After seeing *Pierrot le Fou* five or six times I wanted to be
    Godard, and I still do. If I had a daughter she wouldn't be allowed to date
    someone who didn't like *Pierrot*.' Bill Forsyth, 'British Cinema: 1981 to …',
    Sight and Sound, Autumn 1981, p. 243. Text of paper delivered at a
    symposium organised by the BFI.

15 Set in the 1950s, *Housekeeping* is a delicately crafted story of two orphaned
    teenage girls, Lucille (Andrea Burchill) and Ruthie (Sara Walker), living with
    their eccentric aunt Sylvie (Christine Lahti) in the small town of Fingerbone.
    The theme of loneliness and isolation is once again central but this time is
    defined and explored more subtly through forms of human interaction and
    the ways in which individuals define themselves through their relationships.
    The close bond between the two sisters is eroded then broken by their
    response to Sylvie, an itinerant forced by circumstance into becoming a

reluctant surrogate mother. She is distanced from the conservative social norms of Fingerbone by way of her eccentric dress and behaviour (collecting tin cans and newspapers, watching TV through neighbours' windows, sleeping on park benches in the middle of the day). This alienates the increasingly socially conformist Lucille, but strengthens Sylvie's relationship with Ruthie, a painfully shy gawky adolescent who ultimately identifies more with her aunt's free spirit than the stultifying conventionality of Fingerbone.

16 For a fuller account of the debacle of the production, see Allan Hunter's interview with Forsyth, 'Being Human', *Sight and Sound* August 1994.

17 These were reflected in the respective cinematographic styles, Michael Coulter's soft high-key approach being suited to romantic comedy of the former film whereas the murky winter light captured by Chris Menges visually underscored the underlying despair in the latter.

18 Philip Kemp, review of *Soft Top, Hard Shoulder*, *Sight and Sound*, January 1993, p. 52.

19 Andrew Noble, 'Bill Douglas's Trilogy' in Eddie Dick (ed.), *From Limelight to Satellite: A Scottish Film Book* (London: BFI/SFC, 1990), p. 136.

20 André Bazin, 'The Evolution of the Language of Cinema' in *What is Cinema?* Volume 1 (Berkeley: University of California Press, 1967). Trans. Hugh Gray.

21 John Caughie, 'Don't Mourn – Analyse: Reviewing the Trilogy' in Eddie Dick, Andrew Noble and Duncan Petrie (eds), *Bill Douglas: A Lanternist's Account* (London: BFI, 1993), p. 200.

22 Ibid., p. 202.

23 For a detailed discussion of the film see Duncan Petrie, 'The Lanternist Revisited: The Making of Comrades' in Dick, Noble and Petrie (eds), *Bill Douglas: A Lanternist's Account*.

24 Caughie, 'Don't Mourn – Analyse', p. 197.

25 One of the first intake of the National Film and Television School at Beacons-field, Radford made a number of documentaries on leaving film school.

26 Incidentally this is also the traditional song sung by the old man in the Anderson shelter in *My Childhood*.

27 Sellar was assistant director on the latter film, a role he also fulfilled on several other BFI productions during this period. These include *Winstanley* (Kevin Brownlow and Andrew Mollo, 1975), *Requiem for a Village* (David Gladwell, 1975) and *The Moon Over the Alley* (Joseph Despins, 1975),

28 Rush's original novel, published in 1985, is set in the East Neuk of Fife.

29 Christopher Rush, 'Venus Peter: From Pictures to Pictures' in Eddie Dick (ed.), *From Limelight to Satellite*, pp. 127–8.

30 Roderick Watson, 'Maps of Desire: Scottish Literature in the Twentieth Century' in T.M. Devine and R.J. Finlay (eds.), *Scotland in the 20th Century* (Edinburgh: Edinburgh University Press, 1996), p. 292.

31 Developed by the SFPF and the European Script Fund, *As An Eilean* was co-financed by Channel Four, Grampian Television and Ross & Cromarty District Council to the tune of £750,000. It was shot on Super-16mm in Wester Ross. The CTG was established in 1990 by the Scottish Office to administer a new fund for minority language television and radio production.

32 This question has been recently addressed by Christopher Harvie in his 1992 essay 'Veere and Afterwards: The Tradition of Scotland in Europe' republished in the collection *Travelling Scot: Essays on the History, Politics and Future of the Scots* (Glendaruel: Argyll Publishing, 1999).

33 See for example Colin McArthur, 'In Praise of a Poor Cinema', *Sight and Sound*, August 1993. It is worth noting however that the SFPF investment in *Prague* represented a mere 6.5 per cent of the final £2 million budget. The involvement of members of the film community in this debate is documented by Robin Macpherson, 'Independent film and television in Scotland: a case of independent cultural reproduction?' Unpublished M.Litt dissertation, University of Stirling, 1991, pp. 278–9.

34 Trevor Johnstone, review of *Prague, Sight and Sound*, November 1992, p. 50.

35 Philip Schlesinger, 'Scotland, Europe and Identity' in Eddie Dick (ed.), *From Limelight to Satellite*, p. 230.

Chapter Eight
The New Scottish Cinema: Institutions

A New Dawn?

John Hill has argued (with reference to Britain) that only a national cinema can adequately address the specificities, preoccupations and experience of contemporary cultural life.[1] But the necessary conditions for a sustainable national cinema in a small country like Scotland require more than the production of a handful of films, however accomplished and interesting they may be. Appropriate structures and institutions are needed to provide and maintain the resources for a critical mass of films to be produced, distributed and exhibited on a consistent and regular basis. Without such support structures there can be no national cinema, although there may be isolated film-makers who by default end up carrying the burden of national projection. Such a situation existed in the early 1980s when Scottish cinema was more or less equated with the films of Bill Forsyth. But the situation has changed dramatically since then. The latter half of the 1990s has witnessed unprecedented levels of production in Scotland, providing opportunities for Scottish film-makers to learn and practice their craft in their native country rather than accepting the inevitable move to London or Los Angeles.

The number of feature films made either wholly or partly in Scotland increased dramatically in the 1990s, from five productions in 1991 to an average of more than ten a year from 1994 onwards. While a certain proportion of these are overseas productions attracted by the Scottish landscape for dramatic locations and picturesque backdrops, the major upsurge in production activity has been spearheaded by a number of indigenous low-budget features such as *Shallow Grave* (Danny Boyle, 1995), *Small Faces* (Gillies Mackinnon, 1996), *Trainspotting* (Danny Boyle, 1996), *My Name is Joe* (Ken Loach, 1998), *Orphans* (Peter Mullan, 1999) and *Ratcatcher* (Lynne Ramsay, 1999). This output has been enhanced by a small number of high-profile international productions embracing Scottish subject matter from the Oscar-winning Hollywood epic *Braveheart* (Mel Gibson, 1995), to the innovative Scandinavian/French art film *Breaking the Waves* (Lars von Trier, 1996). The range of recent activity is demonstrated

A new dawn in Scottish production: Christopher Eccleston in *Shallow Grave*

by statistics compiled by Scottish Screen: of a total number of sixty one films made in Scotland between 1991 and 1997, twenty-five were considered to be wholly or partly 'Scottish', fourteen originated from elsewhere in the UK, nine were Hollywood productions, eight European, one a British/European co-production and four originated from elsewhere in the world.[2] The improvement in facilities and other forms of support has also attracted producers seeking to recreate particular locations. A mining museum in Lothian doubled for Nova Scotia in the Canadian film *Margaret's Museum* (Mort Ransen, 1995), parts of Edinburgh were used for late nineteenth-century Oxford in *Jude* (Michael Winterbottom, 1996), and more recently the Victorian architecture of Glasgow has been transformed into turn-of-the-century New York for Terence Davies's adaptation of Edith Wharton's novel *House of Mirth*. Such sustained interest in Scotland as a location or production base has made a vital contribution to the cultivation of an all-important indigenous infrastructure, directly benefiting more specifically local industrial and cultural concerns in the process.

New Institutions/New Opportunities

The upsurge in film production in the 1990s was to a large extent the result of the emergence of a range of important new indigenous sources of film finance. The germ of this process lay in the forceful demand for financial support generated and articulated by initiatives in the late 1970s like 'Film Bang' and 'Cinema in a Small Country'. In 1979 the Scottish Film Council allocated a modest sum of £5,000 for production which paved the way for a joint initiative between the SFC and the Scottish Arts Council. The result was the establishment three years later of the Scottish Film Production Fund with a budget of £80,000 and a remit 'to foster and promote film and video production as a central element in the development of Scottish culture'.[3] The ability of the SFPF to make a real impact was initially hampered by the limitations of its resources, memorably described by Ian Lockerbie, the first chair of the Fund, as 'a state of penury'.[4] But the Fund was subsequently boosted by subventions from Channel Four in 1986 and BBC Scotland in 1989 to more than £200,000 and during its first decade contributed to the development of a number of feature projects including *Living Apart Together*, *Every Picture Tells a Story*, *Play Me Something*, *Venus Peter*, *Silent Scream*, *Prague* and *Blue Black Permanent*. During the same period, the SFPF also supported a number of documentaries, animation projects and graduation films by Scottish Film Students at the National Film and Television School.[5] The 1990s saw a further swelling of the resources available through the participation of Scottish Television and Comataidh Telebhisein Gaidhlig (CTG) in various initiatives, reaching a peak of £735,000 in 1996 (although a substantial amount of this was linked to particular short film schemes that will be discussed below). This growth allowed the SFPF to expand its feature development programme, nurturing a range of projects like *Shallow Grave*, *Small Faces*, *The Near Room* (David Hayman, 1997), *Carla's Song* (Ken Loach, 1997) and *Orphans*. While all of these tend to be low-budget independent British features budgeted at between £1 and £3 million, the Fund also developed the more ambitious *Rob Roy* (Michael Caton-Jones, 1995), a project subsequently bankrolled by United Artists to the tune of £16 million.

The expansion in production activities by the Scottish Film Production Fund was mirrored by an increasingly professional approach to administration, including the appointment in 1989 of a full-time director. The post was filled by an independent producer, Penny Thompson, who resolved to take a more enlightened approach to the issue of project development:

> The priority was to develop scripts to a certain point so they could then go to Channel Four or perhaps the BBC. But there was no sense that in putting that money in early on you were strengthening the producer's position in terms of him or her going out to raise money ... Along with Chris Young [producer of *Venus Peter* and *Prague*] I was a very early participant in EAVE, the European training programme, and a lot of things I had been thinking over received a certain amount of confirmation from people with much more experience. The situation in Scotland was similar to that in Greece, Portugal or even Ireland at the time. And I think we were right to encourage greater co-operation

between producers and writers, there has to be that energy to get them together.[6]

After three years, Thompson was succeeded by a new director, Kate Swan, who began to develop partnerships with other key bodies such as the BBC and the newly established Glasgow Film Fund. After only two years, Swan decided to move on, passing the reins of the SFPF to Eddie Dick, former Education Officer at the Scottish Film Council. While his lack of production experience drew criticism from some quarters, Dick consolidated the gains that had already been made and set vigorously about expanding the Fund's range of activities, placing it at the centre of an emerging and vibrant new production sector in Scotland. With the support of chairman Allan Shiach (the experienced Hollywood-based screenwriter and producer Allan Scott) Dick began restructuring the organisation to take advantage of the major opportunities that were emerging. This included an expansion of the board and the creation of a separate development panel, both moves a reflection of a considerably increased workload brought about by new sources of production finance in Scotland.

The most significant new initiative in this respect was the Glasgow Film Fund, established as a 'cultural industries' initiative aimed at stimulating production activity in and around the city. A key figure in this process was Lenny Crooks, an economic development worker with aspirations to produce films:

I was aware that the Glasgow Development Agency, Glasgow City Council and Strathclyde Regional Council were interested in the film industry but didn't know how to take a handle on it. There came this opportunity in 1992 when European development funding became available not only for capital projects but also for revenue-based projects. And so with a couple of forward-thinking people I put together the idea to create a small venture capital fund for film for a year. The total sum the three agencies could come up with was £80,000, which the European Regional Development Fund were able to match, creating a total fund of £160,000.[7]

The decision was taken to administer this new money through the Scottish Film Production Fund, with the GFF being explicitly geared towards feature projects budgeted at over £500,000 and intended for *theatrical* release. And while the amount available for investment was in industry terms relatively small, it could assist projects considerably in the difficult process of raising money from other sources to complete the financing. As Andrea Calderwood, former BBC Scotland head of drama notes:

at the under £2 million budget on which many British films are made, the investment of around £150,000 per film available from the Glasgow Film Fund can make a significant difference to whether a film can be made on a feature scale, either providing top-up finance to a broadcaster's budget, or representing a respectable contribution which a producer making a film in Glasgow can propose as part of a co-production finance deal.[8]

The first award made by the GFF was to *Shallow Grave*, a £1 million project brought to the table by a then unknown producer called Andrew MacDonald. Although set in Edinburgh, the majority of the production was shot in a temporary studio constructed in an industrial unit in Glasgow. *Shallow Grave* proved to be an unexpected hit, making more than £5 million at the British box office and providing the Glasgow Film Fund with an auspicious beginning, which Crooks suggests represented 'the most successful investment probably of any venture capital fund in Scotland in any industry'.[9] When Eddie Dick became director of the SFPF he immediately argued for greater flexibility in the operation of the GFF in relation to funding decisions, such as the removal of the ceiling of £150,000 to any particular project. The success of *Shallow Grave* strengthened his argument and subsequent investments from the rolling fund have on occasion been as much as £250,000.[10] The initial financial consolidation of the GFF was also assisted by Channel Four, the majority investor in *Shallow Grave*, who gave the fund a privileged recoupment position on the first three films they co-financed.

From this auspicious start, the Glasgow Film Fund has gone on to make an important contribution to an impressive number of recent Scottish features including *Small Faces, The Near Room, Carla's Song, The Slab Boys* (John Byrne, 1997), *Regeneration* (Gillies Mackinnon, 1997), *The Life of Stuff* (Simon Donald, 1998), *My Name is Joe, Orphans, The Acid House Trilogy* (Paul McGuiggan, 1999), *The Debt Collector* (Anthony Neilson, 1999) and *The House of Mirth* (Terence Davies, 2000).[11] But despite this impressive track record, the financial health of the GFF has varied over the years. European funding ceased in 1995 but the GDA and the City Council continued to plough in between £250,000 and £300,000 annually. A final injection of £500,000 of public money is earmarked with the hope that this will help the GFF to attract private investment on the basis of preferential return. And with a total local spend of £11.5 million on film production in Glasgow in 1999, the economic potential of supporting film-making has been clearly established.[12] The GFF has also undergone certain administrative adjustments, deciding to assume direct in-house responsibility for the running of the fund with the absorption in 1997 of the SFPF into a new single integrated agency, Scottish Screen.[13]

Even more significant than the Glasgow Film Fund has been the provision of finance for film production in Scotland from the National Lottery. When devising a policy for the distribution of revenues from the lottery to so-called 'good causes' the British government decided that with regard to benefiting the arts (including film) this new resource would not be administered by a single UK (i.e. London-based) agency but rather would be devolved to the Arts Councils of England, Scotland, Wales and Northern Ireland. Siona Reid, director of the Scottish Arts Council, subsequently approached the SFPF and the Scottish Lottery Film Panel was established in 1995 based on a model adapted from the Glasgow Film Fund. In the first two years of operations, some £12 million of lottery money was awarded to a range of projects, with an average award to feature films of between £500,000 and £1 million, a considerable sum given the average budgets of such productions. The SFPF were paid a service fee for administering the lottery fund and this allowed more resources to be put into development, an area of activity limited by the funds available. But the impact of the lottery has been such that practically all of the major Scottish films to be produced since 1996 have directly benefited. They include *Stella Does Tricks* (Coky Giedroyc, 1997), *The Slab Boys* (which also received funding from the Arts Council of England), *Regeneration, The Winter Guest* (Alan Rickman, 1998), *The Life of Stuff, My Name is Joe, Orphans, The Acid House Trilogy, This Year's Love* (David Kane, 1999), *Ratcatcher, Gregory's Two Girls* (Bill Forsyth, 1999), *Complicity* (Gavin Millar, 2000), *My Life So Far* (Hugh Hudson, 2000), *Daybreak* (Bernard Rudden, 2000) and *House of Mirth*.[14]

The hugely expanded sums of money available soon generated controversy, however. In January 1997, accusations of corruption and 'cronyism' were levelled at the lottery panel, particularly in relation to decisions to back projects in which prominent panel members like Chairman Allan Shiach and Lynda Myles had interests. No actual misdemeanours were proven but a stigma had been attached to the board which resulted in the Scottish Arts Council reassuming direct responsibility for the funding process. As administrator of the lottery during the period, Eddie Dick found his own position undermined by the controversy, paving the way for his subsequent departure to become an independent producer.[15] The greatest setback for the film community, many of whom had publicly supported Forsyth, was the imposition of an annual ceiling of £2.5 million on the funds available with a cap of £500,000 on any one project. The Scottish Arts Council appointed Jenny Attala to administer the fund and act as secretariat to the new panel drawn from a wider cultural constituency than the more industry-oriented SFPF board. This was to prove a short-term solution, however. Around the same time, the various public screen agencies, including the Scottish Film Production Fund, the Scottish Film Council, Scottish Screen Locations, the Scottish Film Training Trust and the Scottish Film and Television Archive were being integrated into a single new agency, Scottish Screen. As such the new body had considerable political clout and immediately set out lobbying the Scottish Office to move responsibility for the lottery money back to Glasgow. This coincided with major developments in London with the establishment of the new Film Council, which, among other responsibilities was to be given control of English lottery money. Consequently, in April 2000 responsibility for the lottery panel was transferred back to Glasgow under the administration of Scottish Screen.

In addition to providing production finance, a number of new lottery-funded schemes have been aimed at nurturing the emerging but still highly fragile production infrastructure in Scotland. These include a project preparation initiative to assist producers with a developed script to put together a viable package with which to approach financiers; an exploitation scheme to help with the marketing and promotion of Scottish-funded films; a short film scheme aimed at assisting companies wishing to commission a series of short films; and a company development award for independent producers developing a slate of projects. The purpose of the latter award is explained by Scottish Screen's production head Steve McIntyre in the following way:

> It is fundamentally posited on the notion that the best way of helping companies is to enable them to take responsibility for their own development. So while an award of £50,000 might not be a lot of money it can help a company decide which projects to prioritise, enabling companies to move forward. It frees producers up from doing lots of script reading, bits of teaching or jobbing producing just to survive. Instead they can put their energies into their company, allowing a certain maturation of the industry in the process.[16]

McIntyre's purpose here is to build on the work of his predecessors by nurturing the screen industries in Scotland, assisting producers interested in running a successful business rather than struggling from hand to mouth, project to project, as was frequently the case in the past. At the time of writing, Scottish Screen control and administer a development budget of £200,000, but McIntyre's priority is to increase the likelihood of projects attracting production finance by placing an even greater emphasis on the role of producers. In addition to script development, this necessarily involves other crucial elements such as putting a deal together, attaching an appropriate director, drawing up a proper budget and schedule, hiring a casting director, taking a project to markets, etc. Some of the new lottery business and company development schemes, adding a further £350,000 of resources,[17] have been created to meet these concerns.

As in the 1980s, the broadcasters have continued to play a crucial role in the funding process. Channel Four remain a major player by virtue of their support for many of the feature films developed by SFPF/Scottish Screen and the decision to finance *Trainspotting* fully to the tune of £1.7 million. But the problem for a distinctively Scottish cinema is that British broadcasting continues to be largely controlled and run from London, with the Scottish broadcasters either reluctant or unable to become substantially involved in film finance.[18] The first major involvement by BBC films in a Scottish production was the £500,000 invested in *Prague*. But under Andrea Calderwood, who succeeded Bill Bryden as head of drama in 1993, BBC Scotland began to make a modest but significant contribution to theatrical production in its own right beginning with *Small Faces* (in which BBC Films were also involved) and *Mrs Brown* (John Madden, 1997), a period drama made ostensibly for the small screen which subsequently found a substantial cinema audience after it was bought by the American distributor Miramax and screened at the 1997 Cannes Film Festival. Calderwood subsequently moved to Pathé Pictures in 1998, a member of one of the three consortia to win major production franchises from the lottery, and was succeeded by Barbara McKissack who collaborated closely with her former boss on the development and production of Lynne Ramsay's debut feature *Ratcatcher*.

McKissack continues to develop single films for both large and small screen as part of a wider slate of production. But being a 'regional' office of a 'national' broadcaster, her ability to realise any particular project depends upon the support of BBC Films, the London-based department who hold the production budget for single features. However, despite this continued impulse to centralisation, McKissack argues that the development of the relationship between BBC Scotland and BBC films in recent years has been beneficial to Scottish production:

> There used to be almost a situation that when a film was released it was branded as a BBC film. Now we brand it as BBC Films, Scotland and I think it is indicative that it is no longer acceptable to say it's all one thing. You have to acknowledge that I don't just work for BBC Scotland, I also work for BBC films. Now if I'm doing that I'm not just working for BBC films in London, I work for BBC Films, Scotland. The Corporation are beginning to recognise that and it's a massive cultural development for them to have released the rein that much. It's due to the fact that we now have the talent at every level, we no longer have to go cap in hand to London looking for producers, for example. They no longer say 'who is the cameraman', they accept you will hire someone good.[19]

The New Significance of Short Films

The BBC have also made a major contribution to the dramatic increase in the number of short films made in Scotland during the 1990s, constituting a significant secondary tier of production activity. But once again the major initiator has been the Scottish Film Production Fund/Scottish Screen. In 1990, Ian Lockerbie expressed regret that so few short films had been supported by the fund, the primary reason given being the lack of opportunities for such work to find an audience.[20] Some vital contributions were made along the way to a number of graduation films from the NFTVS including *Fall From Grace* (Ian Wyse, 1984), *The Riveter* (Michael Caton-Jones, 1986), *Passing Glory* (Gillies Mackinnon, 1986), *Ashes* (Douglas Mackinnon, 1990), *Tin Fish* (Paul Murton, 1990) and *Alabama* (Jim Shields, 1990). By the mid-1990s, however, the Fund was involved in four separate short-film schemes with various funding partners, and in 1996 some twenty-two short films were produced in Scotland with some kind of public support.[21]

The longest running and most successful of these schemes, 'Tartan Shorts', began in 1993 as a collaborative exercise between the SFPF and BBC Scotland. The scheme involves the annual production of three short films of around fifteen minutes in length. The initial budgetary ceiling per film stood at £30,000 but this has since been raised to around double that figure by way of an increased contribution from the BBC and the National Lottery. The scheme was explicitly designed to identify and cultivate new talent and is aimed at writer–director–producer teams yet to make the break into feature films. The films are originated on 35mm and distributed internationally to film festivals in addition to being broadcast by the BBC. 'Tartan Shorts' got off to a spectacular start when one of the first three films commissioned, *Franz Kafka's It's a Wonderful Life*, written and directed by Peter Capaldi, won the Oscar in 1994 for best short film. Since then, various 'Tartan Shorts' have had a very successful profile on the international film festival circuit, winning more than forty awards in the process. Among the most accomplished films to be produced under the scheme are *Fridge* (Peter Mullan, 1995) and *Gasman* (Lynne Ramsay, 1997), both of which helped pave the way for the film-makers concerned to make their first feature.[22] The broader significance of the initiative in relation to the issue of talent development is discussed by Barbara McKissack in the following way: 'I think "Tartan Shorts" is probably the most prestigious short film scheme in Britain. It's got a really good reputation for graduates progressing to features. The question of talent is important at every level, not just in the writing. What you try to ensure is that a short scheme is used to bring on people at all levels. For example promoting a cameraman who hasn't lit or a production manager who hasn't produced.'[23]

In addition to honing their writing and directorial skills, making short films has also enabled film-makers like Mullan and Ramsay to develop close working relationships. While both clearly possess a distinctive style and thematic concerns they also readily acknowledge the importance of collaboration, ensuring that the same creative teams they worked with on their short films graduated with them to the realm of features. Indeed, schemes like 'Tartan Shorts' can be equally important as calling cards for up-and-coming technicians and actors.

The success of 'Tartan Shorts' helped the SFPF to establish two similar initiatives in 1996 with different funding partners. 'Prime Cuts' was set up in collaboration with British Screen and Scottish Television to produce five films on 16mm of around five to seven minutes in length. While 'Gear Ghear', funded by the CTG and BBC Scotland, was envisaged as a Gaelic-language version of 'Tartan Shorts', run with a similar remit and budgetary levels although only two films a year are made under this scheme. The CTG had already contributed to the financing of one major dramatic short film, *Sealladh/The Vision* (1992), Douglas Mackinnon's wry and poetic evocation of a nineteenth-century Highland community during time of famine. STV on the other hand had previously been involved with the Scottish Film Council in establishing 'First Reels', a lower-budget initiative providing entry-level opportunities to aspiring film-makers via small grants to assist the production and completion of their projects.[24] The portfolio of short-film schemes administered by Scottish Screen took a major blow in 1998 with the withdrawal of STV from Prime Cuts and First Reels, demonstrating the fragility of a system dependent of the continuing collaboration of key institutional partners. But the damage was partly compensated by two new initiatives: 'Newfoundland', a scheme to produce six 30-minute films for television, funded by the Scottish Media Group (a conglomerate owning both STV and Grampian television) and 'Cineworks', an entry-level collaboration between Scottish Screen, the Lottery and the Glasgow Film and Video Workshop.[25]

These official schemes do not encompass the totality of short-film production in Scotland, however. The Glasgow Film Fund invests in around five shorts a year, recent examples including *California Sunshine* and *Somersault*, both directed by David Mackenzie, and the Cineworks project *Sex and Death*, written and directed by Cat McKiernan. In addition, UK institutions like the BFI and Channel Four have also had an important impact in this arena, considerably aiding the careers of film-makers like Jim Gillespie, whose BFI 'New Directors' short *Joyride* led to an offer from Hollywood to direct the high-profile cult horror film *I Know What You Did last Summer* (1998). While Morag Mackinnon's award-winning film *Home*, a quirky and poetic triptych of events in the day of a Glasgow council housing officer, was made for the Channel Four 'Short and Curlies' strand after being rejected for 'Tartan Shorts'.

While boasting many successes including the promotion of newcomers like Ramsay, Mullan and others, the short-film schemes have also attracted criticism. The involvement of broadcasters like the BBC and the Scottish Media Group has led to accusations that they are the major beneficiary of such schemes, deriving high-quality programming at a low price; while other critics have attacked the kind of structured apprenticeship for film-makers from entry level schemes through to 'Tartan Shorts' as an overly prescriptive and narrow model serving the interests of the mainstream industry to the detriment of alternative and more challenging modes of cultural film-making.[26] There is also the very real question of just how effective short films actually are as industry calling cards.[27] Producer Paddy Higson explains the situation:

> The big concern I have is that we are setting up expectations and finding lots of new talent, and yet they get to a certain stage and find that it's just as difficult for them to raise money for their next film. They then have to struggle and chances are they will go back to being a PA or an assistant director. Within British television at the moment there is a culture of wanting a director who has done *Eastenders*, a writer who has written two series etc. So you are not able to bring in the person who has directed the best short film and get them on to do a film drama because they haven't proved they can shoot a schedule. I took Peter Mullan on to do three episodes of *Cardiac Arrest* and it counted towards being able to convince financiers that he could do *Orphans*.[28]

In an attempt to begin to tackle the problem of talent development, Higson's production company Antonine have recently established their own short-film scheme, 'Eight and a Half', with funding from the lottery. Up to four films will be produced annually but the major innovation is that the scheme incorporates a major training element and will ensure that everyone involved will be properly paid, one of the major problems in an area of production over-reliant on good will and favours. Rather than taking a production fee, Antonine will sign first script deals with the successful participants, giving them the opportunity to nurture these film-makers through the next difficult stage towards TV drama and feature production.

Economics versus Culture

The developments examined above have created the economic means by which feature films can be funded and produced in Scotland. But the creation of something with aspirations towards being a Scottish 'national cinema', particularly given the central role played by public sources of funding, must be concerned with more than questions of economics. How these initiatives relate to the rather thorny but pressing question of cultural need must also be addressed. Since the early 1980s a sustained and robust line of criticism has been levelled at key institutions like the Scottish Film Council and the Scottish Film Production Fund by Colin McArthur. At the heart of McArthur's critique lies the accusation that the policies of the Scottish screen agencies have embraced an economic conception of film as primarily a commodity while neglecting cultural considerations. In other words the kind of Scottish cinema envisaged, and arguably being realised, is for McArthur an inappropriate one: 'The absence of cultural analysis in the discourses of the SFC and SFPF has meant that they have both been unequipped to think of alternatives to the industrial model, or to recognise the problems relating to national culture and identity that the industrial model might create.'[29]

The emphasis of the agencies is on the creation of a cinema rooted in narrative-based storytelling derived from Hollywood film practice, coupled with market-driven production strategies. For McArthur such a strategy not only drives up production costs, it also fails to address the more pressing cultural and social questions to which an indigenous Scottish cinema ought to be committed. The argument being that the larger the budgets, the greater the necessity that films 'work' internationally, the less they are able to address the specificity of the national culture concerned. As a more appropriate model, McArthur has elaborated the case for a 'Poor Scottish Cinema', a 'low budget, aesthetically austere, indigenously oriented' film-making practice.[30] Using the subsidised workshop sector as a facilitator, and restricting budgets to a maximum of £300,000, he proposes funding conditions which would inspire film-makers to look to alternative aesthetic strategies and production methods, creating a cinema that would by necessity 'be manifestly rooted in the society from which it comes'.[31] Touchstones include individual auteurs like Bill Douglas, Chris Marker, Robert Bresson, Dusan Makavejev and Derek Jarman and 'movements' such as Italian neo-realism, the French *nouvelle vague*, and Brazilian *Cinema Novo*.

McArthur's critique has drawn equally vigorous responses from some of the prime movers in the agencies concerned. In 1982, John Brown, the first part-time director of the SFPF, stated that 'oppositional film-making needs something to oppose, and my own view is that we must also have an indigenous mainstream Scottish Cinema, as an even higher priority.'[32] More recently, Eddie Dick, replying specifically to McArthur, rejected the idea that aesthetic austerity should be a necessity for Scottish cinema, advocating in turn a cinema which can be both austere and flamboyant, incorporating both low-budget innovation and ambitions to work on a larger canvas.[33] While Steve McIntyre, the current head of production at Scottish Screen, adopts an equally unequivocal pro-industry stance:

I don't think it is up to us to take any kind of substantial editorial line.
Obviously we want to support good work, but our view has to be let 1000
flowers bloom. I don't think we can say 'we will prioritise low budget work'. I
don't think it's our job to say that. Our view has to be culturally neutral,
technologically neutral, genre-neutral. If it turns out that a group of film-
makers emerge in that kind of environment and work in a particular way then
that's fine. But it's not up to us to dictate that.[34]

This debate raises some important questions about the relationship between
culture and economics in the development of cinema in a small country like
Scotland. For Colin McArthur, the key is establishing certain strategic priorities which promote particular kinds of cultural film-making and allow the
greatest number of film-makers access to public funding. The argument that in
order to adequately address important cultural questions a national cinema
must necessarily be a poor or dependent cinema has been articulated elsewhere
by John Hill.[35] But as we have seen, Hill's sense of a successful national cinema
offering an alternative to Hollywood is one drawing upon an integration of the
aesthetic strategies, cultural preoccupations and support mechanisms of European 'art' cinema and British public service broadcasting.[36] And such a version
of poverty or dependency necessarily embraces the kind of projects and budgets supported by the agencies and broadcasters mentioned above. It also
accepts the importance of films reaching both a national and an international
audience and, as we have seen, since the early 1980s most British films have
been differentiated and distributed in the international market place with
regard to an expanded concept of 'art cinema': 'In this respect, the adoption of
aesthetic strategies and cultural referents different from Hollywood also
involves a certain foregrounding of "national" credentials. The oft-noted irony
of this, however, is that art cinema then achieves much of its status by circu-
lating internationally rather than nationally.'[37]

The international success of films like *Shallow Grave, Trainspotting, Mrs
Brown, The Winter Guest, My Name is Joe* and *Orphans* can be seen very much
in this context, although even this small range of titles encompasses various different conceptions of Scotland and Scottishness. At the same time, the
involvement of broadcasters ensures that these films also reach a sizeable
domestic audience on television, a medium which, despite increasing concerns
about greater competition, the proliferation of new channels and a 'dumbing
down' of content, continues to engage with and reflect the diversity and complexity of contemporary cultural life.

The need for innovation within the bounds of the feature film is as pressing
as ever and Colin McArthur's argument for certain kinds of innovation has
much to recommend it. But while low-budget experimental production can

BBC Scotland takes the plunge into feature production: *Small Faces*

facilitate unorthodox approaches to form and content, aesthetic frontiers can also be challenged on higher budgets of between £2 and 3 million, as Peter Mullan and Lynne Ramsay have recently demonstrated. A certain diversity of production does seem to be the most appropriate strategy in relation to both cultural and economic arguments. But this must include a space for low-budget innovation, a need that is beginning to be recognised at the policy level with the launch in 1999 of the new Twenty First Films scheme by the Scottish Arts Council and Scottish Screen. The scheme will provide up to 75 per cent of the production costs for projects budgeted at £500,000 or less. While 'Twenty First Films' can be regarded as an initiative designed to promote a 'Poor Scottish cinema', this will effectively complement rather than replace the existing funding mechanisms available, promoting a more mixed economy of indigenous production in the process.

Conclusions: A Devolved British Cinema?

The 1990s has witnessed the emergence of a distinct Scottish film production sector, enabling more and more feature productions to be developed in Scotland and for a considerable proportion of production finance to be raised from indigenous sources. But other institutions outside Scotland have also continued to play a vital role in the new Scottish cinema. Channel Four in particular continues to be a major contributor, investing in a considerable number of the films in question including *Shallow Grave*, *Trainspotting*, *Carla's Song*, *The Slab*

Boys, The Winter Guest, Stella Does Tricks, My Name is Joe, Orphans, The Acid House Trilogy, The Debt Collector and *Gregory's Two Girls*. The centralised BBC Films has also been significant in providing finance for *Prague, Small Faces, Regeneration, Mrs Brown* and *Ratcatcher*. Scottish productions also rely on securing deals with British and overseas distributors; indeed the international success of films like *Trainspotting* and *Mrs Brown* has been considerably aided by the marketing push provided by distributors like Polygram and Miramax respectively. It is equally important to avoid and direct equation of Scottish cinema with a number of key film-makers. In addition to his three Scottish features, *The Conquest of the South Pole, Small Faces* and *Regeneration*, Gillies Mackinnon has also made films in Liverpool, London, the United States, Ireland and Morocco; while the team of Danny Boyle, Andrew MacDonald and John Hodge responsible for *Shallow Grave* and *Trainspotting* have since moved on to more international concerns with *A Life Less Ordinary* (1997) and *The Beach* (2000), made in America and Thailand respectively. On the other hand some recent important films dealing with Scotland have been made by outsiders like Ken Loach (*Carla's Song, My Name is Joe*), Les Blair (the 1998 TV movie *Stand and Deliver*), Alan Rickman (*The Winter Guest*) and Lars von Trier (*Breaking the Waves*). The new Scottish cinema is a distinct and meaningful entity but as yet its status should perhaps be understood in terms of a devolved British cinema rather than fully independent entity.

If there has been an institutional shortcoming it has been the problem of distribution which affected the British film industry more generally. While production levels remain buoyant – the figure of 128 in 1996 representing the highest number of films produced in Britain in a year since 1957, this was mediated by the increasing difficulties many of these films were having finding a distributor in what is their own home market. Of the 78 films produced in the previous year, 24 had still failed to appear in cinemas two years later.[38] Several recent Scottish films have faced such distribution problems: *The Near Room* and *Stella Does Tricks* waited two years before being released while *The Slab Boys* and *The Life of Stuff* received only very minimal cinema exposure. *Orphans* also experienced problems when Channel Four, who, having provided the major part of the production budget, declined to handle the film through their own distribution arm. Luckily, it was picked up by the small independent Downtown Pictures and opened in Britain in May 1999.[39] If a number of films continue to fail to find adequate distribution, then the legitimacy of public funding mechanisms will certainly be brought into question, seriously threatening the green shoots of the new Scottish cinema. However, the new emphasis on business support and on sustaining the viability of Scottish production by agencies like Scottish Screen and the lottery players in the sector suggests that this very real problem is being addressed.

Notes

1   See John Hill, 'The Issue of National Cinema and British Film Production' in Duncan Petrie (ed.), *New Questions of British Cinema* (London: BFI, 1992).

2   Figures from *Scottish Screen Data 1997*, 4th edn (Glasgow: Scottish Screen, 1999). The definition of a 'Scottish' production (p. 13) requires a production to meet at least one of the following criteria:
   – Scottish organisations played a significant role in the development of the film;
   – Scottish organisations played a significant role in production funding;
   – Scottish based film-makers played a significant role in the production.

3   Ian Lockerbie, 'Pictures in a Small Country: The Scottish Film Production Fund' in Eddie Dick (ed.), *From Limelight to Satellite: A Scottish Film Book* (London: BFI/SFC, 1990), pp. 172–3.

4   Ibid., p. 175.

5   Lockerbie's article includes a list of all of the projects supported by the fund between 1982 and 1990.

6   Interview with Penny Thompson, Edinburgh, 23 August 1999.

7   Interview with Lenny Crooks, Glasgow, 21 January 2000.

8   Andrea Calderwood, 'Film and Television Policy in Scotland' in John Hill and Martin McLoone (eds) *Big Picture Small Screen: The Relations Between Film and Television* (Luton: University of Luton Press, 1996), p. 194.

9   Interview with Lenny Crooks.

10 The largest investments made by the GFF have been in *The Near Room* and *Orphans*.

11 According to Lenny Crooks, the most successful GFF films after *Shallow Grave* have been *Small Faces* ('Gillies [Mackinnon] getting into gear as a film-maker'), *Carla's Song* (initiating a productive relationship with the production company Parallax Films who have subsequently made three more feature projects in Glasgow – *Stand and Deliver, My Name is Joe, Hold Back the Night*), and the 1998 Cannes success when the GFF screened three films – *My Name is Joe, The Acid House* and *Orphans* ('All of them are making returns so they are doing a good job at putting us back on the map and giving us a chance to look at other projects'). Interview with Lenny Crooks.

12 Figure provided by Lenny Crooks who is also chief executive of the Glasgow Film Office.

13 A new advisory panel was set up comprising Mark Shivas, Head of BBC Films, Sue Bruce Smith, director of film sales at the BBC and Scottish producer Ian Madden.

14 Not every project backed by the lottery has been realised including two high-profile adaptations of Scottish novels, Alasdair Gray's *Poor Things*, ironically

the very first lottery award made to a feature project in Britain in August 1995, and Neil Gunn's *The Silver Darlings*. A potential solution to this problem is suggested by Steve McIntyre in terms of creating a situation where producers producers can approach the lottery with greater confidence: 'What I am keen on having is a kind of points system around fairly precisely defined eligibility requirements and some kind of automatic funding mechanism. If you had a points system – so many for being a Scottish company, having a Scottish producer, a Scottish writer etc. The value of this is not as a way of getting rid of projects but of providing some kind of structured guidance, the definition of a Scottish film, if you like. But what this does is that it enables companies to feel more confident about getting Lottery money. So you develop a project, a script and business development. The producer can then go out and raise 75 per cent of the money. Helping them to do this should give a fairly high degree of possibility that they will get Lottery money for the last 25 per cent as they already have the proof that the market wants to support the project. What is attractive is that Scottish producers would have money in their pockets. It also means that you are not offering £500,000 to a project that sits on the books and never gets made.' Interview with Steve McIntyre, Edinburgh, 28 August 1999.

15 The controversy generated by the accusations of cronyism also led to the premature departure of Allan Shiach, who was briefly chair of the new integrated Scottish Screen before being succeeded by James Lee, former chief executive of Goldcrest, the production and distribution company that had played a major role in the British 'renaissance' of the early 1980s. The issue this affair highlights, however, is the difficulties in establishing an appropriate board to administer public finance to the film industry. Clearly, there must be a place on such a body for experienced Scottish producers and other industry people. On the other hand if these individuals are active then conflicts of interest will inevitably arise given the significance of sources like the lottery for current Scottish film production.

16 Interview with Steve McIntyre.

17 This includes £200,000 for the project preparation scheme and £150,000 for the business development scheme, co-funded by Scottish Screen and Scottish Enterprise.

18 After a flurry of investments in the early 1980s, STV have only made one other significant contribution to a Scottish feature, *The Big Man* (1990) adapted from the novel by William McIlvanney by writer-director David Leland.

19 Interview with Barbara McKissack, Edinburgh, 19 August 1999.

20 Ian Lockerbie, 'Pictures in a Small Country' in Eddie Dick (ed.), *From Limelight to Satellite*.

21 Figure included in *Scottish Screen Data 1996*, compiled by Jamie Hall and published by Scottish Screen.

22 A poignant black and white essay about life on the margins of society, *Fridge* depicts the struggle faced by two alcoholics to free a young boy who has become trapped in a chest freezer in the back courtyard of a Glasgow tenement block. *Gasman* is equally rich and poetic in its contemplation of an 8-year-old girl's shocking realisation that her father has two children with another woman. The exquisite control of the images affords the film an intense contemplative quality rare in British cinema, inviting the audience to look closely in the attempt to understand the complex emotional landscape being portrayed.

23 Interview with Barbara McKissack.

24 These awards of between £500 and £4,000 effectively functioned as catalysts for the productions, helping pay for film stock and post-production. The film-makers consequently had to rely heavily on the generosity of the industry, particularly the workshop sector, for expertise and equipment and their own pockets. But the scheme did allow some extraordinary work to be produced, including Peter Mullan's first two shorts, *Close* (1993) and *A Good Day for the Bad Guys* (1994), kick-starting his career as a writer-director and paving the way for *Fridge* and then *Orphans*.

25 Providing production awards of up to £10K and £15K, or completion funding up to £5K, and successful projects also receive support, advice, training, production offices and discounted equipment and stock.

26 Colin McArthur, 'Tartan Shorts and the Taming of First Reels', *Scottish Film*, Issue 9, 3rd Quarter, 1994.

27 In addition to Mullan and Ramsay, the relatively small number of film-makers who have graduated from 'Tartan Shorts' to features includes writer-director Peter Capaldi, producer Angus Lamont and director Patrick Harkins.

28 Interview with Paddy Higson, Glasgow, 19 January 2000.

29 Colin McArthur, 'In Praise of a Poor Cinema' *Sight and Sound*, August 1993, p. 31.

30 This is developed principally in the *Sight and Sound* article referenced above and at greater length in 'The Cultural Necessity of a Poor Celtic Cinema' in Paul Hainsworth, John Hill and Martin McLoone (eds), *Border Crossing: Film in Ireland, Britain and Europe*, (Belfast: IIS/Queen's University, 1994).

31 Colin McArthur, 'The Cultural Necessity of a Poor Celtic Cinema' in P. Hainsworth, J. Hill and M. McLoone, (eds) *Border Crossing*, p. 124.

32 John Brown, 'Film Industry Needs Whiz Kids Too', *Glasgow Herald*, 20 July 1982.

33 Eddie Dick, 'Poor Wee Scottish Cinema', *Scottish Film*, Issue 10, 4th Quarter 1994, pp.19–23.

34 Interview with Steve McIntyre.

35 John Hill, 'The Issue of National Cinema and British Film Production', in Petrie (ed.), *New Questions of British Cinema*.

36 See John Hill, 'British Cinema as National Cinema: Production, Audience, Representation' in Robert Murphy (ed.), *The British Cinema Book*, (London: BFI, 1997).

37 Ibid., p. 247.

38 Figures from Nick Thomas, 'UK Film, Television and Video Overview', *BFI Handbook 1998* (London: BFI, 1998).

39 But the significance of the distribution crisis has yet to be properly recognised. It is perhaps instructive that the annual publication 'Scottish Screen Data', an otherwise invaluable source of statistical information on Scottish film and television, should concentrate on production and exhibition while omitting any information relating to the distribution of Scottish films.

Chapter Nine
The New Scottish Cinema: Themes and Issues

The institutional developments examined in the last chapter have facilitated an unprecedented level of film-making activity in Scotland. For the first time ever, there is a sufficient body of work being produced to allow a tentative exploration of the aesthetic and thematic trends defining this important moment in Scottish cultural production. A certain momentum has also been built over the last few years with the result that in 1999 no less than seven Scottish feature films were released in the UK: *The Acid House, This Year's Love, Orphans, The Debt Collector, The Match, Gregory's Two Girls* and *Ratcatcher*, the last noted proving a popular choice to open the 1999 Edinburgh International Film Festival.[1] In a year that also witnessed the restoration of a Scottish parliament after 292 years of direct rule from London, this achievement suggests the beginnings of a devolutionary impetus within the British film industry itself. A greater volume of production has also served to broaden the range of cinematic representations of Scotland, extending and transforming the dominant traditions already explored in this book. While it is premature to talk of identifiable Scottish genres, there are certainly significant thematic and aesthetic issues raised by these films that are clearly central to the cultural engagement of this new Scottish cinema.

The Commercial and Critical Breakthrough

As we have seen, the potential for independent feature production in Scotland had been nurtured in the 1980s by Channel Four and the British Film Institute, resulting in a number of interesting and important films. But the popular profile of Scottish cinema was to be considerably reinvigorated in the mid-1990s by the unprecedented commercial and critical success of two features made by a team of talented newcomers. Andrew MacDonald, the grandson of the great screenwriter Emeric Pressburger, had been working as a production runner since the mid-1980s on a number of films including *Venus Peter*. In 1991, he met John Hodge, a recently qualified doctor who had written his first screenplay, a dark thriller set in Edinburgh. Recognising the potential of this script,

MacDonald set about finding a director, leading him to Danny Boyle, whose impressive track record in theatre and television included the acclaimed BBC period drama series *Mr Wroe's Virgins* (1992). Together the three formed Figment Films and secured finance from Channel Four and the Glasgow Film Fund for their project *Shallow Grave* which was premièred at the 1994 Edinburgh Film Festival

Eschewing the kind of gritty, naturalistic aesthetic models suggested by previous British thrillers, *Shallow Grave*'s novelty lay in its energetic embrace of generic conventions and techniques drawn from an American tradition of style-conscious, low-budget film-making running from *Psycho* to John Carpenter, the Coen Brothers and Abel Ferrara. And despite the distinctive setting of the Edinburgh new town, the intended universality of the film is unequivocally signalled in the opening voice-over: 'This could have been any city – they're all the same.'[2] The basic narrative premise of *Shallow Grave* is a simple one: after finding their mysterious flatmate dead with a suitcase full of money, Alex (Ewan McGregor), David (Christopher Eccleston) and Juliet (Kerry Fox), three obnoxious young Edinburgh professionals, set about erasing all traces of him in order to keep the money. But the emotional strain of dismembering and burying the body generates unbearable tensions and mistrust between the three and order quickly begins to break down. David retreats to the attic with the suitcase, his increasingly deranged behaviour manifests itself in terms of both voyeurism (drilling holes in the ceiling to allow him to spy on Alex and Juliet below) and psychosis (threatening Alex with a drill and bludgeoning to death the two thuggish associates of the dead Hugo who come looking for the money). With the police closing in, Alex attempts to extricate himself from the situation by informing on his flatmates, while Juliet schemes to double-cross David by pretending to be romantically interested in him. The resulting violent and bloody climax culminates in David being stabbed to death by Juliet who makes off with the money leaving Alex pinned to the kitchen floor by a knife. But the final twist in the plot reveals that the suitcase is full of paper, the money having been hidden under the kitchen floorboards by a devious Alex, the film ending on a shot of his triumphant grin.

Shallow Grave announces its arrival with an opening fast-motion, high-energy ride through the streets of the Edinburgh new town, accompanied by the pumping music of techno band Leftfield. Moya Luckett suggests that such an unusual approach to establishing a sense of place 'enhances the stature of the architecture while imbuing it with a new energy and modernity, highlighting Scotland's urban sophistication and producing an emphasis on the surface'.[3] These ideas apply equally to the construction of the domestic space in which the bulk of the action subsequently takes place. Designed by Kave Quinn, the main set is an exaggerated version of a typical Edinburgh flat in the Georgian style, characterised by spacious rooms, high ceilings and bright colourful decor (in this case bold blues, greens and reds). The flat is a stylish and highly desirable environment, something that Alex, David and Juliet use to devastating effect in their ritual humiliation of the various hapless applicants who apply for the vacant room. But the narcissistic obsession with interior design slowly gives way to disorder, the impending disintegration anticipated early on by the seemingly random insertion of unsettling images of extreme violence apparently unrelated to the main action. Once trust breaks down, the flat becomes a claustrophobic battleground within which the three occupants desperately vie for control. The charged atmosphere that gradually comes to permeate the world of *Shallow Grave* owes a great deal to Brian Tufano's inspired noirish lighting – particularly in the dark attic criss-crossed by the rays of light penetrating David's numerous spy-holes – and the incessant prowling camera. These visual effects are augmented by Simon Boswell's chilling keyboard music recalling the incessant unnerving theme of John Carpenter's masterly contribution to the horror genre, *Halloween* (1978). *Shallow Grave* was an overnight sensation when it was released in early 1995, grossing £5 million at the British box office and almost $30 million world-wide.[4] For Channel Four's David Aukin, the most significant aspect of this was 'the fact that it was able to recoup its costs within the UK without its success here being powered by an initial success in the USA, as was the case with *Four Weddings and a Funeral*'.[5]

Flushed with their success, the Figment Films troika turned to Edinburgh writer Irvine Welsh's 1993 cult novel *Trainspotting* for their next project. Sensing an even bigger commercial success, Channel Four had no hesitation in fully funding the production to the tune of £1.7 million, the largest single investment they had made in a feature film to date. Boyle, MacDonald and Hodge reassembled the same team who had made *Shallow Grave*, including Tufano, Quinn and editor Masahiro Hirakubo; while Ewan McGregor was cast in the central role of Mark Renton, a young heroin addict, supported by an ensemble of emerging acting talent including Robert Carlyle, Jonny Lee Miller, Ewan Bremner, Kevin McKidd and Kelly MacDonald.[6] Consequently, *Trainspotting* embraces the same breathless style that distinguished its predecessor, bursting into life in even more memorable fashion with Renton's dash along Edinburgh's Princess Street, the police in hot pursuit, accompanied by the frantic beat of Iggy Pop's 'Lust For Life' and the emblematic 'choose life' mantra, rejecting the trappings of modern consumer culture in favour of the illicit pleasures of heroin. The chase ends with Renton colliding into a car, the image of him grinning through the windscreen at the driver/camera is frozen and the character's name appears on-screen in a manner recalling the credits sequence of Martin Scorsese's *Mean Streets* (1973). The other main characters, Begbie, Sick Boy, Spud and Tommy, are introduced in a similar manner while playing

Edinburgh's finest: Ewan Bremner and Ewan McGregor in *Trainspotting*

a robust game of five-a-side football. But, significantly, none of them are allowed the same direct acknowledgement of the audience. For this is Renton's story and the subsequent action is to be organised according to his consciousness.[7]

The bulk of the narrative is largely constructed around a series of studio-based set pieces charting Renton's experiences: the highs and lows of junk dependency, including an elaborately planned attempt to kick the habit, his brief romance with Diane, the move to London in the attempt to escape the inevitable downward spiral of life in Edinburgh, to the final drug deal which provides the fresh start Renton craves. Although set in Edinburgh, the interiors were, like *Shallow Grave*, filmed in a studio in Glasgow and once again the careful creation of an exaggerated stylised environment was an important consideration for director Boyle:

> When you work with a film crew, you automatically lose about a third of the space you're in because of the lights, the people and all the technical equipment. I wanted to have a bigger space so that we could try to give some sense of environment within a house ... Usually, the other side of the equation is that for a landscape, or geography, you go outside. Britain is so disappointing as a landscape, because we are fed on a diet of American or international landscapes which are massive. Britain feels slightly mundane by

comparison. But when you work inside, you can have more freedom and create bigger spaces.[8]

The neo-expressionist aesthetic of *Trainspotting* draws on a number of inspirations including the paintings of Francis Bacon and Stanley Kubrick's 1971 film *A Clockwork Orange*, transcending the naturalistic limitations of low-key television dramas like Peter McDougall's *Shoot for the Sun*. The film sets out to subvert expectation both at the level of the representation of the experience of pleasure/pain at the heart of the junkie subculture and the depiction of contemporary urban Scotland. John Orr suggests that the supercharged hyperreal quality of *Trainspotting* constructs a mythic Edinburgh environment in which the real is substituted by 'the burning intensity of the copy'.[9] The squalid and minimalist drug den is a slum version of the apartment in *Shallow Grave* with each room once again colour coded – reds, greens, oranges, blues – a space filmed in a proliferation of low-angled shots and floor-level tracking shots representing a world of narcotic oblivion in which the characters spend most of their time on the floor. A humorous contrast to this soporific, shabby environment is provided by the ill-fated group commune with the restorative and romantic beauty of the landscape, inspiring Renton's rant about the shortcomings of being Scottish.[10]

But it is the ensemble playing that gives *Trainspotting* its dynamism, Renton's general amiability aided and abetted by Sick Boy's (Jonny Lee Miller) obsession with Sean Connery and Spud's (Ewan Bremner) speed-fuelled job interview. The one bad apple is Begbie (Robert Carlyle), a psychotic thug who shuns hard drugs but has an over-fondness for mindless violence, and as in *Shallow Grave* the initial camaraderie of the group is gradually eroded, giving way to paranoia, mistrust and exploitation. Boyle acknowledges the importance of his cast in the following way: 'We shaped the film around the actors. You have a big screen. And the wonderful thing about a big screen is that people can select. That's the wonderful thing about Tarantino which nobody says – that he lets you select what you watch. He lets the actors get on with it rather than shape everything all the time.'[11]

The reference to Quentin Tarantino is equally instructive in terms of Boyle's similar emphasis on the audacious manipulation of film form that is central to productions like *Reservoir Dogs* (1992) and *Pulp Fiction* (1994). *Trainspotting* abounds with similar excess including temporal manipulation, intrusive editing, freeze frames, split screen and on-screen subtitles. These techniques are put to effective use in the various set pieces, some of which also use humour, such as Renton's surreal attempt to retrieve opium suppositories from a filthy toilet which leads to him disappearing into the bowl and diving for pearls through clear blue water and the multiple sex scene featuring the split-screen couplings of Renton and Diane, Tommy and Lizzie and Spud and Gail. Other sequences convey some of the harsher aspects of heroin, however. Renton's near-fatal overdose, cut brilliantly by editor Hirakubo to the ironic strains of Lou Reed's 'Perfect Day', is represented by his body sinking into the carpet, his point of view peering up as if from inside a coffin as he is rushed to the emergency unit at the hospital. The subsequent nightmare of withdrawal is punctuated by an incessant vertiginous tunnel effect of moving walls and terrifying hallucinations including a dead baby crawling along the ceiling. But for all the warnings about the dangers of heroin, *Trainspotting* is a resolutely upbeat film, sanitising and rendering more palatable for mass consumption the grimmer excesses of the novel but also losing some of the subtleties and uncertainties in the process. The combination of attractive low-life characters (McGregor's fashionable junkie-waif look is far removed from Welsh's acne-scarred red head), humorous offbeat situations and a soundtrack featuring a roll call of the hippest young British rock and club bands like Blur, Pulp, Primal Scream, Underworld, Leftfield and Sleeper as well as classics by Lou Reed and Iggy Pop constructed *Trainspotting* as the perfect commercial package, a cult movie to order. And, as such, it worked a dream, the most profitable British release of 1996, taking more than £12 million at the domestic box office and over $72 million world-wide.[12]

The *Trainspotting* Effect

The ramifications of *Shallow Grave* and *Trainspotting* for the subsequent development of Scottish cinema in the latter half of the 1990s were considerable. As images of contemporary Scotland they had little direct connections with established cinematic or televisual traditions, rejecting both Celtic romanticism and naturalistic grit. *Trainspotting* in particular had forged a new sophisticated urban aesthetic, the combination of a young cast, edgy subject-matter, vibrant colours, visual pyrotechnics and a pounding soundtrack a direct allusion to the sensory pleasures of club culture, a major influence also on the Scottish novels of both Welsh and Alan Warner.[13] The film in turn paved the way for a spate of energetic, self-conscious British productions, including *Twin Town* (Kevin Allen, 1997), *Lock, Stock and Two Smoking Barrels* (Guy Ritchie, 1998), *Human Traffic* (Justin Kerrigan, 1999), all featuring various combinations of low-life criminal activity, hedonism and hip music. *Trainspotting* also helped to confirm the stars status of both Ewan McGregor and Robert Carlyle who found themselves inundated with projects from both British and American producers.[14] Scotland found itself fashionable in film circles and it was inevitable that the *Trainspotting* effect would prove influential closer to home.

Other than in his cameo appearance as drug-dealing chancer Mikey Forester, Irvine Welsh had very little direct involvement in the production of *Trainspotting*. But in the aftermath of the film's success he was inspired to adapt three short stories from his 1994 collection, *The Acid House*, for the screen. Initially conceived as a series of short dramas for television, the three were cobbled together to construct an episodic feature film with the same title as the volume. The opening story, *The Granton Star Cause*, broadcast on Channel Four before the rest of the film was completed, is a parody of Kafka's *Metamorphosis*[15] in which a hapless amateur footballer, Boab (Stephen McCole), is transformed into a fly by a bitter and vengeful god (Maurice Roeves) whom he encounters in a local pub. This was followed by *A Soft Touch*, charting the fate of another working-class loser, Johnny (Kevin McKidd), whose life with wife Catrina (Michele Gomez) and baby daughter is ruined by the arrival of Larry (Gary McCormack), a preening and narcissistic hard man who moves into the upstairs flat. The concluding episode, *The Acid House*, is a hallucinogenic fantasy in which, during the course of a violent thunderstorm, the consciousness of Hibernian-supporting football hooligan, Coco Bryce (Ewan Bremner), is switched with that of the baby son of respectable middle-class couple Jenny (Jemma Redgrave) and Rory (Martin Clunes).

As befitting the subject matter, the three stories are rendered with a great energy and fidelity to Welsh's vision by director Paul McGuigan. In addition to placing a far greater reliance on real Edinburgh locations, particularly the grim housing schemes on the peripheries of the city, *The Acid House* adopts a visual style that is even more excessive that of *Trainspotting*, utilising a plethora of slow motion and hand-held techniques, distorting lenses, jump cuts, stop motion and audacious point-of-view shots (such as that of Boab transformed into a fly soaring above the derelict housing scheme and Coco's acid trip that culminates in his being struck by lightning). The influence of both hallucinogenic drugs and club culture is highly significant here, Xan Brooks describing the third section as 'tilting at a kind of record deck aesthetic [that] loops and scratches its dialogue like a dance remix set in celluloid'.[16] Once again, the soundtrack is a crucial element in the mix, featuring a heady brew of top acts including The Verve, the Chemical Brothers, Primal Scream, Nick Cave, Beth Orton and Oasis. But this energy is largely dissipated by a misanthropic script that renders the characters as either pathetic losers or contemptible and self-centred, devoid of the nuances and charm of the *Trainspotting* cast. As such, it is a far cry from the complexity, humanity and sharp observation that gave a voice to the Edinburgh underclass and made Welsh's reputation as an novelist in the first place, confirming his decline into shock tactics and self-parody.

The novel of *Trainspotting* had spawned a theatrical adaptation in 1994, a production regarded as part of a new wave of Scottish drama that confronted the nihilism of post-industrial urban life.[17] Another important work in this respect was Simon Donald's acclaimed 1992 play *The Life of Stuff* dealing with a similar shadowy world of drugs, crime and urban desolation. The pedigree of which made it obvious material for a big-screen outing, particularly in the wake of the *Trainspotting* phenomenon. The resulting film, adapted and directed by Donald, clearly bears many similarities with Boyle's production at the level of both content and form. Based around the preparations for a drug-fuelled party thrown by gangster Willie Dobie, *The Life of Stuff* is an ensemble drama confined to a series of surreal interior spaces – including a dungeon-like basement and an Egyptian-style party room – designed by Zoe MacLeod, Kave Quinn's art director on *Shallow Grave*. Donald also uses cinematographer Brian Tufano who once again deploys the trademark 'noir lighting in colour'[18] that was so effective in both *Shallow Grave* and *Trainspotting*. But there the similarities end in that where *Trainspotting* fizzed with energy and surprise, *Life of Stuff* creaks and groans under the weight of its own self-regard. The action is excessively theatrical, the *mise en scène* overly self-conscious in its attempt to convey the hedonistic excess of sex, drugs and violence, and the dramatic shifts too abrupt, culminating in a messy pastiche of styles that conspicuously fails to gel. With Donald's direction sorely lacking the kind of consummate control over the cinematic process demonstrated with such panache by Danny Boyle, even on experienced and talented cast including Ewan Bremner, Gina McKee, Cieran Hinds, Jason Flemyng, and Liam Cunningham fails to make an impact. In commercial and critical terms *The Life of Stuff* proved to be as conspicuous a disaster as *Trainspotting* had been a triumph, earning back a mere 0.2 per cent of its £2 million budget.[19]

The combination of youth culture, popular music and social comment at the heart of *Trainspotting* can also be related to an attempt to resurrect an earlier defining moment in Scottish popular culture. In 1996 John Byrne directed his own adaptation of *The Slab Boys*, the acclaimed stage play that had made his reputation when it was first performed in 1978. Byrne had previously adapted the work for television in 1979, but this time he expanded the focus, incorporating material from both the original play and *Cutting a Rug*, the second part of his *Slab Boys* trilogy. The resulting feature replays the familiar interaction of three young apprentices in the slab room of a Paisley carpet factory in 1957. Stuck in a dirty and monotonous job, they all dream of escaping from their humdrum existence. The geekish Hector Mackenzie (Bill Gardiner) has his eye on promotion to the design department, but the others seek adventure elsewhere. Phil McCann (Robin Laing), magnificent in his rockabilly haircut and drape coat, aspires to become an art student, while George 'Spanky' Farrell (Russell Barr) dreams of playing guitar and emigrating to America. Like Byrne's previous stage and TV work, *The Slab Boys* combines a celebration of the power of imagination, working-class camaraderie and the energy of American popular culture with a recognition of the kind of pain, disappointment and rejection endemic at the bottom of the social ladder: epit-

omised by Phil's failure to get into art school, the TB diagnosis that will prevent Spanky from leaving Scotland and even Hector's unrequited love for
office doll Lucille (Louise Berry). In technical terms *The Slab Boys* is an
impressive achievement, making a virtue of its studio-bound artifice and a
soundtrack comprising an array of rock-and-roll classics performed by contemporary Scottish musicians including the Proclaimers, Edwyn Collins,
Eddie Reader and Pat Kane. But, unfortunately, this is undermined by slack
and monotonous direction and consequently the film lacks the tight control
and pacing that made *Tutti Frutti* such a joy. The material also fails to ressurect
the impact it had when first performed on stage, Byrne's vision of working-
class life having lost its novelty through the emergence of a new generation of
Scottish novelists, playwrights, film-makers and painters over the intervening
two decades.

Tales of the City

Whatever the success or failure of respective films, the kind of cinema emerging in Scotland in the mid-1990s placed a new emphasis on the urban
experience and environment. While many film-makers in the 1980s and early
1990s had contemplated the Scottish rural experience (*Ill Fares the Land, Local
Hero, Another Time, Another Place, Venus Peter, Blue Black Permanent, As An
Eilean*), the new cinema heralded by *Shallow Grave* and *Trainspotting* entailed
a new engagement with the Scottish city, coupled with a new exploration of
artifice and the creation of imaginary worlds. The existence of the Glasgow
Film Fund has also encouraged this trend, extending the range of cinema representations of not only Glasgow but also Edinburgh (a number of productions
such as *Shallow Grave* and *The Acid House* qualifying for funding by using Glasgow locations and/or facilities). And while films like *That Sinking Feeling,
Comfort and Joy* and *Heavenly Pursuits* had previously helped to move the
image of Glasgow beyond its association with heavy industry, hard drinking
and violence, the 1990s witnessed a greater diversity in the cinema's construction of urban scenarios and cityscapes than ever before.

But within this new range there were certain continuities. The confluence of
the crime film and 'hard man' tradition was reworked with liberal helpings of
American *film noir* style by writer Robert Murphy and director David Hayman
in *The Near Room*, a project supported by the GFF. Set in Glasgow, this dark
tale of paedophilia, corruption and murder centres around Charlie Colquhoun
(Adrian Dunbar), a burned-out hack-turned-sleuth, searching for his illegiti-
mate daughter. Along the way he uncovers a sordid child-sex ring involving top
solicitor Harris Hill (David O'Hara) and the bodies begin to pile up as the narrative draws to its final revelation and violent climax. Drawing on the
established tradition of Scottish crime and detection scenarios familiar from

popular television series like *Taggart* and the novels of William McIlvanney and Ian Rankin, *The Near Room* relies heavily on generic familiarity and a range of stock characters, including a cameo by Peter McDougall as a blackmailer and director Hayman as a rather over-the-top tabloid editor. But despite the strong sense of cinematic style and imagination – the Glasgow that Colquhoun uncovers is closer to *Dante's Inferno* than *A Sense of Freedom* – *The Near Room* is flawed by a rather lacklustre central performance and an overdetermined plot that might have been better suited to the greater narrative latitude provided by the extended format of the mini series.

A less convoluted but equally dark vision of urban criminality is conveyed in *The Debt Collector*, written and directed by Anthony Neilson. The film charts the obsessional harassment by an Edinburgh policeman, Gary Keltie (Ken Stott), of Nickie Dryden (Billy Connolly), a criminal he helped to put away for murder twenty years previously. Since being released from prison, Dryden has rebuilt his life with the help of his journalist wife Val (Francesca Annis), establishing himself as a successful writer and sculptor. But Keltie refuses to allow Dryden to forget his violent past as a loan shark, in particular his 'policy' which involved the ruthless punishment of close friends and relatives of defaulting debtors. The animosity between Dryden and Keltie becomes intensified, culminating in a rather overblown and bloody knife fight on the esplanade of Edinburgh Castle during the climax of the military Tattoo. Despite the obvious allusions to the life of Jimmy Boyle, *The Debt Collector* has none of the psychological depth and sophistication of *A Sense of Freedom*. Dryden and Keltie are rather contrived characters, the latter grappling with a surfeit of psycho-sexual hang-ups including an over-attachment to his elderly mother and a pathological attraction to Dryden's middle-class wife. This is all presented in a heavy handed, cliché-ridden manner, devoid of any real insight into the nature of psychotic obsession or the complex moral questions around criminality and redemption. While many of the sequences were actually filmed in Glasgow, certain familiar Edinburgh landmarks such as the Castle, the Balmoral Hotel and the Forth Bridge are utilised to provide a sense of place, demonstrating the continuing association of the city with a sense of 'urban grandeur' (even in a crime film) largely absent from cinematic representations of Glasgow despite its acclaimed architectural status.[20]

The depiction of Glasgow as both physical and social environment is also central to *Carla's Song* and *My Name is Joe*, two productions directed by Ken Loach, a film-maker whose close association with an observational realist style and a political engagement with working-class experience and problems dates back to the mid-1960s. These films can be seen as part of Loach's broader output in the 1990s which John Hill argues share a concern with 'how de-industrialisation, mass unemployment and anti trade union legislation have not only significantly altered the social character of the British working class but have undermined the prospects for self-confident forms of working-class action as well'.[21] Loach's first connection with a Scottish subject came with *Riff Raff* (1991), a film focusing on the pernicious consequences of casualisation in the building trade. Written by the late Bill Jesse, *Riff Raff* introduced Robert Carlyle as Stevie, a young Scottish labourer who arrives in London looking for work. Loach subsequently cast Carlyle in *Carla's Song*, as George the mild-mannered Glasgow bus driver who falls in love with a mysterious young Nicaraguan refugee, Carla (Oyanka Cabezas), who he persuades to return to her country to confront certain traumatic events that occurred during the civil war. George consequently experiences at first hand the continuing struggle of the Nicaraguan people to establish a socialist state in the face of brutal CIA-backed terrorism. Written by Paul Laverty, a Glaswegian who had worked as a civil rights lawyer in Nicaragua, *Carla's Song* celebrates the spirit and necessity of collective political action, conspicuous by its absence in George's Glasgow. But there are compensatory virtues: George and his friend Sammy (Gary Lewis) are warm, generous and honest people, Sammy providing a room for George's mysterious new friend when she is thrown out of her hostel without even a question.

The importance of community is equally central in Loach and Laverty's second collaboration. *My Name Is Joe*, an assured and powerful piece of work that offers a more sustained engagement with contemporary Glasgow. Once again the plot revolves around an unusual and mismatched relationship between Joe

Hope and despair in Glasgow: Ken Loach's *My Name is Joe*

Kavanagh (Peter Mullan), a recovering alcoholic who runs a local no-hoper football team, and Sarah Downie (Louise Goodall), a local health visitor. The two meet through Sarah's clients Liam (David Mackay) and Sabine (Annemarie Kennedy) a young couple with a baby son who are struggling to keep the family unit together. Joe also has a paternalistic interest in Liam who is a member of his team, and he intervenes when the couple fall foul of a ruthless drug dealer and gangster, McGowan (David Hayman). In agreeing to act as a courier for McGowan, Joe alienates Sarah and sends his own life spinning once again out of control. *My Name is Joe* tackles head on the ways in which the lives of those at the bottom of the heap are profoundly circumscribed by restricted opportunity and choice. Aided by the support of his steadfast and loyal friend Shanks (Gary Lewis in what is practically a reprise of his role in *Carla's Song*) Joe is presented as a man whose life entails an ongoing struggle to keep his head above water. The precariousness of his situation is signalled early on by the encounter with the social security snooper who photographs Joe decorating Sarah's flat, resulting in a week's suspension of his dole money. But things are even more desperate for Liam and Sabine trapped in a cycle of drug dependency that leads to Sabine working as a prostitute and ultimately to Liam's suicide.

Joe's relationship with Sarah presents a major dilemma, offering redemption but also opening up intense feelings of insecurity and guilt. We discover that he brutally beat up his previous girlfriend, a traumatic event that triggered his decision to quit drinking. The class barrier prevents Sarah from fully understanding why Joe has become involved with McGowan, suggesting that despite their closeness they continue to inhabit separate universes guided by incommensurate structures of choice and possibility. As Hill has noted, these irresolvable differences rooted in class render *My Name is Joe* Loach's most profoundly pessimistic work.[22] Loach himself has acknowledged the importance of confronting the political and social legacy of the 1980s:

> As Britain emerged from the spell that Thatcher had put on it, I and perhaps some other film-makers felt dissatisfied with ourselves. We felt we hadn't really put on screen the appalling costs in human misery that aggressive Thatcherite politics had brought on everybody. We should have made films in the early 80s that really showed what was happening, but I know that I didn't. I think the last few years have been an attempt to remedy that.[23]

But, despite the deep pessimism, *My Name is Joe* is marked by numerous small moments celebrating the endurance of humanity and even humour (the incongruity of the sight of Joe's rag-bag football team sporting West German and Brazilian shirts adorned with the names of legendary international players like Müller and Pele) in the teeth of adversity. Much of this is attributable to the finely nuanced performance of Mullan which won him the best-actor prize at Cannes. Despite his flaws, Joe, like George in *Carla's Song*, embodies the basic good-heartedness of ordinary people who somehow manage to retain a sense of value in a world riddled with inequality, exploitation and greed. The film also portrays a Glasgow where the last vestiges of community life manage to cling on in the form of small quiet interactions between friends, colleagues and lovers. This is rendered all the more palpable by the detached observational shooting style of cinematographer Barry Ackroyd, serving to place the characters within a defined social and physical environment which is both recognisably Glasgow but is equally applicable to other major British cities. This dialectic allows the inner-city violence represented by McGowan and his gang to be related to wider economic and social processes rather than being simply yet another rehashing of the image of the traditional Glasgow loan shark/hard man.[24]

The familiar theme of urban violence and the Glasgow 'hard-man' figure had been given a fresh re-examination in *Small Faces* in an understated but assured collaboration between director Gillies Mackinnon and his screenwriter/producer brother Billy. A highly personal film inspired partly by childhood experiences and partly by Luchino Visconti's classic tale of familial relationships *Rocco and his Brothers* (1960), *Small Faces* paints an intimate portrait of the relationships between three brothers growing up against a backdrop of conflict between rival teenage gangs in Glasgow in the late 1960s. At the centre of the narrative is Lex McLean (Iain Robertson), a precocious 13-year-old living in a cramped flat in Govan Hill with his brothers Alan (Joe McFadden) and Bobby (J.S. Duffy) and their long-suffering mother Lorna (Claire Higgins). Lex and Alan are both talented artists, distancing them from the emotionally disturbed Bobby who seeks belonging as a member of the Glen, the local gang led by the spivish Charlie Sloan (Garry Sweeney). After Lex unwittingly ignites hostilities with a rival gang, the Garaside Tongs, whose psychotic leader Malky Johnson (Kevin McKidd) he accidentally shoots in the face with an air gun, the conflict becomes progressively serious, culminating in the horrific murder of Bobby on an ice rink. Filtered through the consciousness of Lex, *Small Faces* conveys the anxiety and excitement of someone on the verge of puberty, curious about new worlds of adult possibility yet afraid of the responsibilities maturity entails.

The relationship of art to the allure of the gangs is ambivalent and complex in *Small Faces*. On one level, the two are closely linked: Lex's imaginary map of gangland Glasgow and Alan's assignment as a 'war artist' by Sloan allude to the mythologisation of the Glasgow gangs in Scottish painting and a number of gangland novels.[25] Yet at other points in the film, art seems the antithesis of the mindless violence perpetrated by the Glen and the Tongs, a creative means of escape and self-fulfilment.[26] While Mackinnon avoids any romanticisation of the hard-man figure, presenting Sloane as a pampered thug and Johnson as a vicious psychopath who thinks nothing of laying into his diminutive step-brother Gorbals, it is in the gang-related scenes that his powerful visual sense is most effective. The most horrifying scene being the killing of Bobby at the ice rink, culminating in the shot of his body being dragged across the ice leaving a crimson sweep of blood. But the visceral qualities of these moments are balanced by the poignant and still montage of grief, loss and loneliness in the aftermath of Bobby's killing that ties together the McLeans, with the suffering of various other characters, culminating with the traces of hate, mob mentality and even evil implicit in Alan's drawings which adorn his bedroom wall. The sequence conveys a powerful realisation of the destructive power of the gangs and the need to move beyond such tribal barbarism. The city is also powerfully rendered in terms of a contrast between the traditional sandstone tenements of Lex's neighbourhood and the imposing high-rises, empty waste ground and foreshortened brick walls that constitute 'Tongland', the latter filmed in such a way as to suggest a highly stylised dystopia owing more to the imaginative universe of Lex (and Mackinnon) than modes of documentary realism.

The representation of the city in recent Scottish films also extends beyond Scotland. The southward emigration of generations of Scots, including many involved in contemporary film-making, has given London a particular resonance within the Scottish creative imagination. The tour guide pastiche of the metropolis in *Trainspotting*, with its stereotypical images of red buses, pearly queens and famous landmarks, served to create a playful contrast with the decidedly non-stereotypical representation of Edinburgh.[27] A similar tension between North and South, Glasgow and London, is central to the structure of *Stella Does Tricks*, directed by Coky Giedroyc from a screenplay by the Scottish novelist A.L. Kennedy. The film charts the life of a teenage Scottish prostitute, Stella McGuire (Kelly MacDonald) working the London streets under the control of manipulative sleazy pimp Mr Peters (James Bolam). Stella eventually breaks free from Peters, although not before she is brutally raped by a group of his henchmen, moving in with Eddie (Hans Matheson) a young junkie. Integrated into the narrative are a series of subjective flashbacks to Stella's childhood in Glasgow with her father Francis (Ewan Stewart) and her puritanical aunt Aileen, a place associated with childhood hope but also sexual abuse.

Despite its grim surface naturalism, *Stella Does Tricks* is equally concerned with Stella's inner world and imagination, and the opposition between her objective and subjective worlds is conveyed by the different ways in which the two cities are represented in the film. As Charlotte Brunsdon notes:

London is tightly filmed in medium and medium-long shots – always showing more than the figures on which the frame is focused, but never stretching to give a sense of space or distance. It is a city of seedy hotels and cafés, flats and a dusty inner city park. The camera rarely rises above eye level and we only see the sky briefly in the park ... Glasgow, in appropriate contrast for a city visited in the film mainly in memory or fantasy, is more spacious and is rendered more often in twilight long shots, particularly the pigeon loft, Stella's father's pride and joy.[28]

The loft is also the sight of her abuse by her father and the film ends with a fantasy image of the young Stella, carefree in butterfly wings, torching the strange tower.

The significance of dreams are that they constitute a realm beyond the domination and abuse of others: Peters may have control over Stella's body but her flights of fancy are something he cannot reach. But at the same time they also haunt her. In one disturbing fantasy sequence conveying the particularly Presbyterian dimension of Stella's predicament, her father performs a stand-up routine in a church, recounting a horrific gag concerning the rape of his daughter, while the frigid aunt Aileen accuses her of wantonness and guilt. In her first novel, *Looking for the Possible Dance* (1993), Kennedy explores the complex relationship between a daughter and father with subtlety and depth and in *Stella Does Tricks* maintains the ambivalence felt by Stella towards Francis, avoiding a simple denunciation of him as a fiend. Unlike her father, Stella is a natural raconteur, entertaining her fellow prostitutes in the cafe where they hang out, and after she has taken a fatal overdose, the film ends with a vision of Stella on stage in a club recounting the story of her life and of her dreams to the audience. This engagement with the psychic response to material adversity contrasts with the more objective perspective of Loach, marking out *Stella Does Tricks* as a film arguably embodying a more feminine perspective. In any case, its focus on a young woman provided a welcome alternative to the overtly male-centred narratives that continue to dominate the Scottish cinematic engagement with the city.

A very different but no less interesting depiction of young Scots in London is offered by David Kane's irreverent romantic comedy, *This Year's Love*. Focusing on the various romantic trysts of group of 20-somethings in Camden Town, this ensemble piece is very much in the mould of Kane's previous television film *Ruffian Hearts*. At the centre are three young Scots: tattoo artist Danny (Douglas Henshall) and clothes designer Hannah (Catherine McCormack), whose wedding day is wrecked when it is revealed that Hannah has been sleeping with the best man, and Cameron (Dougray Scott), a painter who spends his time sexually exploiting women who place ads in lonely hearts' columns. The other major characters include lone parent Sophie (Jennifer Ehle), a bitter ex-Roedean drop-out who lives in a barge with her son Caleb, Liam (Ian Hart), Cameron's nerdish and emotionally unstable housemate and Marey (Kathy Burke) who suffers from low self-esteem. The drama charts the various couplings involving this group over a three-year period culminating in the reconciliation between Danny and Hannah. Along the way, the tables are turned on Cameron when Sophie walks out on him, while Liam survives an attempted suicide only to degenerate slowly into madness. As an example of a contemporary romantic comedy, *This Year's Love* demonstrates a bite and a grittiness conspicuously lacking in the better-known and infinitely more 'tasteful' work of Richard Curtis (*Four Weddings and A Funeral*, *Notting Hill*). The pitch-black humour, particularly the blunt acidic dialogue, connects the film with a rich tradition of confrontational and socially engaged Scottish comedy running from Billy Connolly to *Rab C. Nesbitt*, giving *This Year's Love* a depth that is by turns engaging and melancholic, ultimately suggesting that not only are relationships doomed to failure but that human beings learn very little in the process.

Return to the Edge of the World

While the city has achieved a new dominance in representations of Scotland in the 1990s, the familiar image of a wild landscape far removed from modern 'civilisation' did not disappear. The remoteness of the Western Isles from metropolitan London continued to feature as a a plot device in very different scenarios from a bawdy comedy like *Staggered* (Martin Clunes, 1994) to a sensitive period film like *The Governess* (Sandra Goldbacher, 1998). If the Glasgow cityscape continued to reflect the pain, struggle and bewilderment of male characters like Charlie Colquhoun, Joe Kavanagh and the McLean brothers, then the Scottish rural landscape in contrast had a deep connection with female subjectivity. This association, arguably given its most powerful statement in literature by Lewis Grassic Gibbon in *Sunset Song*, had been reworked by films like *Another Time, Another Place* and *Blue Black Permanent* and continued to be explored in the mid-1990s.

One of the most intense engagements with this theme is *Breaking the Waves*, a Scandinavian–French co-production by Danish director Lars von Trier, set on the Western Highland seaboard in the early 1970s. The film tells the tragic story of Bess McNeil (Emily Watson) an emotionally frail young woman who secretly communes with God in the austere Presbyterian church in which women are officially forbidden to talk. Bess's insecurities are exposed by her marriage to Jan (Stellan Skarsgård), an oil worker who, after being paralysed in an accident, encourages Bess to seek out other men for sex so she can come back and tell him about it. Convinced that with God's blessing this will help

On the edge of the world: Emily Watson in *Breaking the Waves*

her husband recover, this promiscuity leads Bess to being shunned by her family and the community and ultimately to her tragic death at the hands of sadistic foreign sailors.

A formally innovative production, *Breaking the Waves* is shot in a hand-held style in conjunction with a extreme widescreen ratio giving the film an unsettling vertiginous quality.[29] The images are also excessively grainy and drained of colour, having been transferred to video for post-production manipulation. This immediacy is in stark contrast to the animated picture postcards of the land and seascape that mark eight chapters into which the narrative is arranged. But beyond the foregrounding of technique, what makes *Breaking the Waves* so interesting is its portrait of a community in the grip of a repressive and authoritarian belief-system that reflects the harshness and unforgiving nature of the environment itself. While the excesses of Calvinism had been contemplated in films like *The Thirty-Nine Steps* and *The Kidnappers*, what *Breaking the Waves* does, by virtue of being a Scandinavian production, is to link the Scottish experience to that of neighbouring countries on the northern edges of Europe similarly shaped by extreme Protestantism.[30] The intense austerity of the images, coupled with the themes of isolation, devotion and doubt recall the work of Ingmar Bergman, while von Trier's big close-ups of Bess talking to God clearly reference Carl Dreyer's breathtaking images of Marie Falconeti in the 1927 silent classic *Jeanne d'arc*. *Breaking the Waves* itself is caught up in a similar profound uncertainty concerning the substance of belief. While it is never totally clear whether or not Bess's voices are delusions, the climactic image of the celestial bells high over the oil rig after her secret burial at sea (a response to the lack of bells in the Presbyterian kirk) suggests a rather different interpretation of her 'madness'.

The intensity of *Breaking the Waves* is echoed in *The Winter Guest*, an equally stylised production directed by Alan Rickman. Adapted by Sharman Mac-Donald from her own play, the film is shaped by a profoundly feminine sensibility characteristic of a writer who had chosen to work primarily in England, Peter Zenziger noting that 'her escape from a male-dominated Scottish culture shows in the almost complete absence of adult men in her plays'.[31] Set in a small Scottish seaside town, *The Winter Guest* revolves around four pairings of characters, at the centre of which is the rather fractious relationship between Frances and her mother Elspeth (played by real-life mother and daughter Phyllida Law and Emma Thompson). Frances mourns her dead husband and plans to leave for Australia while Elspeth, fearful of her own mortality, attempts to rekindle the bond between them that has clearly been lost. Meanwhile, Frances's lonely son Alex (Garry Hollywood) meets the beguiling and sparky Nita (Arlene Cockburn) who helps him to exorcise the ghost signified by the photographs of his dead father. The other characters include two pre-pubescent schoolboys, Sam and Tom, who skip school and explore the frozen coastline, and the elderly eccentrics Lily and Chloe who spend their lives attending funerals.

In different ways each of the dyads allows the exploration of themes of uncertainty, loss, the fear of mortality and the emotional complexity of close relationships. The title of the work invokes death, a presence that is conjured by both character and environment. While the mannered dialogue at times threatens to undermine the verisimilitude of the film, this is countered by the rooting of the action within the real (if digitally manipulated) Fife fishing villages of Pitenweem and Elie, the frozen sea and wintry vistas providing layers of subtlety by reflecting the emotional landscapes of the different characters. The emotional force of *The Winter Guest* is enhanced by cinematographer Seamus McGarvey's liberal use of cold bright light which invokes a sombre, yet deeply tranquil quality again reminiscent of Bergman's more introspective films. This visual sensitivity is matched by Michael Kamen's richly evocative piano score which adds further substance to this highly accomplished film. The recurring metaphor of walking out on the ice, emphasised by the fact that the boundary between land and sea is never clearly defined, not only alludes to the courage needed for relationships to endure. It also functions as a subliminal reminder of Scotland's own peripheral status, a cold country on the edge of Europe tentatively groping its way towards a new and more confident sense of identity and self-determination.

History Lessons

But the contemplation of national identity always involves more than the contemplation of an uncertain future. The past continues to inform the present in
a multitude of ways, providing symbolic and mythical versions of historical
destiny waiting to be fulfilled. At the same moment, films like *Shallow Grave*
and *Trainspotting* were constructing a novel version of a Scottish present, Hollywood was taking an interest in the past, marking a return to a familiar
tradition of romantic heroes and the honourable struggle for freedom. Such a
vision is epitomised by *Braveheart*, Mel Gibson's rendition of the life of William
Wallace, the Scottish patriot who famously defeated the English army at Stirling Bridge in 1297. Financed by 20th Century-Fox, this big-budget epic set
about revitalising a myth closely associated with expressions of Scottish
Nationalism, a fact that led to the image of Gibson as Wallace being appropriated as an emblem by the Scottish National Party.[32] The circumstances of the
production itself were also the subject of some rancour when filming was transferred from Scotland to Ireland due in part to the more favourable Irish system
of tax concessions, although *Braveheart* still played a significant part in giving
a boost to the Scottish tourist industry.[33] The film charts the rise of Wallace as
a leader, his burning desire for Scottish liberation fuelled by the murder of his
father and brother when he was a child. The subsequent execution of his wife
Murren (Catherine McCormack) by an English nobleman moves him to action,
sparking a popular rebellion culminating in the victory at Stirling and a successful campaign in the north of England. Wallace is ultimately undone by the
ruthlessness of the English king, Edward 'Longshanks' (Patrick McGoohan)
and the duplicity of the Scottish nobility including an impressionable young
Robert the Bruce (Angus Macfadyen) manipulated by his scheming leprosy-
ridden father (Ian Bannen). After defeat at Falkirk, Wallace is lured into a trap
and subsequently tried and executed in London. But in true hyperbolic Hollywood fashion, *Braveheart* ends on a high note with the Bruce leading the
Scottish army to victory at Bannockburn, establishing the Scottish independence and freedom Wallace had fought and died for.

Produced at the same time as *Braveheart* was yet another cinematic rendering of the story of Rob Roy MacGregor. Although ostensibly a Scottish project
produced by Peter Broughan, written by Alan Sharp and directed by Michael
Caton Jones, *Rob Roy* was financed by United Artists. Its international aspirations are also clearly apparent in the casting of Liam Neeson (whose star status
had been ensured by *Schindler's List*) as the eponymous hero and Jessica Lange
as Mary MacGregor. Set two years before the 1715 Jacobite rebellion, *Rob Roy*
recounts the by now familiar story of the former cattle thief who falls foul of
the devious Duke of Montrose (John Hurt) and is forced to take to the hills as

a fugitive. At the centre of this version, however, is the villainous presence of a foppish young Englishman, Archibald Cunningham (Tim Roth) who is also a deadly swordsman. With the connivance of Montrose's factor Killearn (Brian Cox), Cunningham steals the £1,000 loan provided to Rob by Montrose and then sets about pursuing the debt, culminating in the brutal rape of Mary and the destruction of the MacGregor homestead. After various encounters – including his memorable escape from capture by leaping over the bridge at Orchy (almost throttling Cunningham in the process) – Rob finally avenges his (and his wife's) honour in a climactic duel with Cunningham.

Braveheart and *Rob Roy* share some remarkable similarities, both featuring outlaw-heroes whose exploits take place against a magnificent Highland back-drop.[34] Neeson's Rob Roy MacGregor is a rugged, towering figure magnificent in his plaid, while Gibson's more diminutive stature as Wallace is more than compensated by his robust physique, piercing blue eyes and war paint. The bodies of both men are tested to the limit, bruised and bloodied in combat, but they ultimately possess the strength, skill and the intelligence to overcome adversity. Rob fights and kills three adversaries in one-on-one encounters, the climactic duel being a particularly spectacular addition to the cinematic annals of sword fighting pitting the ox-like Rob against Cunningham's lightning rapier. Wallace on the other hand is more directly comparable to the Hollywood action hero, slaying dozens of his enemies with impunity both on the battlefield and in surprise ambushes. The ingenuity of his combat skills is matched by the feroc-ity with which he enacts his vengeance, while the final image of Wallace's broadsword, thrust into the ground after the victory at Stirling, is emblematic of the film's excessive use of patriotic symbolism.

The rugged masculinity of the Scottish heroes is contrasted by the effemi-nacy of certain English characters, a familiar association in Scottish cultural production as commentators like Christopher Whyte have demonstrated.[35] Cunningham's foppishness leads Argyll to suggest he is a 'buggerer of boys' unable to 'tell arse from quim',[36] while Longshanks's son and heir Prince Edward (Peter Hanly) is a pathetic, simpering weakling whose sexual procliv-ities are signified by his preference for the company of his friend Phillip over his beautiful French wife Isabelle (Sophie Marceau). The virility of the Scots is underlined in the encounters between Wallace and Princess Isabelle, his brav-ery, honour and masculinity representing everything her husband lacks. Their coupling culminates in Isabelle's gloating news to the dying Longshanks that she is carrying a child which has nothing to do with his son, a twist that also symbolically turns the tables on Edward's initial plan to pacify Scotland by invoking the feudal right of *jus primae noctis*, granting English nobles the right of sexual access to female tenants on their wedding night. *Rob Roy* also ends with a pregnancy which may be a consequence of Mary's rape by Cunningham, but this is used to further demonstrate Rob's personal strength and humanity in his ability to accept the situation and love the child come what may.

While *Braveheart's* representation of Scottish history at times verges on the ludicrous: the Scottish army's defiant lifting of their kilts at the enemy recalling the hilarious 'devils in skirts' in *Carry On Up the Khyber*, *Rob Roy* situates its action within a more complex and subtle acknowledgement of the political power structures of eighteenth-century Scotland. Wallace simply ignores the fractious nobility in assuming command of the Scottish rebellion, but Rob is forced to seek the patronage of the Duke of Argyll to legitimate his reclamation of honour. Staged in a cellar-like chamber the duel itself is constituted as a clandestine prize fight, a gambling opportunity for the rich and powerful rather than an open and honourable setting of scores, Rob may return a hero to his wife and family but the limitations of his scope of influence have been clearly demonstrated. If *Braveheart* at times resembles a medieval action adventure, inspired by Gibson's previous screen incarnations in the successful *Mad Max* and *Lethal Weapon* series, *Rob Roy* suggests a certain affinity with the revenge western with its themes of cattle rustling, struggling communities, rivalry between powerful landowners and duels of honour. Indeed, Alan Sharp's reputation as a Hollywood screenwriter had been forged by a direct engagement with the genre in *Ulzana's Raid* (Robert Aldrich, 1972) and *Billy Two Hats* (Ted Kotchef, 1973).

The mid-1990s saw further engagements with these two defining moments in Scottish history, but on a rather different scale to the international Hollywood gloss of *Braveheart* and *Rob Roy*. *Chasing the Deer* (Graham Holloway, 1995), a recounting of the ill-fated Jacobite rebellion of 1745, and *The Bruce* (Bob Caruthers and David McWhinnie, 1996), a biopic of the victor of Bannockburn, were produced on the minuscule budgets of £460,000 and £500,000 respectively, raised from a number of private small investors who also appear as extras in the films. The ingenuity of this funding scheme, coupled with the explicit commercial orientations of the film-makers concerned to make low-budget mainstream product, render these productions a fascinating contribution to the new Scottish cinema. But, unfortunately, the mismatch between ambition and resources is plain to see, both marred by overly contrived plots, unconvincing performances, poorly staged set pieces, a general lack of narrative tension, and a diminished sense of scale. *Chasing the Deer* revolves around a father and son, Alistair and Euan Campbell, who end up on different sides at the battle of Culloden. The critical portrayal of the 1745 rebellion echoes Peter Watkins's *Culloden*, but this sits uncomfortably with the cloying sentimentality of a plot that culminates in the tragic death of father and son on Culloden moor, followed by the upbeat coda of the birth of Euan's child to his sweetheart Mary. *The Bruce* depicts the rise of its eponymous hero, overcoming the treachery of his rival Comyn and the indifference of the nobles to claim the crown of Scotland and lead the army to victory at Bannockburn. There are echoes of *Braveheart* throughout (the Bruce even resorts to a similar evocation of 'freedom' to rouse his troops on the battlefield), while the motif of the Bruce's heart, cast among the Saracens by Scottish crusaders, directly mirrors the symbolism of Wallace's sword. But the climactic battle is painfully devoid of the scale and spectacle of Gibson's Stirling Bridge: the final confrontation between Bruce and the English noble De Bouwn (Michael van Wijk, better known as Wolf in the TV series *Gladiators*), the kidnapper of the Bruce's family and slayer of his beloved mentor Bishop Wishart (Oliver Reed), one of the most unconvincing sword fights in cinema history.

A rather different image of history is provided by the BBC film *Mrs Brown*, directed by John Madden. Ostensibly a Scottish contribution to the popular 'heritage film', the production focuses on the relationship between Queen Victoria and her Scottish ghillie John Brown that developed during her long period of grief after the death of Prince Albert. In typical heritage style, *Mrs Brown* conveys an acute attention to Victorian period detail and the rituals of upper-class social etiquette. But such *longeurs* are overshadowed by the energetic performance of Billy Connolly as Brown, his presence a veritable whirlwind of irreverent energy breezing through the stifling social niceties of the court, represented by the Queen's private secretary Henry Ponsonby (Geoffrey Palmer), her physician Doctor Jenner (Richard Pasco) and her son, the effete Bertie, Prince of Wales (David Westhead). While this strategy invokes a familiar nature–culture opposition between the Scots and the English,[37] but the tragedy of the drama lies in the subtle way in which his restorative energies give way to an inappropriate obsession with the queen (Judi Dench). This in turn exposes Brown's vulnerability, allowing powerful and jealous enemies to engineer his downfall. Much of the action takes place at Balmoral and the hills and glens of Deeside are constructed very much as Brown's domain. Yet while the film touches on the growing republican impulse fanned by Victoria's seven-year absence from participating in state duties following Prince Albert's death in 1861, it has little to say about Victoria's active role in the promotion of a particular nineteenth-century vision of the Highlands.[38]

One major historical event almost totally ignored by cinematic representations of Scotland is the First World War despite the terrible consequences it had for the Scottish population. As historian T.M. Devine notes, 26.4 per cent of the Scottish men who enlisted were killed, compared with a figure of 11.8 per cent for the rest of the British army, and only the Serbs and Turks having higher fatality rates.[39] The symbolic resonance of the loss of a generation is conveyed by the countless war memorials adorning practically every town and village across Scotland. But the conflict also looms large in Scottish writing from Lewis

Grassic Gibbon and Neil Gunn, to Alan Sharp and Alasdair Gray. As Cairns Craig observes:

> The First World War, much more than the Second, haunts Scottish novelists because it gives particular definition to Scotland's relationship to the historical. However destructive the experience, it represents the possibility of a new beginning, a new engagement in the forces of history, a reconnection of Scotland with the real dynamics of the external world.[40]

In this way, Craig suggests that the Great War has a similar symbolic function for lowland Scotland as the 1745 Jacobite rebellion and the clearances do for the Highlands in its similar erasure of the past.

The destructive force of the conflict is explored in *Regeneration*, Allan Scott's adaptation of Pat Barker's novelisation of the experiences of the war poets Siegfried Sassoon and Wilfred Owen at the Craiglockart Hospital outside Edinburgh. Sensitively directed by Gillies Mackinnon, the film depicts the attempts of Dr William Rivers (Jonathan Pryce) to treat officers suffering from shell shock. In addition to Owen (Stuart Bunce) and Sassoon (James Wilby), the latter committed for expressing anti-war sentiments, Rivers's patients include Billy Prior (Jonny Lee Miller), a working-class officer suffering from mutism. This disorder is apparently confined to the lower social ranks in contrast to officers' greater propensity for stammering, a condition suffered by Rivers himself. In different ways, both Prior and Sassoon force Rivers to confront his complacency about the war with regard to both the iniquities wrought by the class system and the political justification for the continued mass slaughter at the front. While the regenerative theme is further explored by way of the blossoming friendship between Owen and Sassoon, marking the former's emergence as an important poet encouraged by the established writer to engage more directly with his first-hand experience of war. But, ultimately, *Regeneration* leaves the particular historical resonance of the Great War to Scotland undeveloped, being motivated more by a concern with issues of class and masculinity than nation.

Iconoclastic Visions

In addition to the broad thematic tendencies identified above, Scottish cinema has also continued to embrace the more personal tradition of art cinema, culminating in three films by distinctive writer-directors that link the achievements of the recent past with a new burst of creative achievement. In 1999, Bill Forsyth marked a welcome return to a Scottish subject after a fifteen-year absence. *Gregory's Two Girls* is a sequel to the film that had done so much to make his reputation in the early 1980s. Gregory Underwood (portrayed as in the original *Gregory's Girl* by John Gordon Sinclair) is now in his mid-thirties and teaching

English at his old school in Cumbernauld. But he continues to suffer from a profound inability to deal with women, his emotional complications being provided by the 'two girls' of the title: Frances (Carly McKinnon), a 16-year-old pupil Gregory has an unbearable crush on, and Bel (Maria Doyle Kennedy), a sexually voracious colleague actively pursuing him. Consequently, much of the drama revolves around Gregory's difficulty in confronting his responsibilities as an adult, a situation complicated by feelings of guilt and fear engendered by his transgressive fantasies on the one hand and his rejection of a legitimate emotional and physical relationship on the other. This delicate study of masculine evasion and introspection – a stultifying inwardness that might also be regarded as a critique of national character traits – is slightly undermined by a rather convoluted sub-plot involving a South American political refugee and the revelation that a local businessman is supplying torture equipment to oppressive regimes around the world. But, on balance, *Gregory's Two Girls* marks a welcome return to the cinema of astute observation that made Forsyth's reputation in the first place, using humour to explore the complexities of inappropriate and unrequited obsession, while studiously avoiding the puerile approach to sexual desire that continues to be the stock-in-trade of too many British films.[41]

In addition to connecting with a previous significant moment in the development of Scottish cinema, 1999 also witnessed the emergence of arguably the

Family ties: Douglas Henshall and Stephen McCole in *Orphans*, Peter Mullan's acclaimed debut feature

most iconoclastic and exciting Scottish film-makers since Bill Douglas and Bill Forsyth. Peter Mullan and Lynne Ramsay had both won critical acclaim for short films like *Fridge* and *Gasman*, but the creative vision demonstrated in these 'miniatures' was to be surpassed by two of the most accomplished feature debuts in Scottish cinema history. Mullan's film *Orphans* charts the experiences of four siblings, Thomas (Gary Lewis), Michael (Douglas Henshall), John (Stephen McCole) and the wheelchair-bound Sheila (Rosemarie Stevenson), during the twenty-four hours before the funeral of their beloved mother. As night falls over Glasgow, a storm brews, providing an appropriately excessive elemental backdrop to the bizarre and extreme events that follow as the orphans attempt to deal with their devastating sense of grief and loss. The stubborn Thomas makes good a promise to his dying mother, steadfastly remaining with her coffin in the Catholic church where the funeral will take place. This dedication to duty leads him to neglect the needs of Sheila, who is rescued by a young girl dressed as a fairy princess after her wheelchair has broken down in a dark street. Meanwhile, Michael, who has been stabbed in a pub brawl, waits for the morning so he can claim bogus industrial injury compensation for a wound that is slowly draining the life blood out of him. The youngest brother, John, spends the night trying to find a gun with which he can kill his brother's assailant. For each of the characters, the night represents a descent into very different types of hell and the Glasgow portrayed is an expressionistic, carnivalesque world where literally anything can happen.

Orphans offers an honest and refreshing meditation on problem of contemporary Scottish masculinity. None of the men in the film are able to deal with their grief: Thomas retreats into himself, Michael equally spends the night running away from his emotions, his failure as a husband and father, while John is prepared to sacrifice university and his own liberty by committing murder in the name of a misplaced sense of family honour. But unlike the pessimism and defeat at the heart of Peter McDougall's studies of masculinity in crisis, or even of more recent films like *My Name is Joe*, Mullan's resolution offers hope and redemption in the reintegration of the family by their mother's graveside, a scene shot in bright sunlight. *Orphans* is also distinguished by Mullan's cinephilic use of an eclectic array of aesthetic styles and references ranging from the stillness of Bill Douglas or Terence Davies, the surrealism of Buñuel and the carnivalesque energy of Fellini to the audacious magical realism of Emir Kusturica.[42] There are also a range of more deeply rooted references running from Shakespeare to the New Testament to the scatological humour of Billy Connolly. This cultural richness at times recalls Alasdair's Gray's extraordinary first novel *Lanark* (1981), Roderick Watson's assessment of which might equally apply to *Orphans* in spirit if not in letter: '*Lanark* allowed us to reassess the Scottish penchant for dealing with other realms, mixing metaphysical questions and fantastic inner experience with terror, black bawdry and political satire, all expressed with an extraordinary textual energy.'[43]

But unlike the breathless intertextuality of a film like *Trainspotting*, the energy and drive of *Orphans* is derived from the way in which Mullan raids the expressive store of cinema history to find the right kind of image or technique to convey specific ideas or emotions. Consequently, the film is replete with memorable moments – a statue of the Virgin smashing into hundreds of pieces, the wind ripping the roof off the church where Thomas holds his vigil, a delirious Michael floating down the Clyde on a pallet, Thomas buckling under the weight of his mother's coffin as he attempts to carry it to the graveside – in what amounts to a celebration of the cinema's rich creative palette.

In contrast to the excesses of *Orphans*, *Ratcatcher* is an exercise in restrained austerity recalling the brooding contemplation and paired-down aesthetic of Bill Douglas. Like Douglas's trilogy, Ramsay's film is an intense and melancholic study of childhood dislocation, confusion and loneliness. Set during the 1973 Glasgow refuse workers' strike, *Ratcatcher* depicts the experiences of 12-year-old James Gillespie (William Eadie), a loner morbidly drawn to the canal where his friend, Ryan Quinn, accidentally drowns at the beginning of the film. Feeling responsible for the tragedy, James keeps his secret even from his friend Margaret Anne (Leanne Mullan), a 14-year-old whose own profound alienation has led her into an abusive relationship with the local gang of boys. The Gillespie home is blighted by James's father's drinking and his mother's increasingly desperate wait for the family to be rehoused by the council. His own desire for escape leads him to the discovery of a greenfield building site on the outskirts of the city. In addition to providing a sanctuary beyond the overcrowded dingy tenements surrounded by the rubbish strewn streets and courtyards, the new houses also overlook an expanse of green fields, the image framed by the window like a cinema screen in what functions as practically a fantasy of freedom and possibility for the young boy. Ramsay's poignant images are reinforced by her skilful direction of both professional actors like Tommy Flannagan and Mandy Matthews (as James's parents) and non-professionals, including members of her own family.[44] The understated performances by Eadie and Mullan in particular lend *Ratcatcher* an understated naturalism. In conventional narrative terms very little happens in the film, yet the audience is invited to experience a rich palate of experiences and emotions from James's guilt and loneliness to moments of spontaneous bliss when he runs through the open fields, or in the tender scene in which he innocently takes a bath with Margaret Anne.

The central force of *Ratcatcher* is in the access it provides into an emotional landscape characterised by significant places, objects and interactions, forcing the viewer to look, to listen, to feel and ultimately to understand. As Ramsay commments:

I'm very interested in focusing in on details and making audiences see things they don't normally see. What I do a lot in *Ratcatcher* is frame something so that it's what you don't see that's important. I try to be economical, to show the bare minimum and leave the rest to the imagination. Maybe that makes the film harder for audiences but I think it makes it a more rewarding experience, creating a kind of mystery and tension.[45]

This approach is apparent from the opening sequence in which Ryan Quinn's distracted reverie, wrapped in a net curtain, is broken by a sudden slap in the face from his mother who appears out of nowhere. Ryan runs off leaving the camera's gaze on the twisted curtain as it slowly unwinds, facilitating contemplation of a small moment of innocent pleasure disrupted by violence and pain. While the stillness of this moment and many others clearly evoke the intensity of Bill Douglas, Ramsay's visual style is far more eclectic in its use of camera angles, jump cuts and subtle manipulation of focal depth. There are even occasional touches of the absurd, such as Kenny's mouse floating off in a red balloon accompanied by a musical reference to a similar moment in Terrence Malick's *Badlands* (1973). After the eclectic magical-realism of *Orphans*, the representation of Glasgow in *Ratcatcher* marks a return to a more familiar image of a shabby and neglected proletarian city, a backdrop to unrealised dreams and wasted lives. This is consistent with Ramsay's resolutely downbeat ending in which James drowns himself, the image of his body suspended in the murky water juxtaposed with the hopeless fantasy of his family walking through the wheat field to a new home.

The various films discussed in this chapter not only gave substance to the idea of a new Scottish cinema, they also served to rework the dominant representational traditions of the past. While no less reliant on the imaginative powers of myth, these images of Scotland have placed a new emphasis on the city as the heart of contemporary Scottish experience. The cinematic projection of Glasgow transformed from a rather narrow association with shipbuilding, slums and violence, by way of a diverse range of representations in the process. But, at the same time, important continuities were retained, most notably in the kind of working-class energy and camaraderie glimpsed in films like *Floodtide* and even *The Gorbals Story*. The focus on male anxiety that had been so central to the Scottish contribution to serious television drama in the 1970s continued to be an important theme, but this was complemented by a greater acknowledgement of feminine subjectivity and experience, particularly outside the domain of the post-industrial city. This also served as a reminder of the rich but often neglected feminine dimensions of the cinema's historical engagement with Scotland, particularly in terms of the virtues of popular fantasy and desire. Such a consideration also locates the first major attempts to resurrect a romantic vision of Scottish history as spectacle by a film like *Braveheart* that succeeded in delighting the popular audiences and enraging the intelligentsia in equal measure. Above all, the new Scottish cinema provided an unprecedented range of images that worked against any simple reductionism, a reflection of the creative potential of the medium and the cultural and the new-found ambition of its Scottish practitioners.

Notes

1 While this was proclaimed as the first Scottish film to open the festival since Forsyth's *Comfort and Joy* some fifteen years previously, *The Big Man* had provided a similar function in 1990.

2 This actually resulted in the film being criticised in some quarters for being insufficiently Scottish. See Robert McCall, 'Shallow Grave: A Worthy Standard-Bearer for Scotland?', *Scottish Film*, Issue 9, 3rd Quarter, 1994, pp. 15–17.

3 Moya Luckett, 'Image and Nation in 1990s British Cinema' in Robert Murphy (ed.), *British Cinema of the 90s* (London: BFI, 2000), p. 92.

4 Figures drawn from Angus Finney, *The State of European Cinema: A New Dose of Reality* (London: Cassell, 1996), p. 174.

5 David Aukin in Duncan Petrie (ed.), *Inside Stories: Diaries of British Film-Makers at Work* (London: BFI, 1996), p. 3.

6 This recalls the importance of earlier ensemble casting of films like *The Gorbals Story* (1949) and *The Brave Don't Cry* (1952) with players drawn respectively from the Glasgow Unity Theatre and the Citizens' Theatre.

7 This organisation of the narrative is one of the major departures from Welsh's original novel which gives direct access to the subjective worlds of several of the characters. The film also lacks any explanation of the otherwise enigmatic title. The novel features a scene set in the disused Leith central station in which the pointless idea of trainspotting in that empty shell symbolises the lack of human connection for those on society's margins' experience. For a discussion of the scene, see Cairns Craig, *The Modern Scottish Novel: Narrative and the National Imagination* (Edinburgh: Edinburgh University Press, 1999), pp. 97–9.

8 Danny Boyle quoted by Angus Finney, *The State of European Cinema*, p. 179.

9 John Orr, *Contemporary Cinema* (Edinburgh: Edinburgh University Press, 1998), p. 15.

10 John Hill explores the ways in which *Trainspotting* subverts traditional assumptions about space and place in 'British Cinema as National Cinema' in Robert Murphy (ed.), *The British Cinema Book* (London: BFI, 1997), pp. 251–52.

11 Danny Boyle interviewed by Geoffrey MacNab, *Sight and Sound*, February 1996, p. 10.

12 Figures from Nick Thomas, 'UK Film, Television and Video: Overview' in *The BFI Film and Television Handbook 1998* (London: BFI, 1998), p. 41.

13 The fusion of club and drug culture is central to Irvine Welsh's second novel *Maribou Stork Nightmares* (1995) and the short story collection *The Acid House* (1994) and also to Alan Warner's debut novel *Morvern Callar* (1995).

14 This has ranged from similar low-budget British films to big-budget international productions, including McGregor's appearance in *The Phantom Menace* (George Lucas, 1999) and the casting of Carlyle as the villain in the James Bond vehicle *The World is Not Enough* (Michael Apted, 1999).

15 Also the inspiration behind the Scottish Oscar-winning 'Tartan Short' *Franz Kafka's It's a Wonderful Life* (1993), written and directed by Peter Capaldi.

16 Xan Brooks, Review of *The Acid House*, *Sight and Sound*, January 1999, p. 40.

17 See for example, Peter Zenziger, 'The New Wave' in Randall Stevenson and Gavin Wallace (eds), *Scottish Theatre Since the Seventies* (Edinburgh: Edinburgh University Press, 1996).

18 Brian Tufano interviewed by Andrew O. Thompson, 'A Cosmopolitan Celebration of Cinema', *American Cinematographer*, December 1997.

19 Brian Pendreigh, 'It was billed as the new Trainspotting. It made £4,438. What went wrong?', *The Guardian*, 15 January 1999.

20 The architectural diversity of Glasgow is much more central to *Taggart*. Indeed as Ian Spring points out, the association of the series' eponymous hero with the city embraces a wide variety of locations and situations. Ian Spring, *Phantom Village: The Myth of the New Glasgow* (Edinburgh: Polygon, 1990), pp. 80–2.

21 John Hill, 'Failure and Utopianism: Representations of the Working Class in British Cinema of the 1990s' in Robert Murphy (ed.), *British Cinema of the 90s*, p. 179.

22 Ibid.

23 Ken Loach quoted by Graham Fuller in Fuller (ed.) *Loach on Loach* (London: Faber & Faber, 1998), p. 111.

24 Indeed a very similar figure appears in Loach's earlier feature *Raining Stones* (1993) set in Manchester.

25 Andy O'Hagan identifies the key works in this tradition as including *No Mean City* (1937), *Glasgow Keelie* (1940), *Cut and Run* (1962) and *Laidlaw* (1977) and the television plays of Peter McDougall, 'Gangs in the Hood', *Sight and Sound*, July 1995.

26 This also informs Byrne's *The Slab Boys* to Alasdair Gray's seminal 1981 novel *Lanark*, both of whom like Gillies Mackinnon attended the Glasgow School of Art.

27 Although as Moya Luckett points out, the film subsequently undermines this tourist gaze, suggesting more of an affinity between London and Edinburgh. 'Image and Nation in 1990s British Cinema' in Robert Murphy (ed.), *British Cinema of the 90s*, p. 92.

28 Charlotte Brunsdon, 'Not Having it All: Women and Film in the 1990s' in Robert Murphy (ed.), *British Cinema of the 90s*, p. 170.

29 The experience of this filming process, from an actor's point of view is conveyed by Katrin Cartlidge in her diary in Duncan Petrie (ed.), *Inside Stories*, pp. 102–7. The film's unorthodox technique also anticipates some of the key ideas of the Dogme 95 manifesto drawn up by von Trier and his colleagues.

30 Von Trier had originally planned to make the film on the west coast of Jutland. See Stig Björkman, 'Naked Miracles', *Sight and Sound*, October 1996, p. 12.

31 Peter Zenziger, 'The New Wave' in Randall Stevenson and Gavin Wallace (eds), *Scottish Theatre Since the Seventies*, p. 135.

32 See Marinell Ash, 'William Wallace and Robert the Bruce: The Life and Death of a National Myth' in Raphael Samuel and Paul Thompson (eds.), *The Myths We Live By* (London: Routledge, 1990).

33 The Scottish Tourist Board calculated that the articles generated by the production of *Braveheart* and *Rob Roy* brought in the equivalent of £11,450,000 of free advertising. Among a poll of overseas visitors to Scotland, 15 per cent claimed that seeing *Braveheart* had been a major factor in influencing their decision to come. See *Scottish Screen Data '96* (Glasgow: Scottish Screen, 1998), compiled by Jamie Hall, pp. 30–1.

34 The locations for *Rob Roy* included Glen Coe and Glen Nevis, the latter also used to great effect in *Braveheart* before the production relocated to Ireland.

35 Whyte explores traditions of misogyny and homophobia in twentieth-century Scottish literature in the introduction to his edited collection, *Gendering the Nation: Studies in Modern Scottish Literature* (Edinburgh: Edinburgh University Press, 1995).

36 But as Liz Lochhead notes, such sentiments are proven to be false in that Cunningham is in fact deadly both in sex and war, 'The Shadow', *Sight and Sound*, p. 16. A certain homophobic tendency is identified in Alan Sharp's earlier novels by Berthold Schoene in his essay 'Angry Young Masculinity and the Rhetoric of Homophobia and Misogyny in the Scottish Novels of Alan Sharp', in Christopher Whyte (ed.), *Gendering the Nation*.

37 An opposition which is also frequently used in relation to women and men. But interestingly in this instance the vitality of Brown's noble savage is coded as superior to the languid formality of the English court.

38 For a discussion of this construction, see Trevor R. Pringle, 'The Privation of History: Landseer, Victoria and the Highland Myth' in Denis Cosgrove and Stephen Daniels (eds), *The Iconography of Landscape* (Cambridge: Cambridge University Press, 1988).

39 T.M. Devine, *The Scottish Nation 1700–2000* (London: Penguin, 1999), p. 309. Christopher Harvie notes that the Scottish casualties numbered around 100,000 dead. *No Gods and Precious Few Heroes: Scotland 1914–1980* (London: Edward Arnold, 1981), p. 24.

40 Cairns Craig, 'The Body in the Kit Bag' in *Out of History: Narrative Paradigms in Scottish and British Culture* (Edinburgh: Polygon, 1996), p. 35.

41 This would appear to be a minority view however. *Gregory's Two Girls* met with a hostile critical reception and had a very limited exposure in British cinemas.

42 Mullan has alluded to a broad range of cinematic influences in various interviews – 'The tradition I come from is experimental and very un-British. I like expressionist cinema, Spanish surreal cinema and silent cinema.' 'Tearing the Roof Off: Liese Spencer talks to Peter Mullan about *Orphans*', *Sight and Sound*, April 1999, p. 14.

43 Roderick Watson, 'Maps of Desire: Scottish Literature in the Twentieth Century' in T.M. Devine and R.J. Finlay, *Scotland in the 20th Century* (Edinburgh: Edinburgh University Press, 1996), pp. 285–6.

44 Ramsay's brother James, who plays the father of Ryan Quinn in *Ratcatcher*, had appeared in all of her previous three short films, *Small Deaths*, *Kill the Day* and *Gasman*. While her niece, Lynne Jnr, in the role of James's younger sister Anne Marie, had been previously cast in *Small Deaths* and *Gasman*.

45 Lynne Ramsay, interviewed by Liese Spencer, 'What Are You Looking At?', *Sight and Sound*, October 1999, p. 18.

Conclusion
Into the Twenty-First Century

The new millennium dawned with Scottish cinema seemingly going from strength to strength. Not only had 1999 been a particularly auspicious year in terms of film production, including a new record spend in Scotland of nearly £30 million achieved without the assistance of a major Hollywood production, the devolution of political power from Westminster to Edinburgh carried major implications given the increasingly vital role played by public agencies in stimulating and supporting film-making in Scotland. The new Scottish Executive has already given clear indications of its interest in the field, convening an MSPs film group and instigating a new cultural strategy review under the new junior minister for culture, Rhona Brankin, with the interests of film being represented on the steering group by John Archer, the chief executive of Scottish Screen.[1]

Scottish Screen itself appear to be well placed to continue to promote for the interests of the film-making sector in Scotland. The creation in 1997 of an integrated single agency with an ambitious mission 'to establish Scotland as a major screen production centre and project (Scottish) culture to the world',[2] anticipated subsequent developments south of the border with the establishment of the Film Council two years later. But unlike the London-based Film Council, which is primarily involved in production, Scottish Screen also incorporate training within its remit as well as education, exhibition and archives.[3] While concerns have been expressed about increasing centralisation, the creation of Scottish Screen would appear to have provided a new sense of purpose and an increasingly professional engagement with the expanding sector now collectively labelled the 'Scottish Screen industries'. The expressed aim to help nurture companies involved in an increasingly diverse range of projects and activities is a reflection of the reality of independent production in Scotland. Unlike the narrow focus of the past, whether it be on the notoriously uncertain domain of feature production, or the rather more modest area of sponsored documentary, the emphasis is now on diversification as a means to create greater stability and continuity with the independent sector. As John Archer puts it:

I think during 1999 it became possible to talk about a Scottish Film Industry

without having to use quotation marks around the 'industry' bit. That's
because there is a sufficient body of production companies working across
television drama and film, pursuing projects, making shorts and so on to justify
talking about an independent sector which is also a Scottish film industry.[4]

The leading lights in this sector themselves convey a sense of the diversity of
Scottish production. They include an established company like Antonine, set
up in the early 1980s by Paddy Higson, with a track record in cinema features
(*The Girl in the Picture, Silent Scream, Orphans*); large independents like Ideal
World and Wark/Clements specialising in making a range of programmes for
television have begun to increase their involvement in cinema projects through
key individuals like Angus Lamont and Julie Fraser; and a number of new
companies currently developing ambitious slates of production, such as Gabriel
Films run by Catherine Aitken and Roz Borland, and Eddie Dick's Makar Productions. Scottish Screen's increasing interest in nurturing the business side of
this sector has been further enhanced by the establishment in Glasgow of the
Channel Four's Regions and Nations research centre explicitly to assist and support independent producers.

But a successful industry also requires appropriate facilities, one of the major
problems in this respect being the lack of major studio space in Scotland. There
had been attempts to establish a viable studio in the past. In 1984 Paddy Higson purchased a building in the east end of Glasgow for £60,000 in the attempt
to alleviate some of the problems involved in operating on a project by project
basis with no permanent production facilities: 'On every film I had done we
had had to move into an office, buy furniture, install telephone systems and try
to find a workshop where we could build bits of sets. And then when we'd finished we would move out again. I though it would be wonderful if we could
have somewhere we could do it all from.'[5]

The result was Black Cat studios where Higson subsequently produced the
features *The Girl in the Picture* and *Silent Scream*. A number of independent
productions were also made at Black Cat including the Channel Four drama
Brond, the music and arts programme *Half Way to Paradise* and numerous
commercials and music videos. But despite a reasonable throughput of business, Higson was unable to generate enough revenue to pay off her initial loan
with the result that Black Cat was forced to close in 1991. The cruel irony being
that the initiative came a decade too early: the upsurge in film-making activity
in the 1990s necessitating the construction of temporary studio spaces for productions like *Shallow Grave* and *Trainspotting*, while the Glasgow Film and
Television Studio, a converted scenery construction workshop in Maryhill provided a base for *Gregory's Two Girls* and *Complicity*. But the present provision
needs to be considerably enhanced if Scotland's production capacity is to be

expanded and, consequently, at the time of writing various bodies are investigating the possibility of establishing a new studio to meet the ever-increasing demand for such a facility.

The other key area of opportunity concerns the creative possibilities offered by new technology, particularly in the area of digital video production. The impact of a number of high-profile low-budget features shot wholly or partly on video, including the first Dogme 95 productions *The Idiots* (Lars von Trier, 1998) and *Festen* (Thomas Winterberg, 1998), and *The Blair Witch Project* (Daniel Myrick and Eduardo Sanchez, 1999) has generated a great deal of excitement verging on the hyperbolic. However, the new technology offers both greater accessibility to film-makers in terms of a significant reduction in production costs, and flexibility with regard to the technical properties of new video formats (portability of camera equipment, sensitivity to low light levels, desktop editing on a PC) and the creative freedom that working on a micro budget entails.[6] The primary aim of the new Scottish Arts Council Lottery Fund and Scottish Screen funding scheme, Twenty First Films, is to encourage new and innovative ways of telling stories using the new technologies.

At the time of writing, the first wave of Scottish feature productions using digital video have already materialised. This includes the first production to be made under the banner of Film Lab, another new-low budget initiative, launched by Film Four. Co-financed by the Scottish Lottery and the German company Kinowelt, *Daybreak* is a contemporary thriller set in an Edinburgh world of night clubs, hallucinogenic drugs and Internet porn. The film is also the debut feature of writer-director Bernard Rudden, whose previous work includes the unsettling black and white short *The Hunger Artist*, and is produced by James Mackay and Jim Hickey. The former has long been an advocate of video technology, pioneering its use for post-production on such innovative collaborations with Derek Jarman as *The Last of England* (1987) and *The Garden* (1990). As he noted in 1992:

> I have been profoundly influenced by experiments with video as a production
> medium such as Antonioni's *Oberwald Mystery* and by the work that Coppola
> was doing on the use of electronic images in cinema. These experiments gave
> us all the courage to get to something like *The Last of England* by creating a
> way of working as much as finding the small amount of money to make the
> film. Apart from providing a highly sophisticated and flexible method of
> editing and applying visual effects to footage generated on Super-8 or 16mm
> film, what I believe video post-production can do is make the kind of magic
> that cinema had in its wonderful Technicolor days.[7]

Produced on a budget of £800,000, *Daybreak* is a relatively conventional low-budget film in terms of subject-matter, construction and the organisation of the production process. What the Sony Digital Video system afforded the film-makers was the opportunity to shoot on location in Edinburgh, including a number of night-time sequences, more economically than would have been possible using film. Even more important for Mackay is the fact that Digital Video allowed the production to be made almost entirely in Edinburgh, with the exception of the sound recording and the transfer to film, rather than depending heavily on London-based post-production facilities.

But *Daybreak* was not the first digital feature to be shot in Edinburgh. In 1997 Don Boyd had directed *Lucia*, a romantic drama inspired by Donizetti's opera *Lucia di Lammermoor* in which the lives of the characters come to resemble the plot of the opera they are preparing. Like Mackay, Boyd is an expatriate Scot whose career has been largely based in London where in the late 1970s he helped to pioneer a new vitality in British production with his company Boyd's Co, laying the ground for the subsequent emergence of a new generation of dynamic independents like Palace Productions and Working Title. A more radical exploration of the potential of Digital Video is offered by *One Life Stand*, a micro-budget feature written and directed by May Miles Thomas, a Glaswegian film-maker highly experienced in the world of commercials and music video. Yet in contrast to the frenetic styles associated with such production, *One Life Stand* adopts an austere black and white minimalism more reminiscent of Bill Douglas to render its intimate working-class domestic drama. Making her film on Digital Video for a reported £60,000 afforded Thomas total control over every stage of the production process, including the editing which was done on a PC in her home. Owning the film also placed her in a very advantageous position in terms of securing a distribution deal for *One Life Stand*.

Such pioneering experiments not only open up new realms of creative possibility for Scottish film-makers, they also suggest a new vitality and diversity in film culture. In some senses, the emergence of digital technology and schemes like Twenty First Films could be seen as constituting the first moves in the creation of the kind of culturally driven innovative low-budget space long advocated by critics like Colin McArthur. But it is important not to create the illusion of a new utopia. The domain of digital production is subject to the same industrial structures and conventions as film. The level of excitement and anticipation generated by the project make it unlikely that *One Life Stand* will fail to find a distributor. But while it may be relatively easy to make a micro-budget film on DV that doesn't mean it will necessarily be any easier to get the finished work shown. Indeed, the evidence so far from America and Europe suggests that DV production will encourage a mixed bag of inspiration and amateurism. On the other hand, the mainstream, the form of the Film Lab, is already making moves to colonise the new margins, siphoning off the emerging talent to allow such a market-oriented player as Film Four to claim that it is actively involved in promoting genuine creative innovation.

But what is clear is that Scottish film-making is entering the new millennium with unprecedented levels of confidence, achievement and ambition. The emergence of a distinctive Scottish cinema has been just one element of the rich and diverse fermentation of creativity and cultural expression in Scotland over the last quarter century that has done so much to forge a new culture of possibility. As many commentators have suggested, this outpouring was in direct response to political disappointment including the sabotaging of the 1979 devolution referendum and the election in the same year of Margaret Thatcher's Conservative government that very quickly demonstrated its antipathy towards the aspirations of the majority of Scots. Two decades on, the situation has changed: a new parliament sits in Edinburgh consolidating Scotland's growing sense of cultural self-determination. The new Scottish cinema has an opportunity not only to project Scotland to the rest of the world but also to play an important role at the heart of a revitalised national culture in reflecting the diversity of contemporary Scottish experience, interpreting and reinterpreting the past, and providing a space for social criticism and the imagination of alternative possibilities. Despite the pressures towards homogenisation exerted by increased globalisation in the moving-image markets, the new Scottish cinema represented by *Trainspotting, Small Faces, My Name is Joe, Orphans, Ratcatcher* and *Daybreak* continues to demonstrate the expression of cultural specificity in terms that are both resolutely national and international in their relevance and appeal.

Notes

1   *Celebrating Scotland: A National Cultural Strategy*, published by the Scottish Executive, August 1999.
2   Taken from Scottish Screen's *Annual Review 1998/99*, p. 4.
3   These functions are the domain of the industry training body Skillset and the British Film Institute respectively.
4   Interview with John Archer, Glasgow, 19 January 2000.
5   Interview with Paddy Higson, Glasgow, 19 January 2000.
6   For a useful summary of the technical opportunities offered by Digital Video (DV), see Peter Broderick, 'DIY=DVC', *Media Watch '99*, a supplement published by *Sight and Sound*, March 1999, pp. 6–9.
7   James Mackay, 'Low Budget British Production: A Producer's Account' in Duncan Petrie (ed.), *New Questions of British Cinema* (London: BFI, 1992), p. 59.

Appendix One
Institutional Funding for Scottish Production

1. Features Developed by the Scottish Film Production Fund/Scottish Screen

Living Apart Together (Charles Gormley, 1983)
Every Picture Tells a Story (James Scott, 1984)
Venus Peter (Ian Sellar, 1989)
Play Me Something (Timothy Neat, 1989)
Silent Scream (David Hayman, 1990)
Prague (Ian Sellar, 1992)
Shallow Grave (Danny Boyle, 1995)
Rob Roy (Michael Caton-Jones, 1995)
Small Faces (Gillies McKinnon, 1996)
Carla's Song (Ken Loach, 1997)
The Near Room (David Hayman, 1997)
Orphans (Peter Mullan, 1999)

2. Features Supported by the Glasgow Film Fund

Shallow Grave (Danny Boyle, 1995) £150,000
Small Faces (Gillies Mackinnon, 1996) £150,000
The Near Room (David Hayman, 1997) £251,000
Carla's Song (Ken Loach, 1997) £150,000
The Slab Boys (John Byrne, 1997) £170,000
Regeneration (Gillies Mackinnon, 1997) £71,000
The Life of Stuff (Simon Donald, 1998) £150,000
My Name is Joe (Ken Loach, 1998) £100,000
Orphans (Peter Mullan, 1999) £250,000
The Acid House (Paul McGuigan, 1999) £75,000
The Debt Collector (Anthony Nielson, 1999) £200,000
The House of Mirth (Terence Davies, 2000) £200,000

3. Features Supported by the Scottish Arts Council National Lottery Fund

The Slab Boys (John Byrne, 1997) £550,000
Regeneration (Gillies Mackinnon, 1997) £1,000,000
The Winter Guest (Alan Rickman, 1998) £500,000
The Life of Stuff (Simon Donald, 1998) £1,000,000
Stella Does Tricks (Coky Giedrocyk, 1998) £137,178
My Name is Joe (Ken Loach, 1998) £500,000

The Acid House (Paul McGuigan, 1999) £370,000
This Year's Love (David Kane, 1999) £750,000
Orphans (Peter Mullan, 1999) £900,000
Gregory's Two Girls (Bill Forsyth, 1999) £1,000,000
Complicity (Gavin Millar, 2000) £500,000
My Life So Far (Hugh Hudson, 2000) £1,000,000
Daybreak (Bernard Rudden, 2000) £399,054
House of Mirth (Terence Davies, 2000) £500,000
Aberdeen (Hans Petter Moland, 2000) £325,000

Appendix Two
The Short-Film Schemes

1. Short Films made under the *Tartan Shorts* Scheme

1993

Franz Kafka's Its a Wonderful Life — Producer: Ruth Kenley-Letts; Writer and Director: Peter Capaldi

Rain — Producer: Amanda Partridge; Writer: James Mavor; Director: Jim Shields

A Small Deposit — Producer: Paul Holmes; Writer: Danny McCahon; Director: Eleanor Yule

1994

Daddy's Gone a Hunting — Producer: Julie Fraser; Writer: Kathy Crombie; Director: Morag Fullerton

Latin For a Dark Room — Producer: Catherine Aitken; Writer: Liz Lochhead; Director: Joe Aherne

Narance — Producers: Jo Spreckley, John McVay; Writer: Toby Kurnow; Director: Patrick Harkins

1995

Dancing — Producer: Pamela Wilson; Writer and Director: Stevan Rimkus

Fridge — Producer: Frances Higson; Writer and Director: Peter Mullan

The Pen — Producer: Barbara McKissack; Writer: Ian Heggie; Director: Bill Pryde

1996

Dead Sea Reels — Producer: Oscar Van Heek; Writer: Sergio Casci; Director: Don Coutts

Initiation — Producer: Angus Lamont; Writer and Director: Martin McCardie

The Star — Producers: Ildiko Kemeny, Stephen Marsh; Writer: John Milarky; Director: David Moore

1997

Candy Floss — Producer: Marnie Anderson; Writers: Hannah Robinson, Maria MacDonell; Director: Hannah Robinson

Gasman — Producer: Gavin Emerson; Writer and Director: Lynne Ramsay

Karmic Mothers — Producer: Charlie Stuart; Writer: Kate Atkinson; Director: John Tiffany

1998

Duck — Producer: Robin Macpherson; Writer: Des Dillon; Director: Kenny Glenaan

First It's Dark — Producer: Wendy Griffin; Writer and Director: Jon Love

Spitting Distance — Producer: Miglet Crichton; Writer and Director: Brian Ross

1999

Billy & Zorba — Producer: Gaynor Holmes; Writer: Ed McCardie; Director: Brian Kirk

Marcie's Dowry — Producer: Glynis Robertson; Writer: Bill Chamberlain; Director: David Mackenzie

Poached — Producer: Mark Grindle; Writer and Director: Justin Molotnikov

2000

Birthday — Producer: Hannah Lewis; Writer and Director: Morag McKinnon

The Lovers — Producer: Paul Welsh; Writer and Director: Ewan Morrison

Rice Paper Wars — Producer: Becky Lloyd; Writer and Director: Andy Goddard

2. Short Films made under the *Gear Ghearr* Scheme

1996

An Iobairt (The Sacrifice) — Producer: Lucy Conan; Writer: Aonghas MacNeacail; Director: Gerda Stevenson

Roimh Ghaoth Agheamhraidh (Before Winter Winds) — Producer: Margaret Mary Murray; Writer and Director: Bill MacLeod

1997

Ag Iasgash (Fishing) — Producer: John J. MacIsaac; Writer and Director: Roddy Cunningham

A Bhean Eudach (The Jealous Sister) —

Producer: John Smith; Writer and Director: Domhnall Ruadh

1998

Dathan — Producer: Ann Morrison; Writer and Director: Iain F. MacLeod

Keino — Producer: Catherine Macdonald; Writer: Norman Maclean; Director: Iseabail Maciver

Mac — Producer: Seumas Mactaggart; Writer and Director: Alasdair Maclean

3. Short Films made under the *Prime Cuts* Scheme

1996

The Beauty of the Common Tool — Producer: Matthew Zajac; Writer: May Eakin; Director: Owen Thomas

Dancing Some Days — Producer: Jane Skinner; Writer: Marianne Carey; Director: Katrina Macpherson

Dead Eye Dick — Producer: David Muir; Writer: Paul Gallagher; Director: Nicola Black

Fantoosh — Producer: Hannah Lewis; Writer: Colin McLaren; Director: Morag McKinnon

Hard Nut: A Love Story — Producer: Martin McCardie; Writer: Ed McCardie; Director: Jim Twaddale

Here's Johnny — Producer: Gill Parry; Writers: Tom Shankland, Brian Kirk; Director: Brian Kirk

1997

Bite — Producer: Sue Bainbridge; Writer: Andrea Gibb; Director: Brian Ross

Friendly Voices — Producer: Simon Mallinson; Writers: Dilys Rose, Jack Wyper; Director: Jack Wyper

Little Sisters — Producer: Nic Murison; Writer and Director: Andy Goddard

Santa Claws — Producer: Carolynne Sinclair Kidd; Writers: Jack Lothian, Saul Metzstein; Director: Saul Metzstein

Thicker Than Water — Producer: Sue Porter; Writer: Frances Bell; Director: Elly M. Taylor

Waterloo — Producer: Wendy Griffin; Writer and Director: Margaret Reeves

1998

Horsehair — Producer: Jolyon White; Writers: Duncan Nicoll, Joylon White; Director: Duncan Nicoll

The Nightsweeper — Producer: Paul Welsh; Writer: Asim Ullah; Director: Rachel Sieffert

No-One Sees Black — Producer: Bert Ross; Writer and Director: Chris Dooks

Panfried — Producer: Susan Kemp; Writer and Director: Justin Molotnikov

Sonny's Pride — Producers: Carole Sheridan, Gaynor Holmes; Writer: Barry Gornell; Director: Brian Kelly

4. Short Films made under the *New Found Land* Scheme

2000

I Saw You — Producer: David Muir; Writer: Ewan Morrison; Directors: Ewan Morrison and John Dingwall

Long Haul — Producer: Jonnie Turpie; Writer: Janet Paisley; Director: Bob Blagden

Nan — Producer: Pamela Hanson; Writer: Colin Hough; Director: Alison Peebles

Night Swimmer — Producer: Paul Welsh; Writer: Chiew-Siah Tei; Director: Hannah Robinson

The Only True Comedian — Producer: Angus Lamont; Writer: Ian Rankin; Director: Andy Goddard

To a Mouse — Producer: Angus Lamont; Writer and Director: Davie McKay

Bibliography

1. Books

Ian Aitken, *Film and Reform: John Grierson and the Documentary Film Movement* (London: Routledge, 1990).

Ian Aitken (ed.), *The Documentary Film Movement: an Anthology* (Edinburgh: Edinburgh University Press, 1998).

John Barnes, *The Beginnings of the Cinema in England, 1894–1901*: Revised Volume 1 (Exeter: University of Exeter Press, 1999).

John Barnes, *The Beginnings of the Cinema in England 1894–1901: Volume 2, 1897* (Exeter: University of Exeter Press, 1996).

Charles Barr, *Ealing Studios* (London: Cameron & Tayleur/David & Charles, 1977).

Craig Beveridge and Ronald Turnbull, *The Eclipse of Scottish Culture: Inferiorism and the Intellectuals* (Edinburgh: Polygon, 1989).

Craig Beveridge and Ronnie Turnbull, *Scotland After Enlightenment* (Edinburgh: Polygon, 1997).

James Beveridge (ed.), *John Grierson: Film Master* (New York: Macmillan, 1978).

David Bruce, *Scotland the Movie* (Edinburgh: Polygon/SFC, 1996).

Peter Bruce, *100 Years of Glasgow's Amazing Cinemas* (Edinburgh: Polygon, 1996).

Angus Calder, *Revolving Culture: Notes from the Scottish Republic* (London: I.B. Tauris, 1994).

John Caughie, *Television Drama: Realism, Modernism and British Culture* (Oxford: Oxford University Press, 2000).

S.G. Checkland, *The Upas Tree: Glasgow 1875–1975* (Glasgow: University of Glasgow Press, 1976).

Ian Christie, *Arrows of Desire: The Films of Michael Powell and Emeric Pressburger* (London: Waterstone, 1985).

Ian Christie (ed.), *Powell, Pressburger and Others* (London: BFI, 1978).

Linda Colley, *Britons: Forging the Nation 1707–1837* (Yale University Press, 1992).

Pam Cook, *Fashioning the Nation: Costume and Identity in British Cinema* (London: BFI, 1996).

Gladys Cooper, *Gladys Cooper* (London: Hutchison, 1931).

John Corner and Sylvia Harvey (ed.), *Enterprise and Heritage: Cross Currents of National Culture* (London: Routledge, 1991).

Cairns Craig, *Out of History: Narrative Paradigms in Scottish and British Culture* (Edinburgh: Polygon, 1996).

Cairns Craig, *The Modern Scottish Novel: Narrative and the National Imagination* (Edinburgh: Edinburgh University Press, 1999).

James Curran and Jean Seaton, *Power Without Responsibility: The Press and Broadcasting in Britain*, 3rd edn (London: Routledge, 1988).

T.M. Devine and R.J. Finlay (eds), *Scotland in the 20th Century* (Edinburgh: Edinburgh University Press, 1996).

T.M. Devine, *The Scottish Nation 1700–2000* (London: Penguin, 1999).

Eddie Dick (ed.), *From Limelight to Satellite: A Scottish Film Book* (London: BFI/SFC, 1990).

Eddie Dick, Andrew Noble and Duncan Petrie (eds), *Bill Douglas: A Lanternist's Account* (London: BFI, 1993).

Margaret Dickinson, *Rogue Reels: Oppositional Film in Britain, 1945–90* (London: BFI, 1999).

Margaret Dickinson and Sarah Street, *Cinema and State: The Film Industry and the British Government 1927–84* (London: BFI, 1985).

Alan Eyles, *ABC: The First Name in Entertainment* (London: Cinema Theatre Association/BFI, 1993).

Angus Finney, *The State of European Cinema: A New Dose of Reality* (London: Cassell, 1996).

Graham Fuller (ed.) *Loach on Loach* (London: Faber & Faber, 1998).

Dennis Gifford, *A Pictorial History of Horror Movies* (London: Hamlyn, 1973).

Forsyth Hardy (ed.), *Grierson on Documentary*, 1st edn (Glasgow: Collins, 1946), 2nd edn (London: Faber & Faber, 1966).

Forsyth Hardy, *John Grierson: A Documentary Biography* (London: Faber & Faber, 1979).

Forsyth Hardy (ed.), *John Grierson's Scotland* (Edinburgh: Ramsay Head Press, 1979).

Forsyth Hardy, *Scotland in Film* (Edinburgh: Edinburgh University Press, 1990).

Stephen Harvey, *Directed by Vincente Minnelli* (New York: MOMA, 1989).

Sylvia Harvey and Kevin Robbins (eds), *The Regions, the Nations and the BBC: The BBC Charter Review Series, Volume 3* (London: BFI, 1993).

Christopher Harvie, *Scotland and Nationalism* (London: Allen & Unwin, 1977).

Christopher Harvie, *No Gods and Precious Few Heroes: Scotland 1914–1980* (London: Edward Arnold, 1981).

Christopher Harvie, *Travelling Scot* (Glendaruel: Argyll Publishing, 1999).

John Herdman, *The Double in Nineteenth-Century Fiction* (London: Macmillan, 1990).

Andrew Higson, *Waving the Flag: Constructing a National Cinema in Britain* (Oxford: Clarendon Press, 1995).

Andrew Higson and Richard Maltby (eds), *'Film Europe' and 'Film America'* (Exeter: University of Exeter Press, 1999).

John Hill, *British Cinema in the 1980s* (Oxford: Oxford University Press, 1999).

John Hill and Martin McLoone (eds), *Big Picture, Small Screen: The Relations Between Film and Television* (Luton: University of Luton Press, 1996).

Jeremy Issacs, *Storm Over 4: A Personal Account* (Weidenfeld & Nicolson, 1989).

Philip Kemp, *Lethal Innocence: The Cinema of Alexander Mackendrick* (London: Methuen, 1991).

Michael Korda, *Charmed Lives: A Family Romance* (New York: Random House, 1979).

Karol Kulik, *Alexander Korda: The Man Who Could Work Miracles* (London: W.H. Allen, 1975).

Maurice Lindsay and David Bruce, *Edinburgh: Past and Present* (London: Robert Hale, 1990).

Rachael Low, *The History of the British Film 1906–1914* (London: Allen & Unwin, 1949).

Rachael Low, *The History of the British Film 1918–1929* (London: Allen & Unwin, 1971).

Rachel Low, *Documentary and Experimental Films of the 1930s* (London: Allen & Unwin, 1975).

Rachael Low, *Film-Making in 1930s Britain* (London: Allen & Unwin, 1985).

Michael Lynch, *Scotland: A New History* (London: Pimlico, 1992).

Colin McArthur, *Television and History*, BFI Television Monograph no. 8 (London: BFI, 1980).

Colin McArthur (ed.), *Scotch Reels: Scotland in Cinema and Television* (London: BFI, 1982).

Janet McBain, *Pictures Past: Scottish Cinemas Remembered* (Edinburgh: Moorfoot, 1985).

Janet McBain (ed.), *Scotland in Silent Cinema: A Commemorative Catalogue to Accompany the Scottish Reels Programme at the Pordenone Silent Film Festival, Italy 1998* (Glasgow: Scottish Screen, 1998).

David McCrone, *Understanding Scotland: The Sociology of a Stateless Nation* (London: Routledge, 1992).

David McCrone, Angela Morris and Richard Kiely, *Scotland the Brand: The Making of Scottish Heritage* (Edinburgh: Edinburgh University Press, 1995).

Kevin MacDonald, *Emeric Pressburger: The Life and Death of a Screenwriter* (London: Faber & Faber, 1994).

Don Macpherson, *Traditions of Independence* (London: BFI, 1980).

Robin Macpherson, 'Independent film and television in Scotland: a case of independent cultural reproduction?' Unpublished MA dissertation, University of Stirling, 1991.

Karl Miller, *Doubles: Studies in Literary History* (Oxford: Oxford University Press, 1985) .

Sheridan Morley, *The Other Side of the Moon: The Life of David Niven* (London: Weidenfeld & Nicolson, 1985).

Michael S. Moss and John R. Hume, *Workshop of the British Empire: Engineering and Shipbuilding in the West of Scotland* (London: Heinemann, 1977).

Robert Murphy (ed.), *British Cinema of the 90s* (London: BFI, 2000).

Tom Nairn, *The Break-Up of Britain*, 2nd expanded edn, (London: Verso, 1981).

David Niven, *The Moon's a Balloon* (London: Book Club Associates/Hamish Hamilton, 1972).

Charles Oakley, *Fifty Years at the Pictures* (Glasgow: Scottish Film Council, 1946).

John Orr, *Contemporary Cinema* (Edinburgh: Edinburgh University Press, 1998).

Duncan Petrie (ed.), *New Questions of British Cinema* (London, BFI, 1992).

Duncan Petrie (ed.), *Screening Europe: Image and Identity in Contemporary European Cinema* (London: BFI, 1992).

Duncan Petrie, *The British Cinematographer* (London: BFI, 1996).

Duncan Petrie (ed.), *Inside Stories: Diaries of British Film-Makers at Work* (London: BFI, 1996).

David Pirie, *A Heritage of Horror: The English Gothic Cinema 1946–1972* (London: Gordon Fraser, 1973).

Murray Pittock, *The Invention of Scotland: The Stuart Myth and Scottish Identity, 1638 to the Present* (London: Routledge, 1991).

Michael Powell, *A Life in Movies* (London: Heinemann, 1986).

Michael Powell, *Edge of the World: The Making of a Film* (London: Faber & Faber, 1990).

S.S. Prawer, *Caligari's Children: The Film as Tale of Terror* (Oxford: Oxford University Press, 1980).

John Pym, *Film on Four: A Survey 1982/1991* (London: BFI, 1992).

Jeffrey Richards, *The Age of the Dream Palace: Cinema and Society in Britain 1930–39* (London: Routledge & Kegan Paul, 1984).

Jeffrey Richards, *Films and British National Identity: From Dickens to Dad's Army* (Manchester: Manchester University Press, 1998).

John Russell Taylor, *Hitch: The Autrhorised Biography of Alfred Hitchcock* (London: Faber & Faber, 1978) .

Tom Ryall, *Alfred Hitchcock and the British Cinema* (London: Athlone, 1986).

Scott Salwolke, *The Films of Michael Powell and the Archers* (Lanham, MD: The Scarecrow Press, 1997).

Jo Sherrington, '*To Speak Its Pride*': The Work of the Films of Scotland Committee (Glasgow: SFC, 1996).

Irene Shubick, *Play for Today: The Evolution of Television Drama* (London: Davis-Poynter, 1975).

Joel E. Siegel, *Val Lewton: the Reality of Terror* (London: Secker & Warburg/BFI, 1972).

Anthony Slaven, *The Development of the West of Scotland 1750–1960* (London: Routledge & Kegan Paul, 1975).

T.C. Smout, *A Century of the Scottish People 1830–1950* (London: Collins, 1986).

Ian Spring, *Phantom Village: The Myth of the New Glasgow* (Edinburgh: Polygon, 1990).

Randall Stevenson and Gavin Wallace (eds), *Scottish Theatre Since the Seventies* (Edinburgh: Edinburgh University Press, 1996).

Paul Swan, *The British Documentary Film Movement 1926–1946* (Cambridge: CUP, 1989).

Michael Thompson, *Silver Screen in the Silver City* (Aberdeen: Aberdeen University Press, 1988).

Derek Threadgall, *Shepperton Studios: An Independent View* (London: BFI, 1994).

Various, *Film Bang* (Glasgow: Film Bang, 1976).

Various, *New Edinburgh Review*, 'Scottish Cinema?', vol. 34, no. 2, 1976.

Patricia Warren, *British Film Studios: An Illustrated History* (London: B.T. Batsford, 1995).

Roderick Watson, *The Literature of Scotland* (Basingstoke: Macmillan, 1984).

Harry Watt, *Don't Look at the Camera* (London: Paul Elek, 1974).

Christopher Whyte (ed.), *Gendering the Nation: Studies in Modern Scottish Literature* (Edinburgh: Edinburgh University Press, 1995).

Norman Wilson, *Representing Scotland: A Film Survey* (Edinburgh: Edinburgh Film Guild, 1945).

Brian Winston, *Reclaiming the Real: The Documentary Film Revisited* (London: BFI, 1995).

Peter Womack, *Improvement and Romance: Constructing the Myth of the Highlands* (London: Macmillan, 1989).

2. Articles

Ian Aitken, 'John Grierson, Idealism and the Inter-War Period', *Historical Journal of Film, Radio and Television*, vol. 9, no. 3, 1989.

Marinell Ash, 'William Wallace and Robert the Bruce: The Life and Death of a National Myth' in Raphael Samuel and Paul Thompson (eds), *The Myths We Live By* (London: Routledge, 1990).

André Bazin, 'The Evolution of the Language of Cinema' in *What is Cinema?*, Vol. 1 (Berkeley: University of California Press, 1967).

Ronan Bennett, 'Lean Mean and Cruel', *Sight and Sound*, January 1995.

Stig Björkman, 'Naked Miracles', *Sight and Sound*, October 1996.

David Bordwell, 'The Art Cinema as a Mode of Practice', *Film Criticism*, vol. 4, no. 1, Autumn 1979.

Xan Brooks, Review of *The Acid House*, *Sight and Sound*, January 1999.

John Brown, 'Film Industry Needs Whiz Kids Too', *Glasgow Herald*, 20 July 1982.

John Brown, 'A Suitable Job for a Scot', *Sight and Sound*, Summer 1983.

John Brown, 'Land Beyond Brigadoon', *Sight and Sound*, Winter 1983/84.

Edward Buscombe, 'Sound and Colour', in Bill Nichols (ed.), *Movies and Methods, Volume 2* (Berkeley: University of California Press, 1985).

John Caughie, 'Broadcasting and Cinema: Converging Histories' in Charles Barr (ed.), *All Our Yesterdays: 90 Years of British Cinema* (London: BFI, 1986).

John Caughie, 'Progressive Television and Documentary Drama' in Tony Bennett *et al.* (eds), *Popular Television and Film* (Oxford: Oxford University Press/BFI, 1981).

Cairns Craig, 'Visitors From the Stars', *Cencrastus*, no. 11, New Year 1983.

Robert Crawford, 'Dedefining Scotland' in Susan Bassnett (ed.), *Studying British Culture: An Introduction* (London: Routledge, 1997).

David Daiches, 'Stevenson and Scotland' in Jenni Calder (ed.), *Stevenson and Victorian Scotland* (Edinburgh: Edinburgh University Press, 1981.

Eddie Dick, 'Poor Wee Scottish Cinema', *Scottish Film*, Issue 10, Fourth Quarter, 1994.

Kathryn Dodd and Philip Dodd, 'Engendering the Nation: British Documentary Film, 1930–1939' in Andrew Higson (ed.), *Dissolving Views: Key Writings on British Cinema* (London: Cassell, 1996).

Richard J. Finlay, 'National Identity in Crisis: politicians, Intellectuals and the "End of Scotland"', *History*, vol. 79, no. 256, June 1994.

Bill Forsyth, 'British Cinema: 1981 to …', *Sight and Sound*, Autumn 1981.

Carl Gardner and John Wyver, 'The Single Play: From Reithian Reverence to Cost-Accounting and Censorship', *Screen*, vol. 24, nos. 4–5, 1983.

John Grierson, 'Preface', Paul Rotha, *Documentary Film*, 3rd edn (London: Faber & Faber, 1952).

Thomas Guback, 'Hollywood's International Market' in Tino Balio (ed.), *The American Film Industry*, revised edn (Madison: University of Wisconsin Press, 1985).

Sue Harper, 'Bonnie Prince Charlie Revisited: British Costume Films in the 1950s' in Robert Murphy (ed.), *The British Cinema Book* (London: BFI, 1997).

Hugh Herbert, 'Tutti Frutti' in George W. Brandt (ed.), *British Television Drama in the 1980s* (Cambridge: Cambridge University Press, 1993).

Andrew Higson, 'Re-Presenting the National Past: Nostalgia and Pastiche in the Heritage Film' in Lester Friedman (ed.), *British Cinema and Thatcherism* (London: UCL Press, 1993).

John Hill, 'Every Fuckin' Choice Stinks', *Sight and Sound*, November 1998.

John Hill, 'British Cinema as National Cinema: Production, Audience, Representation' in Robert Murphy (ed.), *The British Cinema Book*, (London: BFI, 1997).

Allan Hunter, 'Being Human', *Sight and Sound*, August 1994.

Trevor Johnstone, review of *Prague*, *Sight and Sound*, November 1992.

Philip Kemp, review of *Soft Top Hard Shoulder*, *Sight and Sound*, January 1993.

A.L. Kennedy, 'Edging Close to the Bone', *Sight and Sound*, December 1996.

Harlan Kennedy, 'Kiltspotting: Highland Reels', *Film Comment*, July–August 1996.

Liz Lochhead, 'The Shadow', *Sight and Sound*, June 1995.

Colin McArthur, 'The Maggie', *Cencrastus*, no. 12, Spring 1983.

Colin McArthur, 'In Praise of a Poor Cinema', *Sight and Sound*, August 1993.

Colin McArthur, 'Tartan Shorts and the Taming of First Reels', *Scottish Film*, Issue 9, Third Quarter, 1994.

Colin McArthur, 'The Cultural Necessity of a Poor Celtic Cinema' in Paul Hainsworth, John Hill and Martin McLoone (eds), *Border Crossing: Film in Ireland, Britain and Europe* (Belfast: IIS/Queen's University, 1994).

Robert McCall, 'Shallow Grave: A worthy standard-bearer for Scotland?', *Scottish Film*, Issue 9, Third Quarter, 1994.

M.K. MacMurragh-Kavanagh, ' "Drama" into "News": Strategies of Intervention in "The Wednesday Play" ', *Screen*, vol. 38, no. 3, Autumn 1997.

Linda McKenney, 'The People's Story: 7:84 Scotland' in Randall Stevenson and Gavin Wallace (eds), *Scottish Theatre Since the Seventies* (Edinburgh: Edinburgh University Press, 1996).

Alastair Michie, 'Scotland: Strategies of Centralisation' in Charles Barr (ed.), *All Our Yesterdays: 90 Years of British Cinema* (London: BFI, 1986).

Steve Neale, 'Art Cinema as Institution', *Screen*, vol. 22, no. 1, 1981.

Andy O'Hagan, 'Gangs in the Hood', *Sight and Sound*, July 1995. .

Andy O'Hagan, 'The Boys are Back in Town', *Sight and Sound*, February 1996.

Jean Oppenheimer, 'Adding Chills to the Winter Guest', *American Cinematographer*, December 1997.

Brian Pendreigh, 'It was billed as the new Trainspotting. It made £4,438. What went wrong?', *The Guardian*, 15 January 1999.

David Pirie, review of *Burke and Hare*, *Monthly Film Bulletin*, vol. 39, no. 457, February 1972.

Julian Poole, 'Independent Frame', *Sight and Sound*, Spring 1980.

Trevor R. Pringle, 'The Privation of History: Landseer, Victoria and the Highland Myth' in Denis Cosgrove and Stephen Daniels (eds.), *The Iconography of Landscape* (Cambridge: Cambridge University Press, 1988).

Nick Roddick, 'The British Revival' in Fenella Greenfield (ed.), *A Night at the Pictures: Ten Decades of British Film* (Bromley: Columbus Books/British Film Year, 1995).

Adrienne Scullion, 'Geggies, Empires, Cinemas: The Scottish Experience of Early Film', *Picture House*, no. 21, Summer 1996.

Mark Sinker, 'Temporary Gentlemen', *Sight and Sound*, December 1997.

Liese Spencer, ' Tearing the Roof Off', *Sight and Sound*, April 1999.

Liese Spencer, 'What Are You Looking At?', *Sight and Sound*, October 1999.

Nick Thomas, 'UK Film, Television and Video Overview', *BFI Handbook 1998* (London: BFI, 1998).

Andrew O. Thompson, 'Trains, Veins and Heroin Deals', *American Cinematographer*, August 1996.

Andrew O. Thompson, 'A Cosmopolitan Celebration of Cinema', *American Cinematographer*, December 1997.

Roderick Watson, 'Introduction' to Robert Louis Stevenson, *Shorter Scottish Fiction* (Edinburgh: Canongate Classics, 1995).

Christopher Williams, 'The Social Art Cinema: a Moment in the History of British Film and Television Culture', in Williams (ed.), *Cinema: the Beginnings and the Future* (London: University of Westminster Press, 1996).

List of Illustrations

Whilst considerable effort has been made to identify correctly the copyright holders this has not been possible in all cases. We apologise for any apparent negligence and any omissions or corrections brought to our attention will be remedied in any future editions.

Chapter Two: *I Know Where I'm Going!* © Archers Film Productions/Independent Productions; *The Brothers* © Triton Films; *Whisky Galore* © Canal Plus (Ealing Studios)

Chapter Three: *Rob Roy* © Gaumont Company/Westminster Film Company (Carlton); *Rob Roy – the Highland Rogue* © Walt Disney Productions; *Culloden* © BBC; *The Kidnappers* © Group Film /Nolbandov-Parkyn Productions

Chapter Four: *The Flesh and the Fiends* © Triad Productions; *Floodtide* © Aquila Film Productions; *The Brave Don't Cry* © Group 3

Chapter Five: *Drifters* © New Era Films/Empire Marketing Board Film Unit; *Flash the Sheepdog* © International Film Associates/Children's Film Foundation

Chapter Six: *Ill Fares the Land* © Portman Productions/Scottish and Global TV/ Channel Four; *Another Time, Another Place* © Umbrella Films/Rediffusion Films/Channel Four/Scottish Arts Council; *Just Another Saturday* © BBC

Chapter Seven: *Silent Scream* © BFI/ Film Four International/Antonine Productions /Scottish Film Production Fund; *Gregory's Girl* © National Film Trustree Company/ Luke /National Film Finance Corporation /Scottish TV; *My Childhood* © BFI Production Board; *Venus Peter* © BFI/ Channel Four/Scottish Film Production Fund/Orkney Islands Council/British Screen

Chapter Eight: *Shallow Grave* © Figment Films/Channel Four; *Small Faces* © BBC Films/BBC Scotland/ Glasgow Film Fund

Chapter Nine: *Trainspotting* © Channel Four/Figment Films/Noel Gay Motion Picture Company Ltd/Universal; *My Name is Joe* © Parallax (Joe) Ltd/Road Movies Vierte/Produktionen GmbH; *Breaking the Waves* © 1996 Zentropa Entertainments ApS and La Sept Cinema; *Orphans* © Channel Four Television Corporation/Antonine Green Bridge

Jacket: *Ratcatcher* © Pathé Fund Limited/Les Productions Lazennec; *Whisky Galore* © Canal Plus (Ealing Studios)

Index